SHAMBHALA DRAGON EDITIONS

The dragon is an age-old symbol of the highest spiritual essence, embodying wisdom, strength, and the divine power of transformation. In this spirit, Shambhala Dragon Editions offers a treasury of readings in the sacred knowledge of Asia. In presenting the works of authors both ancient and modern, we seek to make these teachings accessible to lovers of wisdom everywhere.

THE
MYSTICISM OF
SOUND AND MUSIC

REVISED EDITION

Hazrat Inayat Khan

SHAMBHALA
Boston & London
1996

Shambhala Publications, Inc.
Horticultural Hall
300 Massachusetts Avenue
Boston, MA 02115
www.shambhala.com

15   14   13   12   11   10   9   8   7

Printed in the United States of America

♾ This edition is printed on acid-free paper
that meets the American National Standards
Institute z39.48 Standard

Distributed in the United States by Random House, Inc.,
and in Canada by Random House of Canada Ltd

Library of Congress Cataloging-in-Publication Data
Inayat Khan, 1882–1927.
The mysticism of sound and music/Hazrat Inayat Khan.—Rev. ed.
    p.   cm.—(Shambhala dragon editions)
Consists principally of lectures previously published as The Sufi
message of Hazrat Inayat Khan (v.2); portions also published as
Music, The mysticism of sound, and Cosmic language. Also includes
unpublished material.
Includes index.
Contents: Music—Aphorisms—The mysticism of sound—Cosmic
language—The power of the word—Phrases to be repeated.
ISBN-13 978-1-57062-231-1 (alk. paper)
ISBN-10 1-57062-231-0
1. Music—Philosophy and aesthetics.   2. Music—Religious aspects—
Sufism.   3. Sound—Religious aspects—Sufism.   4. Language and
languages—Religious aspects—Sufism.   5. Music—India—History and
criticism.   6. Music, Influence of.   I. Title.   II. Series.
ML3800.I53   1996   96-22762
781'.12—dc20   CIP

CONTENTS

PREFACE

THIS BOOK is a revised and enlarged edition of the second Volume in the series of 'The Sufi Message of Hazrat Inayat Khan'. It contains a Sufi vision on music, sound, language and the power of words.

The present text, established after a careful examination of the original documents, attempts to follow Hazrat Inayat Khan's own words and his personal, mostly oral, style as closely as possible. Almost all chapters of this book – 'The Mystery of Sound' excepted – were originally lectures and addresses, delivered in various circumstances. Some were addressed to pupils and students who were already acquainted with the Sufi teachings; others were public lectures, and some reports show that an address was given on the occasion of a musical performance.

In the early years of his journeys throughout Europe and the U.S.A. Hazrat Inayat Khan used to introduce Sufism by means of music as well as by his lectures, as is shown by his words: 'Our work is not only to speak to you, to lecture for you, to bring you the Sufi message in the form of books and lectures, but to bring it to you also in music: to play for you, to sing for you, to bring you the truth in the realm of music'.

Soon, however, Hazrat Inayat Khan felt that he had to give up music in the sense of singing and playing, and from then on he often explained how one should consider life itself as music. All his teachings reveal to us the harmony of the universe, and show the part that each individual, each creature, has to play in this symphony. How he gave up his music he himself describes in the Prologue.

In the first edition of this series the intention was already to leave intact, as far as possible, the flow of mystical inspiration and poetical expression which add so much to the spell of these teachings, and without which a significant part of his message would be lost.

In the preface to this earlier edition it was also explained that 'no attempt has been made to transform Inayat Khan's highly personal and colourful language into idiomatically unimpeachable English. Already so much is necessarily lost by the transfer of the spoken word to the printed page, that every effort has been made, as it should, to preserve the Master's melodious phrasing, the radiance of his personality, and the subtle sense of humour which never left him'.

Nevertheless in this earlier edition different lectures were frequently joined together; parts of them were thus omitted and other passages, mostly taken from questions and answers raised after the lectures, were inserted on suitable places. This had the advantage that some repetitions – for instance a story told more than once – could be avoided. The present edition does not adopt this system; keeping even more closely to the original intention, it preserves Hazrat Inayat Khan's lectures intact in their natural rhythm and with their authentic sequence. In some rare cases, however, where an often repeated sentence, or a duplicated passage could be omitted without disturbing the logical and harmonious flow of Hazrat Inayat Khan's words, this has been done. A collection of copies of the complete original documents, transcripts, shorthand and longhand reports of the lectures that constitute the present book is kept and can be consulted.

In the first part of the present edition, 'Music', a few chapters – not published before – are now added, as for instance 'The Connection between Dance and Music', 'The Mysticism of Sound' and 'The Mystery of Sound', a second chapter on 'The Mystery of Colour and Sound', and also two articles formerly published in magazines: 'Esoteric Music' and 'The Influence of Music upon the Character of Man'. The second part of this book reproduces 'The Mysticism of Sound', one of Hazrat Inayat Khan's earlier written works. In ancient magazines – 1918 – it was announced as about to appear in three parts, each of seven chapters. The first edition, however, appeared only in 1923 in the same form as shown here. It is not known what has become of the earlier plan, nor could we discover why it was changed.

The book 'Cosmic Language' forms the third part of this Volume. It consists of a series of lectures given during the Summer School in Suresnes, France, in 1924. During these three months' sessions Hazrat Inayat Khan used to treat subjects more extensively and profoundly, so that they could easily be published afterwards in the form of books. A close study of the two reports of the lectures, available in the archives, has enabled us to make some corrections in the formerly published text. Several sentences have thus become clearer.

The fourth and last part of this Volume II consists of lectures on 'The Power of the Word', to which we have added the chapter 'The Word', formerly published in Volume XII, and the hitherto unpublished lectures 'The Word that was lost 2' and 'The Value of Repetition and Reflection'.

After reading and studying this work, and learning about the power and value of words and their repetition, we can understand why Hazrat Inayat Khan used to give his pupils words and phrases to be repeated, which might be helpful and beneficial in their lives. Such sentences which he was inspired to compose are published at the end of this book. They may be used by those who desire to penetrate more deeply into this world of music, sound and vibrations, for as it was said by Hazrat Inayat Khan in a lecture:

'Another effect of this repetition is that the word is reflected upon the universal Spirit, and the universal mechanism then begins to repeat it automatically. In other words: what man repeats, God then begins to repeat, until it is materialized and has become a reality in all planes of existence'.
(From 'Suggestion by Word and Voice', Summer, 1926)

THE TRANSCRIPTION OF ORIENTAL TERMS

IN THE transcription of the Oriental terms from Arabic origin, often employed by Hazrat Inayat Khan, the standard Orientalist system of transliteration has frequently – even though reluctantly – been dispensed with. In texts, despite their ease of diction calling for close attention, diacritical signs and unusual literal clusters are likely to disorient the general reader, while being superfluous to the specialist. Ease and clarity have been aimed at rather than formal consistency.

Thus modern practice has been followed in familiar words like Panjab, whereas e.g. jemal, kemal, derwish continue an earlier mode of rendering such words into forms most akin to their Turkish version, and as such long familiar in Western writing.

These, moreover, usually are identical with, or very close to the shape they assume when transcribed from Hindustani – Inayat Khan's original language – then India's lingua franca, that has since been separated in Urdu and Hindi, but was in his time everywhere written in the scripts locally current. These, in his case, were the Gujerati and Devanari alphabets.

Earlier editions of Hazrat Inayat Khan's works have, therefore, usually offered transliterations deriving from these scripts (as evinced e.g. by Nagari intercalic *a*). In the circles of his followers words like zat, zikar, have hence long been familiar. On the other hand, with today's vastly increased general acquaintance with technical Sufi terms from popular surveys and standards-work alike, such forms might now well be found confusing as well as imprecise.

In the present edition, therefore, in such cases the terms concerned have been rendered from the original language, and are followed by the traditional Nagari derivation in brackets. Thus in the case of the two above mentioned Arabic words: dhat (zat) and dhikr (zikar).

In this context it is important to remember the words spoken by Hazrat Inayat Khan at the end of the lecture "The power of the word".

PROLOGUE

I GAVE up my music because I had received from it all I had
to receive. To serve God one must sacrifice the dearest thing,
and I sacrificed my music, the dearest thing to me.

I had composed songs, I sang, and played the vina.
Practising this music I arrived at a stage where I touched
the music of the spheres. Then every soul became for me
a musical note, and all life became music. Inspired by it I
spoke to the people, and those who were attracted by my
words listened to them instead of listening to my songs.

Now, if I do anything, it is to tune souls instead of
instruments, to harmonize people instead of notes. If there is
anything in my philosophy, it is the law of harmony: that one
must put oneself in harmony with oneself and with others.

I have found in every word a certain musical value, a
melody in every thought, harmony in every feeling, and I
have tried to interpret the same thing with clear and simple
words to those who used to listen to my music.

I played the vina until my heart turned into the same
instrument. Then I offered this instrument to the divine
Musician, the only musician existing. Since then I have
become His flute, and when He chooses He plays His music.
The people give me credit for this music which, in reality, is
not due to me, but to the Musician who plays on His own
instrument.

MUSIC

CHAPTER I

Music

WHY IS music called the divine art, while all other arts are not so called? We may certainly see God in all arts and in all sciences, but in music alone we see God free from all forms and thoughts. In every other art there is idolatry. Every thought, every word has its form. Sound alone is free from form. Every word of poetry forms a picture in our mind. Sound alone does not make any object appear before us.

1

Music, the word we use in our everyday language, is nothing less than the picture of the Beloved. It is because music is the picture of our Beloved that we love music. But the question is: What is our Beloved, or where is our Beloved? Our Beloved is that which is our source and our goal. What we see of our Beloved before our physical eyes is the beauty which is before us. That part of our Beloved which is not manifest to our eyes is that inner form of beauty of which our Beloved speaks to us. If only we would listen to the voice of all the beauty that attracts us in any form, we would find that in every aspect it tells us that behind all manifestation is the perfect Spirit, the Spirit of wisdom.

What do we see as the principal expression of life in the beauty visible before us? It is movement. In line, in colour, in the changes of the seasons, in the rising and falling of the waves, in the wind, in the storm, in all the beauty of nature there is constant movement. It is this movement which has caused day and night, and the changing seasons. This movement has given us the comprehension of what we call time. Otherwise there would be no time – for it is eternity. This teaches us that all we love and admire, observe and comprehend, is the life hidden behind, and that life is our being.

It is owing to our limitation that we cannot see the whole Being of God, but all that we love in colour, line and form, or personality – all that is beloved by us – belongs to the real Beauty who is the Beloved of all.

When we trace what attracts us in this beauty that we see in all forms, we shall find that it is the movement of beauty: the music. All forms of nature, the flowers so perfectly formed and coloured, the planets and stars, the earth – all give the idea of harmony, of music. The whole of nature is breathing, not only living creatures, but all nature. It is only our tendency to compare that which seems more living with that which to us seems not so living which makes us forget that all things and all beings are living one perfect life. And the sign of life that this living beauty gives is music.

What makes the soul of the poet dance? Music. What makes the painter paint beautiful pictures, the musician sing beautiful songs? It is the inspiration that beauty gives. The Sufi has called this beauty *Saqi*, the divine Giver, who gives the wine of life to all. What is the wine of the Sufi? All beauty: in form, line and colour, in imagination, in sentiment, in manners – in all this he sees the one Beauty. All these different forms are part of the Spirit of beauty which is the life behind, always blessing.

As to what we call music in everyday language – to me architecture is music, gardening is music, farming is music, painting is music, poetry is music. In all the occupations of life where beauty has been the inspiration, where the divine wine has been poured out, there is music. But among all the different arts, the art of music has been especially considered divine, because it is the exact miniature of the law working through the whole universe.

For instance, if we study ourselves we shall find that the beats of the pulse and of the heart, the inhaling and exhaling of the breath, are all the work of rhythm. Life depends upon the rhythmic working of the whole mechanism of the body. Breath manifests as voice, as word, as sound. The sound is continually audible, the sound without and the sound within ourselves: that is music. This shows that there is music outside and music within ourselves.

Music inspires not only the soul of the great musician, but every infant, the instant it comes into the world, begins to move its little arms and legs with the rhythm of music. Therefore it is no exaggeration to say that music is the language of beauty, the language of the One whom every living soul has loved. And we can understand that, if we realize and recognize the perfection of all this beauty as God, our Beloved, then it is natural that this music, which we see in art and in the whole universe, should be called the Divine Art.

2

Many in the world take music as a source of amusement, a pastime; to many music is an art, and a musician an entertainer. Yet no one has lived in this world, has thought and felt, who has not considered music as the most sacred of all arts. For the fact is that, what the art of painting cannot clearly suggest, poetry explains in words, but that, which even a poet finds difficult to express in poetry, is expressed in music.

By this I do not only say that music is superior to painting and poetry: in fact music excels religion, for music raises the soul of man even higher than the so-called external form of religion. But it must not be understood that music can take the place of religion, for every soul is not necessarily tuned to that pitch where it can really benefit from music, nor is every music necessarily so high that it will exalt a person who hears it more than religion will do. However, for those who follow the path of the inner cult, music is most essential for their spiritual development. The reason is that the soul who is seeking for truth is in search of the formless God. Art*, no doubt, is most elevating, but it contains form; poetry has words, names suggestive of forms; it is music only which has beauty, power, charm, and at the same time can raise the soul beyond form.

That is why in ancient times the greatest prophets were great musicians. For instance, in the lives of the Hindu prophets one finds Narada, the great prophet who was at the same time a great musician, and Shiva, a godlike prophet who was the inventor of the sacred *vina*. Krishna is always pictured with a flute.

There is a well-known legend of the life of Moses which tells how Moses heard a divine command on Mount Sinai in

* Hazrat Inayat Khan often used 'art' in the restricted sense of painting, drawing and sculpture.

the words: *'Musa ke!'* – Moses hear, or Moses ponder – and the revelation that thus came to him was of tone and rhythm. He called it by the same name: *musake*. Words such as 'music', or 'musik' have come from that word.* David, whose song and whose voice have been known for ages, gave his message to the world in the form of music. Orpheus of the Greek legends, the knower of the mystery of tone and rhythm, had through this knowledge power over the hidden forces of nature. The Hindu Goddess of learning, of knowledge, whose name is Sarasvati, is always pictured with the *vina*. What does this suggest? It suggests that all learning has its essence in music.

Besides the natural charm that music has, it has a magical power, a power that can be experienced even now. It seems that the human race has lost a great deal of the ancient science of magic, but if there remains any magic it is music.

Music, besides power, is intoxication. When it intoxicates those who hear it, how much more must it intoxicate those who play or sing it themselves! And how much more must it intoxicate those who have touched the perfection of music, and those who have contemplated upon it for years and years! It gives them an even greater joy and exaltation than a king feels sitting on his throne.

According to the thinkers of the East there are four different intoxications: the intoxication of beauty, youth and strength; then the intoxication of wealth; the third intoxication is of power, of command, the power of ruling; and the fourth is the intoxication of learning, of knowledge. But all these four intoxications fade away just like stars before the sun in the presence of the intoxication of music. The reason is that it touches the deepest part of man's being. Music reaches farther than any other impression from the external world can reach. The beauty of music is that it is the source of creation and the means of absorbing it. In other words, by music the world was created, and it is again through music that the world is withdrawn into the source that has created it.

In support of this you may read in the Bible that first was

---

* This story, part of the Indian popular tradition, should not be understood as an etymological explanation. For Hazrat Inayat Khan language was a form of music, and what interested him was to discover the music hidden in words.

the word, and the word was God. That word means sound, and from sound you can grasp the idea of music. There is an Eastern legend that has come from centuries ago that, when God made man out of clay and asked the soul to enter, the soul refused to enter into this prison-house. Then God commanded the angels to sing, and as the angels sang the soul entered, intoxicated by the song.

In the scientific and material world we also see an example of this kind. Before a machine – a mechanism – will run, it must first make a noise. First it becomes audible, and then it shows its life. We can see this in a ship, in an aeroplane, in an automobile. This idea belongs to the mysticism of sound.

Before an infant is capable of admiring a colour or form, it enjoys sound. If there is any art that can charge youth with life and enthusiasm, with emotion and passion, it is music. If there is any art in which a person can fully express his feeling, his emotion, it is music which is best fitted for it. At the same time it is something that gives man that force and that power of activity that make soldiers march to the beats of the drum and the sound of the trumpet.

In the traditions of the past it was said that on the Last Day there will be the sound of the trumpet before the end of the world. This shows that music is connected with the beginning of creation, with its continuity, and with its end.

The mystics of all ages have loved music most. In almost all the circles of the inner cult, in whatever part of the world they are, music seems to be the centre of their cult, or ceremony, or ritual. Those who attain to that perfect peace which is called *nirvana*, or in the language of the Hindus *samadhi*, do so more easily through music. Therefore the Sufis, especially those of the Chishti school of ancient times, have taken music as a source of their meditation. And by meditating thus they derive much more benefit from it than those who meditate without the help of music.

The effect that they experience is the unfoldment of the soul, the opening of the intuitive faculties. Their heart, so to speak, opens to all the beauty that is within and without, uplifting them and at the same time bringing them that perfection for which every soul yearns.

3

Speaking of the harmony of music, I should like to say that the true harmony of music comes from the harmony of the soul. That music alone can be called real which comes from the harmony of the soul, its true source, and when it comes from there it must appeal to all souls.

Every soul differs in its choice in life, in its choice of the path it should follow. This is owing to the difference of the minds, for souls, in their essence, do not differ. Therefore, whatever means be chosen to bring the different minds of people together, there cannot be a better means of harmonizing them than music. It would be no exaggeration if I said that music alone can be the means by which the souls of races, nations and families, which are today so apart, may one day be united. The musician's lesson in life is therefore a great one. Music is not expressed through language, but through beauty of rhythm and tone which reach far beyond language. The more the musician is conscious of his mission in life, the greater service he can render to humanity.

As to the law of music which exists in different nations, there are of course different methods, but in the conception of beauty there is no difference. The differences come when the music is man-made; there is no difference in the soul-made music. Suppose a man comes from the far East, the extreme North, South, or West; wherever he sees the beauty of nature he cannot help admiring and loving it. So it is with the music lover. From whatever country he comes, and whatever music he hears, if the music has a soul, and if he seeks for the soul in music, he will appreciate and admire all music.

Furthermore, music has a mission not only with the multitudes, but with individuals. And its mission with the individual is as necessary and great as its mission with the multitude. All the trouble in the world and all the disastrous results arising out of it – all come from lack of harmony. This shows that the world to day needs harmony more than ever before. So if the musician understands this, his customer will be the whole world.

When a person learns music, he need not necessarily learn

to be a musician, or to become a source of pleasure and joy to his fellow-men. No! By playing, loving and hearing music he should develop music in his personality. The true use of music is to become musical in one's thoughts, words and actions. One should be able to give the harmony for which the soul yearns and longs every moment. All the tragedy in the world, in the individual and in the multitude, comes from lack of harmony, and harmony is best given by producing it in one's own life.

There are different kinds of music, each kind appealing to certain souls according to their evolution. For instance, children in the street are very pleased when beating the time, because that rhythm has a certain effect upon them. But as a person evolves, so he longs for a finer harmony. Why people like or dislike each other is owing to their different stages of evolution. For instance, one person is at a stage where he appreciates a certain kind of music, another one, whose evolution is greater, wants music appropriate to his evolution.

It is the same in religion. Some stick to certain beliefs and do not wish to evolve beyond. So it is possible that the lover of music may be tempted to keep to a certain sort of music and will not rise further. The true way of progressing through music is to evolve freely, to go forward, not caring what others think, and in this way, together with one's development in music, to harmonize the life of one's soul, one's surroundings and one's affairs.

During my travels throughout the world I have heard the music of many different places, and I have always felt that intimate friendship and brotherhood existing in music; I have always had a great respect for music and for the devotee of music. There is one thing I believe and of which I have been convinced time after time in India when meeting those who have touched some perfection in music: that one can feel the harmony which is the real test of perfection not only in their music, but in their lives.

If this principle of music were followed, there would be no need for an external religion. Some day music will be the means of expressing universal religion. Time is wanted for this, but there will come a day when music and its philosophy will become the religion of humanity.

CHAPTER II

Esoteric Music

ACCORDING TO the esoteric standpoint, music is the beginning and end of the universe. All actions and movements made in the visible and invisible world are musical. That is: they are made up of vibrations pertaining to a certain plane of existence. Music is called *sangita* in Sanskrit, signifying three subjects: singing, playing and dancing. These three are combined in every action. For instance, in the action of speech there is the voice signifying singing, the pronunciation of words signifying playing, and the movements of the body as well as the expression of the face signifying dancing.

Oriental music is based entirely upon a philosophical and spiritual basis. Its inventor was Mahadeva, the Lord of Yogis, and its great performer Parvati, his beloved consort. Krishna, the incarnation of God, was an expert musician who charmed both worlds by the music of his flute, making the Yogis dance. Bharata Muni, the greatest Hindu saint, was the first author of music. Mystics, such as Narada and Tumbara, were great musicians. In the heaven of the Hindus the God Indra is entertained by the classical singing of the *Gandharvas* and the dancing of the *Apsaras*. The Goddess of music is Sarasvati who is also the Goddess of wisdom; she is a great lover of the *vina*. The whole system of Hindu religion and philosophy is based on the science of vibration and is called *Nada Brahma*, Sound-God.

The poet Shams-e-Tabriz, writing of the creation, says that the whole mystery of the universe lies in sound. This fact is expressed in the Qur'an as well as in the Bible.

Fine vibrations through action become grosser in their degrees, which form the different planes of existence, ending in the physical manifestation. As water, when frozen, turns into snow, so more activity materializes the vibrations. Less activity etherealizes them, showing that spirit and matter are the same in the higher sense. Spirit descends into matter by the law of vibration, and matter may also ascend toward spirit. The great Yogis and Sufis have always progressed by the help of their practices toward the highest state of perfection by etherealizing through the knowledge of vibrations.

The material sound of instruments, or of the voice produced by the human organs of sound, is really the outcome of the universal sound of the spheres which can only be heard by those in tune with it. This state is called *anahad nada* by Yogis, and *sawt-e-sarmad* by Sufis.

The musician and the music lover become refined and are led on to the higher world of sound. Sufis lose themselves in sound and call it ecstasy, or *masti*. Psychic and occult powers come after experiencing this condition of ecstasy, and knowledge of the visible and invisible existence is disclosed. This bliss of happiness and peace is available only to the Yogis and Sufis interested in the divine art of music.

Almost all the great musicians in the Orient have become great saints through the power of music. The more recent musicians in India, such as Tansen and Maula Bakhsh, have been great examples of spiritual perfection through music.

CHAPTER III

The Music of the Spheres

1

BY THIS title I do not wish to encourage any superstition, or any ideas that might attract people into the fields of curiosity; but through this subject I wish to direct the attention of those, who search for truth, towards the law of music which is working throughout the whole universe and which, in other words, may be called the law of life, the sense of proportion, the law of harmony, the law which brings about balance, the law which is hidden behind all aspects of life, which holds this universe intact, and works out its destiny throughout the whole universe, fulfilling its purpose.

Music as we know it in our everyday language is only a miniature: that which our intelligence has grasped from that music or harmony of the whole universe which is working behind us. The music of the universe is the background of the little picture which we call music. Our sense of music, our attraction to music, shows that music is in the depth of our being. Music is behind the working of the whole universe. Music is not only life's greatest object, but music is life itself.

Hafiz, our great and wonderful poet of Persia, says: 'Many say that life entered the human body by the help of music, but the truth is that life itself is music'. I should like to tell you what made him say this. There exists in the East a legend which relates that God made a statue of clay in His own image, and asked the soul to enter into it. But the soul refused to enter into this prison, for its nature is to fly about freely, and not be limited and bound to any sort of captivity. The soul did not wish in the least to enter this prison. Then God asked the angels to play their music and, as the angels played, the soul was moved to ecstasy. Through that ecstasy – in order to make this music more clear to itself – it entered this body.

It is a beautiful legend, and much more so is its mystery. The interpretation of this legend explains to us two great laws. One is that freedom is the nature of the soul, and for the soul the whole tragedy of life is the absence of that freedom which belongs to its original nature. The next mystery that this legend reveals to us is that the only reason why the soul has entered the body of clay or matter is to experience the music of life, and to make this music clear to itself. And when we sum up these two great mysteries, the third mystery, which is the mystery of all mysteries, comes to our mind: that the unlimited part of ourselves becomes limited and earthbound for the purpose of making this life, which is the outward life, more intelligible. Therefore there is one loss and one gain. The loss is the loss of freedom, and the gain is the experience of life which is fully gained by coming to this limitation of life which we call the life of an individual.

What makes us feel drawn to music is that our whole being is music: our mind, our body, the nature in which we live, the nature that has made us, all that is beneath and around us – it is all music. As we are close to all this music and live and move and have our being in music, it therefore interests us. It attracts our attention and gives us pleasure, for it corresponds with the rhythm and tone which are keeping the mechanism of our whole being intact. What pleases us in any of our arts, whether drawing, painting, carving, architecture, or sculpture, and what interests us in poetry, is the harmony behind them which is music. It is music that poetry suggests to us: the rhythm in the poetry, or the harmony of ideas and phrases.

Besides this, in painting and in drawing it is our sense of proportion and our sense of harmony which give us all the pleasure we gain in admiring art. What appeals to us in being near to nature is nature's music, and nature's music is more perfect than that of art. It gives us a sense of exaltation to be moving about in the woods, to be looking at the green, to be standing near the running water which has its rhythm, its tone and its harmony. The swinging of the branches in the forest, the rising and falling of the waves – all has its music. Once we contemplate and become one with nature, our hearts open to its music. We say: 'I enjoy nature', and what is it in nature that we enjoy? It is its music. Something in us has been touched by the rhythmic movement, by the perfect harmony which is so seldom found in this artificial life of ours. It lifts one up and makes one feel that it is this which is the real temple, the true religion. One moment standing in the midst of nature with open heart is a whole lifetime, if one is in tune with nature.

When one looks at the cosmos, the movements of the stars and planets, the laws of vibration and rhythm – all perfect and unchanging – it shows that the cosmic system is working by the law of music, the law of harmony. Whenever that harmony in the cosmic system is lacking in any way, then in proportion disasters come about in the world, and its influence is seen in many destructive forces which manifest in the world. If there is any principle upon which the whole of astrological law is based – and the science of magic and mysticism behind it – it is music.

Therefore, for the most illuminated souls who have ever lived in this world, as for the greatest of all the prophets of India – their whole life was music. From the miniature music which we understand, they expanded themselves to the whole universe of music, and in that way they were able to inspire. The one who finds the key to the music of the whole working of life – it is he who becomes intuitive; it is he who has inspiration; it is he to whom revelations manifest, for then his language becomes music. Every object we see is revealing. In what form? It tells us its character, nature and secret. Every person who comes to us tells us his past, present and future. In what way? Every presence explains to us all that it contains. In what manner? In the form of music – if only we can hear it. There is no other language: it is rhythm, it is tone. We hear it, but we do not hear it with our ears. A friendly person shows harmony in his voice, his words, his movements and manner. An unfriendly person, in all his movements, in his glance and expression, in his walk, in everything, will show disharmony – if only one can see it. I used to amuse myself in India with a friend who became cross very easily. Sometimes when he visited me I would say: 'Are you cross to-day?' He would ask: 'Now how do you know that I am cross to-day?' I replied: 'Your turban tells me. The way you tie your turban does not show harmony'.

One's every action shows a harmonious or inharmonious attitude. There are many things you can perceive in handwriting, but the principal thing in reading handwriting is the harmonious or inharmonious curves. It almost speaks to you, and tells you the mood in which the person wrote. Handwriting tells you many things: the grade of evolution of the writer, his attitude towards life, his character. You do not need to read the letter, you only have to see his handwriting; for line and curve will show him either to be harmonious or inharmonious – if only you can see it.

In every living being you can see this, and if you look with an open insight into the nature of things, you will read even in the tree – the tree that bears fruit or flower – what music it expresses.

You can see from the attitude of a person whether that person will prove to be your friend, or will end in being your enemy. You need not wait until the end, you can see at the first glance whether he is friendly inclined or not, because every person is music, perpetual music, continually going on day and night. Your intuitive faculty can hear that music, and that is the reason why one person is repellent and the other attracts you so much: it is the music he expresses. His whole atmosphere is charged with it.

There is a story of Umar, the well-known *khalif* of Arabia. Someone who wanted to harm Umar was looking for him, and he heard that Umar did not live in palaces – although he was a king – but that he spent most of his time with nature. This man was very glad to think that now he would have every opportunity to accomplish his objective. As he approached the place where Umar was sitting, the nearer he came, the more his attitude changed, until in the end he dropped the dagger which was in his hand, and said: 'I cannot harm you. Tell me, what is the power in you that keeps me from accomplishing the objective which I came to carry out?' Umar answered: 'My at-one-ment with God'. No doubt this is a religious term, but what does that at-one-ment with God mean? It is being in tune with the Infinite, in harmony with the whole universe. In plain words, Umar was the receptacle of the music of the whole universe.

The great charm that the personality of the holy ones has shown in all ages has been their responsiveness to the music of the Whole Being. That has been the secret of how they became the friends of their worst enemies. But this is not only the power of the holy ones; this manifests in every person to a greater or less degree. Everyone shows harmony or disharmony according to how open he is to the music of the universe. The more he is open to all that is beautiful and harmonious, the more his life is tuned to that universal harmony, and the more he will show a friendly attitude towards everyone he meets, his very atmosphere will create music around him.

The difference between the material and the spiritual point of view is that the material point of view sees matter as the first thing, from which intelligence, beauty and all else evolved afterwards. From the spiritual point of view we see the intelligence and beauty first, and from them comes all that exists. From a spiritual point of view we see that what one considers last is the same as first. Therefore in the essence of this Whole Being – as its basis – there is music, as one can see that in the essence of the seed of the rose there is the rose itself, its fragrance, form and beauty. Although in the seed it is not manifest, at the same time it is there in essence. The one who tunes himself not only to the external but also to the inner being and to the essence of all things, gets an insight into the essence of the Whole Being, and therefore he can find and enjoy that fragrance and flower which he sees in the rose, to the same extent even in the seed.

The great error of this age is that activity has increased so much that there is little margin left in one's everyday life for repose. Repose is the secret of all contemplation and meditation, the secret of getting in tune with that aspect of life which is the essence of all things. When one is not accustomed to take repose, one does not know what is behind one's being. This condition is experienced by first preparing the body, and also the mind, by means of purification. And by making the senses finer one is able to tune one's soul with the Whole Being.

It seems complex, and yet it is so simple. When one is open to one's tried friend in life, one knows so much about him. It is only the opening of the heart; it is only at-one-ment with one's friend; we know his faults and his merits. We know how to experience and to enjoy friendship. Where there is hatred and prejudice and bitterness, there is loss of understanding. The deeper the person, the more friends he has. It is smallness, narrowness, lack of spiritual development which makes a person exclusive, distant and different from others. He feels superior, greater and better than others; his friendly attitude seems to have been lost. In that way he cuts himself apart from others, and in this lies his tragedy. That person is never happy.

The one who is happy is he who is ready to be friends with all. His outlook on life is friendly. He is not only friendly to persons, but also to objects and conditions. It is by this attitude of friendship that man expands and breaks down those walls which keep him in prison. And by breaking down those walls he experiences at-one-ment with the Absolute. This at-one-ment with the Absolute manifests as the music of the spheres, and this he experiences on all sides: beauties of nature, colour of flowers, everything he sees, everyone he meets. In the hours of contemplation and solitude, and in the hours when he is in the midst of the world, always the music is there, always he is enjoying the harmony.

2

There are many in this world who look for wonders. If one only noticed how much there is in this world which is all phenomena! The deeper one sees into life, the wider life opens itself to one, and then every moment of one's life becomes full of wonders and full of splendours. What we call music in everyday language is only a miniature of that which is behind this all, and which has been the source and origin of this nature. It is therefore that the wise of all ages have considered music to be a sacred art; for in music the seer can see the picture of the whole universe, and in the realm of music the wise can interpret the secret and nature of the working of the whole universe.

This idea is not a new idea; at the same time it is always new. Nothing is as old as the truth, and nothing is as new as the truth. Man's desire to search for something traditional, for something original, and man's desire for something new – all these tendencies can be satisfied in the knowledge of truth.

In the *Vedas* of the Hindus we read: *Nada Brahma* – sound, being the Creator. In the works of the wise of ancient India we read: 'First song, then *Vedas* or wisdom'. When we come to the Bible, we find: 'First was the word, and the word was God', and when we come to the Qur'an we read that the word was pronounced, and all creation was manifest. This shows that the origin of the whole creation is sound.

No doubt the word, in the way it is used in our everyday language, is a limitation of that sound which is suggested by these Scriptures. Language is made up of names of comparable objects, and that which cannot be compared has no name. Truth is that which can never be spoken and, what the wise of all ages have spoken, is what they have tried their best to express, little as they were able to do so.

There is in Persian literature a poem by Hafiz who tells us that, when God commanded the soul to enter the human body, which is made of clay, the soul refused. Then angels were asked to sing and on hearing the angels sing the soul entered the body which it had feared to be a prison. It is a philosophy which is poetically expressed in this story. Hafiz remarked: 'People say that on hearing the song the soul entered into the body, but in reality the soul itself was song'.

Those who have probed the depth of material science as far as modern science can reach, do not deny the fact that the origin of the whole creation is in movement, in other words: in vibration. It is this original state of the existence of life which is called in the ancient tradition sound, or the word. The first manifestation of this sound is therefore audible, the next manifestation visible. In the forms of expression of life, life has expressed itself first as sound, next as light. This is supported by the Bible where it is said that first was the word, and then came light. Again one finds in a *Sura* of the Qur'an: 'God is the light of the heaven and the earth'.

The nature of the creation is the doubling of one, and it is this doubling aspect which is the cause of all duality in life. This doubling aspect represents one positive part, the other part being negative; one expressive, the other responsive. Therefore, in this creation of duality, spirit and nature stand face to face. And as there is the first aspect, which I have called sound, and the next, which I have called light, at first in these opposite nature aspects, or responsive aspects, only the light works, and if the creation goes still deeper there is sound. In nature, which is face to face with spirit, what is first expressed is light – or what man first responds to is light, and what man responds to next is what touches him deeper: it is sound.

The human body is a vehicle of the spirit, a finished vehicle which experiences all the different aspects of creation. This does not mean that all other forms and names that exist in the world – some as objects, others as creatures – are not responsive to the expression of the spirit. Really speaking, every object is responsive to the spirit and to the work of the spirit which is active in all aspects, in all names and forms of this universe. One reads in the great work of Maulana Rumi, a Persian poet and mystic, that earth, water, fire and air before man are objects, but before God are living beings: they work at His command – as man understands living beings working under the command of a master.

If the whole creation can be well explained, it is by the phases of sound or vibration, which have manifested in different grades in all their various forms in life. Objects and names and forms are but the expression of vibrations in different aspects. Even all that we call matter or substance, and all that does not seem to speak or sound – it is all in reality vibration.

The beauty of the whole creation is this, that creation has worked in two ways; in one way it has expressed, and in the other way it has made itself a mould in order to respond. For instance, there is substance – matter to touch – and there is a sense to feel touch. There is a sound, and at the same time there is the sense of hearing to perceive the sound. There is light, there is form, there are colours, and at the same time there are eyes to see them.

What man calls beauty is the harmony of all he experiences. What after all is music? What we call music is the harmony of the audible notes. In reality there is music in colour, there is music in lines, there is music in the forest where there is a variety of trees and plants, in the way in which they correspond with each other. The more widely one observes nature, the more it appeals to one's soul. Why? Because there is a music there. And to the extent to which one sees more deeply into life and observes life more widely, one listens to more and more music – the music which answers the whole universe.

But the one whose heart is open – he need not go as far as the forest; in the midst of the crowd he can find music. At this time human ideas are so changed, owing to materialism, that there is no distinction of personality. But if one studies human nature one finds that even a piano of a thousand octaves cannot produce the variety that human nature represents: how people agree with one another, how they disagree; some become friends after a contact of one moment, and some in thousand years cannot become friends. If one could only see to what pitch the different souls are tuned, in what octave different people speak, what standard different people have! Sometimes there are two persons who disagree, and there comes a third person and all unite together. Is this not the nature of music? The more one studies the harmony of music, and then studies human nature – how people agree, and how they disagree, how there is attraction and repulsion – the more one sees that it is all music.

But now there is another question to be understood. What man knows is generally the world that he sees around himself. Very few people trouble to think that there is something beyond that which they realize around themselves. To many it is a story, when they hear that there are two worlds. But if one looks deep within oneself, there are not only two worlds, there are so many worlds that it is beyond expression. That part of one's being which is receptive is mostly closed in the average man. What he knows is to express outwardly and to receive from this same sphere as much as he can receive by himself. For instance, the difference between a simple man and a thinking person with deeper understanding is that, when the simple person has received a word only in his ears, the thinking person has received the same word as far as his mind. So the same word has reached the ears of the one, and the heart of the other. This man whose ears the word has touched has only seen the word, but he whose heart the word has touched has seen deeper. If this simple example is true, it can be understood that one person lives only in the external world, while another lives in two worlds, and a third person may live in many worlds at the same time. When one asks: Where are those worlds? Are they above the sky, or down below the earth? – the answer is: All these worlds are in the same place as we are. As a poet has said: 'The heart of man, if once expanded, becomes larger than all the heavens'.

The deep thinkers of all ages have therefore held one principle of awakening to life, and that principle is: emptying the self. In other words, making oneself a clearer and fuller accommodation in order to accommodate all experiences more clearly and more fully. All the tragedy of life, all its sorrows and pains belong mostly to the surface of the life in the world. If one were fully awake to life, if one could respond to life, if one could perceive life, one would not need to look for wonders, one would not need to communicate with spirits; for every atom in this world is a wonder for the one who sees with open eyes.

In answer to the question: What is the experience of those who dive deep into life, and who touch the depth within? – there is a verse in Persian by Hafiz who has said: 'It is not known how far is the destination, but so much I know: that music from afar is coming to my ears'. The music of the spheres, according to the point of view of the mystic, is like the lighthouse in the port that a man sees from the sea; it promises him that he is coming nearer to the destination.

Now one may say: What music may this be? If there were no harmony in the essence of life, life would not have created harmony in this world of variety. Man would not have longed for something which was not already in his spirit. Everything in this world which seems to lack harmony is in reality the limitation of man's own vision. The wider the horizon of his observation becomes, the more harmony of life he enjoys. In the very depth of man's being the harmony of the working of the whole universe sums up in a perfect music. Therefore, the music which is the source of creation, the music which is found near the goal of creation, is the music of the spheres. And it is heard and enjoyed by those who touch the very depth of their own lives.

CHAPTER IV

The Mysticism of Sound

Before its incarnation the soul is sound.
It is for this reason that we love sound.

THE MAN of science says that the voice comes from the spine,
the diaphragm, the abdomen and the lungs. The mystic says
that sound comes from the soul, the heart and the mind. Let us
see whether this is true. Before we sing or speak the thought
of singing or speaking comes. If we have not the thought we
cannot sing or speak, and before the thought there is the feeling
that causes the thought. In order to make the thought concrete
we must speak.

The sound goes through the ear to the mind, the heart and
the soul. When the feeling, when the thought is spoken, its
power becomes greater. If a person speaks of his sorrow, if
he tells his grief to another, often he may begin to cry. While
he kept the feeling in his heart, the thought in his mind, he did
not cry, but when he spoke he wept. Sometimes a humorous
person, when telling something funny that he has seen, begins
to laugh at his own words. While he only thought of it he did
not laugh, but when he speaks of it he laughs. If we keep a
thought in our mind, it has not the strength that it has when
we speak it out.

If you repeat: flower, flower, flower, your mind will be
much more impressed than if you only think of the flower.
This is why the Sufis repeat the name of God, and do not only
think of God. There are Sufis who repeat the ninety-nine
names of God. There is the *wazifa*, the *namaz*; there are different ways of repeating the name of God. The effect produced is
in accordance with the soul and the heart from which the sound
comes. If there are four violinists, all of whom have studied for
the same length of time, and they all play the same piece of
music one after the other, they will each play very differently.
Each will play in accordance with his musical temperament,

his heart and his soul. Therefore it is very necessary for a musician that his heart and soul should be trained.

The shopman, after he has given us the change, says: 'Thank you'. That 'thank you' is forgotten before we have gone two steps, because it comes from the lips. A grateful person may say: 'Thank you' – only that, but it goes to the heart, because it comes from the heart. One singer may sing just one note, and all the audience is moved. Another sings dozens of notes, and no effect is made.

The force of the sound is in proportion to its duration. If we strike a stone, it gives out a short sound that has no effect. If we strike a bell, the sound is more lasting and the effect greater. If we prolong a tone the effect is greater, for the life is greater. Sound is breath, the breath which is life. If there is a bell and a stone, and if an organ is played or a piano, the bell will give out a sound, but the stone will not. That which is alive gives out a sound that is alive. That which is dead gives none. The soul which is dead gives no sound. That is why in the ordinary song there are many notes, but not one note that lives. All are dead sounds. The music of the great composers lives still. Its echo has come down to us; the echo of the great souls is still here. Thousands who have never thought of anything but the self have gone, and we do not even know that they have existed. The dead souls, the ordinary people, go to hear that dead song. The living soul hears the music that is alive.

The finer people go to see the tragedy where they are moved and shed a few tears. The ordinary people go to the moving picture where they laugh. The heart finds a joy in feeling, in sorrow. It feels that it is used, and in that there is a happiness. The Sufi trains the heart in feeling. There are assemblies among them where *qawl* is sung and played, the music of devotion and praise, the music that arouses feeling, the feeling of devotion, of sorrow, of repentance: to think how foolish we are, how stupid we are, how many mistakes we make. Every feeling is practised. When the heart is made capable of feeling, it can feel the sorrow and joy of others. Every thing touches it, every little sign of mercy, every feeling of admiration. In this there is happiness.

Our feeling must be in our power. A person says: 'I spoke like that because I was angry!' – Yes, but why was he angry?

One says: 'I cry because I am sad. I cannot help being sad; the sadness comes' – or: 'I laugh because I feel humorous'. Sorrow and mirth should be under control. The feeling of kindness must be kept as long as we wish, whatever obstacle we meet with. When this control is learned, then no sorrow can come near.

Then there is the music of the soul. In this there is no feeling, no devotion. There are few words, the syllables have a hidden meaning.[1] It is to awaken the soul, to make the soul conscious of its immortal life.

The longer the thought is kept in the mind, the stronger it becomes. The mystic keeps one thought in the mind for ten minutes, for twenty minutes. He practises this. He practises it with music. First he impresses one *Raga* upon his mind until it is fixed in his mind like a picture. Then he improves upon the *Raga* and looks at that picture like a painter who paints and then looks at his picture. Then he practises the sound only, without melody, one sound or – to break the monotony – two sounds, or three sounds. After that he hums. He keeps all feeling away. There is no anger, no bitterness, no prejudice, no attachment, nothing that keeps him bound to the ego. Then there is no outward sound; he keeps the sound in his mind. Then he begins to hear the sound of the breath, the fine sound that the ears cannot hear.

A very materialistic person has a loud breath, audible to all. The finer a person, the finer is his breath. He hears the sound of his heart: what it speaks, and he hears what the heart of another speaks. This is thought-reading. First he must hear what his own heart says; then he hears what is in the heart of others – in their presence and in their absence. We are accustomed to call that which our ears hear sound, but there is also the sound of the mind, of the heart, of the soul.

Why do we all like to be alone? We may think that we like to be where we have some company, to talk, to be in the society of others, but we are not happy unless we are alone, away from the town, sitting by some stream or lake. It is because then, unconsciously, we hear the sound of the soul. This sound the Sufi hears in the *shagl*, in the *qasb**. It is very difficult, because

---

* Mystical breathing exercises.

for this all the tubes and veins must be open. The soul is a finer essence, and if the veins and tubes are blocked by the fluids, by very much eating and drinking, by alcoholic substances, by very much sleep, by very much comfort and luxury, this sound cannot enter.

The Vedanta speaks of *Nada Brahma*, the Sound-God, the sound that is God, of which all things are made. Sufis call it *sawt-e-sarmad*, the sound that intoxicates man. The Qur'an says: '*Kun fa-yakun* – when God said "Be", it became'. Before this world was, all was in sound, God was sound, we are made of sound. That is why we like music. That is why you are listening to this*, because it is your element. Although it has been dimmed by manifestation, your thought, your mind, is made of sound.

---

* These words show that this address was probably given after a musical performance.

CHAPTER V

The Mystery of Sound

SOUND IS perceptible activity of the all pervading life. Different sounds differ in their outer expression, but within it is one and the same activity which directs all sounds. It is in expression that sounds differ, because of the different instruments through which they are expressed. The deeper we penetrate into the mystery of sound, the more we are able to trace the link that connects all sounds. This link is what the musician calls harmony, and it is in harmony that is hidden the secret of joy and peace.

As one sound is directed by another sound, so every motion is caused by another motion. Therefore no activity can take place without a directing activity, and that activity which directs all is called God. This supports the argument of the fatalist that all is done by God, and it also proves the view of the metaphysician that there is no such thing as chance. At the same time it explains that freewill remains, since each sound, in its outward manifestation, hides within itself its directing activity, so that behind what man calls freewill there is hidden God's will.

As sound takes varying manifestations through different instruments, one sound helps another, harmonizes with another, and one sound differs from another, or covers it. All this is merely caused by the instruments, their response to the directing power within, and their relation to each other.

This symbolism explains all different aspects of life, and shows that good and evil, pleasure and pain, right and wrong, all come from one source. Thus the chief consolation of the thinker is the understanding of the mystery of life, which understanding affords contentment under all kinds of conditions.

The mystic need not follow the principle of contentment unless for convenience. The mystic must be able to rise to the cause instead of laying himself helpless at the feet of the effect. It is that mastery which is called *walayat* in Sufi terms.

It has been shown how every external activity is directed by an inner motion and how, at the source of it, there is a principal cause. It must be understood that every wave of life which is set in motion by the principal cause, works toward a purpose. With its every motion the purpose becomes more definite, and at its every stage of evolution it adjusts itself, making a perfect harmony – although in a limited space this same activity may appear inharmonious. Therefore good and evil, right and wrong, when viewed by the keen sight, correspond with a certain purpose, and thus prove harmonious from the standpoint of the perfect Whole.

Every life-wave which starts from the innermost part of life becomes stronger with its every succeeding motion. It is a gentle impetus given to a wheel that sets it in motion, and every revolution increases its power. The Sufi recognizes three stages of movement. These three stages need not be the same in all aspects of life, since every activity adopts the form of a circle, a wheel, and it is according to its circumference that it covers the ground. Thus these three stages may be called slow, moderately fast, and fast.

At the same time every activity forms a habit which limits each motion to a certain interval of time, and it is this character of life which forms rhythm. Just as it is necessary that motion should be the source and sustaining power of life, so it is necessary that rhythm should exist in every activity. No motion can exist without rhythm. Rhythm, when of an even nature, is felt by everybody, but when uneven it is not perceived.

There are two elements in rhythm, mobility and regularity. The former has a forward, and the latter a lateral movement. The form taken by the movement of rhythm can be seen by observing light which, to the vision of the concentrative mind, is shown to have the form of the cross.

The variety found in all aspects of life results mainly from these three stages of rhythm and its two main elements. But out of these two main elements there arises a third chaotic motion in which mobility and regularity clash together. By recognizing its rhythm the mystic understands from the character of every activity the cause and result of that particular activity.

The first element in rhythm – mobility – is gentle, productive, creative and progressive. The second element is
active, supporting and controlling. It is also productive and
creative in a more advanced state of things, and it is sustaining.
The third element leads to inactivity, decay, destruction and
death. The idea of *Trimurti* – three aspects of God – is the
symbol among the Hindus of these three powers working
as main principles in life. They are named *Brahma* – Creator,
Vishnu – Sustainer, *Shiva* – Destroyer.

There are two stages in every activity, action and result.
Action manifests itself in audibility, and results in visibility.
In the Bible there is a statement about this: that first there
was the word and then there came light. The Qur'an in this
connection says that first the word was spoken, and then all
became manifest. This is seen in some form or other in every
activity which descends from the invisible to the visible. The
preparatory stage of all things is audible, and when finished
they are visible. In other words, from the world of sound
there came the world of forms. Therefore the Hindus call
Nada Brahma, the Sound-God, the Creator.

All things can be studied and understood by understanding the nature of the perfect life. God can be studied and
understood by the study and understanding of human nature,
and man can be studied and understood by the study and
understanding of God.

Since all things are made by the power of sound, of
vibration, so every thing is made by a portion thereof, and
man can create his world by the same power. Among all
aspects of knowledge the knowledge of sound is supreme,
for all aspects of knowledge depend upon the knowing of
form, except that of sound, which is beyond all form. By the
knowledge of sound man obtains the knowledge of creation,
and the mastery of that knowledge helps man to rise to the
formless. This knowledge acts as wings for a man; it helps him
to rise from earth to heaven, and he can penetrate through the
life seen and unseen.

The whole manifestation being the phenomenon of sound,
the knowledge of sound is the key to the mystery. The
knowledge of sound acts as a guide in the maze of names
and forms. That is the reason for the great importance attached

by the Yogis to *mantrayoga* which to the Sufis is dhikr (Zikar). There is nothing man cannot accomplish by the power of *dhikr*, if only he knows which *dhikr*, how to use it, and for what purpose. Just as there is creative power in sound, so is there also destructive power, as in the Scriptures the expression 'the blast of the last trumpet' signifies the destructive power of the sound.

CHAPTER VI

The Mystery of Colour and Sound

1

THE ATTRACTION that one finds in colour and in sound makes one wonder if there is a mystery hidden behind them, if there is a language of colour and sound which could be learned. The answer is that the language of colour and sound is the language of the soul, and that it is our outward language which makes us confused as to the meaning of that inner language. Colour and sound are the language of life. Life expresses itself on all different planes of existence in the form of colour and sound, but the outward manifestations of life are so rigid and dense that the secret of their nature and character becomes buried underneath.

Why is the world called an illusion by the mystics? Because the nature of manifestation is such that it envelops its own secret within itself, and stands out in such a rigid form that the fineness, the beauty, and the mystery of its character are hidden within itself. Therefore the seekers after the truth of life, the students of life, strike two opposite paths. The one wishes to learn from the external appearance, the other wishes to find out the secret which is hidden behind it. The one who learns from the external gets the knowledge of the external, which we call science. The one who finds out from the within, from that which is hidden within this manifestation – he is the mystic; the knowledge he gains is mysticism.

The first question that comes to the mind of the intelligent person is: What is it in colour and in sound that appeals to us? It is the tone and rhythm, of colour as well as of sound, which have an influence on the tone and rhythm of our being. Our being is our capacity for the resonance of the tone and rhythm which come from sound and colour. This capacity enables us to be influenced by sound and colour. Thus some have a liking for a certain colour, others have a liking for another colour. In the way of sound some are attracted to a certain kind of sound. In the range of voice some are attracted to the baritone or to the bass voice, others are attracted to the tenor and soprano. There are some to whom the deep sound of the cello appeals; there are others who are interested in the sound of the violin; some can enjoy even the thick sound of the horn and the trombone; others can enjoy the flute. What does this show? It shows that there is a certain capacity in our hearts, in our being, and it depends upon that particular capacity what kind of sound appeals to us.

At the same time, it depends upon man's grade of evolution, his character, his nature – whether he is gross or fine – also upon his temperament – whether he has a practical nature or is dreamy, whether he loves the drama of life, or whether he is absorbed in the ordinary things of life. According to man's condition, his temperament and his evolution, colour and sound affect him, and the proof of this is that man so often changes his fancy in regard to colour. There is a time when he is so fond of red; there are times when he longs to see purple, or when he dreams of mauve. And then there comes a time when he takes a fancy to blue; he craves for yellow, for orange. There are some who like deep colours, others light colours. It all depends on their temperament and their grade of evolution.

There is always someone to whom music of any kind appeals; the best or the worst, somebody likes it! Have you not seen how children can enjoy themselves with a little tin can and a stick? The rhythm comes within their capacity of enjoyment. Human nature is such that it takes in everything, all put together, from the highest to the lowest. It has such a wide capacity that there is nothing left out; everything has its place, and all is assimilated by human nature.

At the same time there is action and reaction. It is not only his grade of evolution that makes man change his fancy to different colours and tones, but it is also the different colours and tones that help him in his evolution, and that change the speed of his evolution.

Very often man gives great importance to colour and tone – so much so that he forgets that which is behind them, and that leads him to many superstitions, fancies and imaginations. Many people have fooled the simple ones by telling them what colour belonged to their souls, or what note belonged to their lives. Man is so ready to respond to anything that can puzzle him and confuse his mind! He is so willing to be fooled! He enjoys it so much if somebody tells him that his colour is yellow, or green, or that his note is C, D, or F on the piano. He does not care to find out why. It is like telling somebody: 'Wednesday is your day, and Tuesday some other person's'.

In point of fact all days are ours, all colours are ours. It is man who is the master of all manifestation. It is for man to use all colours and tones; they are at his disposal, for him to use and make the best of. It would be a great pity if we were subjected to one colour and tone. There would be no life in this; it would be a form of death. The staircase is made for us to ascend, not for us to continue stepping in one place. Every step is our step, if only we take it.

Coming to the mystical point of view, the first aspect that makes Intelligence conscious of the manifestation is sound. The next aspect is light or colour. All the mystics and prophets and great thinkers of the world, when expressing the history of creation, have in all periods of history given the first place to sound. The scientist of today says the same thing. He calls it radiance, atom, electron, and after going through all the different atoms of substance he arrives at a substance that he calls movement. Movement is vibration. It is only the effect of motion which we call sound. Motion speaks, and we call speech sound because it is audible. When it is not audible, this is because there is no sufficient capacity to make it audible. But the cause of sound is movement, and movement is always there. This means that the existence of movement does not depend upon capacity.

Colour also is movement, and its capacity makes colour concrete to our vision. At the same time, although we may call a colour green or red or yellow, every colour is different to each person. In fine shades of colour people do not see alike, because the capacity is different in each of them. The tone is according to the capacity. In other words, it is not the tone or the colour which differ in value; they become different when we sense them, when we feel them: in their relation to us they are different.

The conception of the five elements, which the mystics have held at all times, cannot be explained in scientific terms, because the mystics have their peculiar meaning. Although the elements may be called water, fire, air, earth and ether, this must not be taken as such. Their nature and character, according to the mystics, are different. But as words are few, one cannot give other names to the elements, although in Sanskrit there are different words for these. 'Ether' is not ether in scientific terms, it is capacity. 'Water' is not water as we understand it in everyday language, it is liquidity. 'Fire' is understood differently; it means glow, or heat, or dryness, or radiance, all that is living. All of these words suggest something more than what is meant by earth, fire, water, etc.

The working of these five elements is distinguished by different colours and sounds. The five elements are represented by sound in the musical scales which are called *Ragas*. In India and China the *Raga* of five notes is considered the most appealing, and I myself have experienced that the scale of five notes is much more appealing than the scale of seven notes. The scale of seven notes lacks some vital influence that the scale of five notes possesses. In ancient times the scales by which miracles were performed were mostly the scales of five notes.

There is a relation between sound and colour. When he hears something, the first tendency a man has is to open his eyes to try to see the colour of it. That is not the way to see it. Colour is a language. The very life which is audible is visible also. But where? It is visible on the inner plane. The mistake is that man looks for it on the outer plane; when he hears music he wants to see the colour before him. Every activity of the outer world is a kind of reaction; in other words, a shadow of the activity which is behind it and which we do not see. Also there is a difference in time. An activity which has taken place twelve hours earlier is now visible in colour on the outer plane, and it is the same with the effect of dreams on life. Of something that one has perhaps seen in a dream at night, one will see the effect in the morning, or a week later. This shows that there is some activity which takes place behind the scenes and is reflected on the outer life, according to how the activities of the outer life are directed.

This is the reason why a seer or mystic is often able to know beforehand his own condition, and the condition of others – what is coming, or what has passed, or what is going on at a distance; for he knows the language of sound and colour. Now the question is: On which plane does he know the language of sound and colour? In what way do they manifest to him? One cannot restrict this to a certain law, and at the same time it has a certain law. Where does he see it? He sees it in his breath.

The whole culture of spiritual development, therefore, is based upon the science of breath. What makes the Yogis, the mystics, see happenings of the past, present and future? Some law behind the creation. A certain working of the mechanism which is a finer mechanism. How can it be seen? By opening one's vision to one's self.

According to the mystics there are five capacities of one's being which may be called five *akashas*. The one capacity which everybody knows and is conscious of, is what may be called the receptacle of food, which is the body. The second, which is more or less recognized, is the receptacle of sense, which is in the senses. The third capacity is called the receptacle of life, and this capacity is a world in itself where one is conscious of the finer forces of life which are working within oneself. They can convey to one a sense of the past, present, or future, for the reason that they are clear to one's vision: one sees them.*

But one may ask: 'How can a man find out the condition of another?' It is not so that he can know more about others, for he is made to know most about himself. But many are unconscious of the third receptacle, that of life. The one who is conscious of his receptacle of life is able to empty the capacity he has, and to give a chance to the life of another person to reflect upon it. This he does by focusing upon the life of another, and by that he covers the past, present and future: he only has to make the camera stand in the right place.

It is exactly like photography. The plate is there; it is clear because man is able to empty his own capacity. The black cloth that the photographer puts over the camera and over his head is concentration. When man has mastered concentration

* For a complete explanation of the five akashas see 'The Story of Lot's Wife' in Volume IX.

he becomes the photographer. He can focus all the light upon one spot. It is all scientific when we understand it in this way, but it becomes a puzzle when it is put before us as a mystery. All is mystery when we do not know it; when we know it all is simple. The true seekers after truth are lovers of simplicity. The right road is simple, clear and distinct. There is nothing vague about it.

The more one follows the path exploring the mystery of life, the more life becomes revealed to one. Life begins to express its secret, its nature. What is required of man is an honest following of life's law, and nothing in this world is more important than the knowing of human nature and the study of human life. That study lies in the study of self, and it is the study of self which is really the study of God.

Question: What is the difference between sound and colour?
Answer: Sound and colour are one, they are two aspects of life. Life and light are one. Life is light, and light is life, and so colour is sound, and sound is colour. But where sound is colour it is most visible and least audible, and where colour is sound it is most audible and least visible. You can find the unity of colour and sound by studying and practising the science of the culture of breath.

2

Both from the point of view of the Sufi and that of all mystics the original state of the whole creation is vibration, and vibration manifests in two forms, or stages. In its original condition vibration is inaudible and invisible, but in its first stage towards manifestation it becomes audible, and in its next step visible.

In its audible stage it is called *nada* in Vedantic terms – a word which means sound – or *Nada Brahma* which represents: Sound the Creator, Sound the creative Spirit. The next stage is called *jatanada* – a word which means light. It is the different degrees of that light and their comparison with one another which give rise to the various colours. Colours are only the different shades of light; compared with one another they are colours, but in reality the light makes all colours. This is shown by the light of the sun which has no particular colour of its own, but the light of which plants partake manifests in the colours of their flowers. These colours seem to be the colours of flowers, vegetables and leaves, whereas in reality they are the colours of the sun.

In the case of souls we may also realize that the manifestation of such a variety among them is an illusion too. One forgets that all the various faces and endless forms of human beings belong to one Spirit and are the manifestatons of that one Spirit. When one begins to understand the theory of colour and sound, one can begin to understand that too. For instance, what is sound? The different notes are the various degrees of breath: human breath, or the echo coming from a vessel, an instrument, or a bell, for that also is breath – the breath of human beings as well as the breath of objects. From the one breath many sounds manifest; so that takes one back again to the idea of unity. All this variety of colours and forms and sounds proceeds from one single source.

Associated with this there is the question of the mysticism of number. This is the idea of rhythm. Every movement must have its rhythm. There cannot be movement without rhythm. By rhythm we imagine the intervals of time, such as hour or minute, or in music crochet, quaver, semibreve. All these arise from our habit of dividing time into rhythm. We do this because our life itself depends on rhythm. The beating of the pulse, of the heart, in the head – all show life's rhythm.

The science of numbers comes from the science of rhythm. A certain number comes to denote a certain duration of time; every action or movement requires a certain time and has a corresponding effect. Every effect which is produced by colour, sound or number depends upon their harmonious or inharmonious effect. If the sound is not harmonious, it has not a desirable effect upon us; if a colour is not harmonious it also has an undesirable effect. This shows that it is not the particular number or sound which gives the desirable effect, but the harmony. That is why a knowledge of the effect of sound, colour or number is insufficient without a development of a sense of harmony in oneself, so that one can understand the harmonious effect of these things.

The mystics have seen five *tatwas*, or elements, working behind both the sound and the rhythm, although musicians consider seven notes in a scale. The original scale known to the mystics had five numbers, and there were five kinds of scales among the ancient people, with five different classes of rhythm. They took five colours to represent the five elements.

People often say: 'This colour is lucky and that one is unlucky. This number is lucky and that one is unlucky'. But it is not the particular colour or number in itself, it is the harmony of the situation which is lucky or unlucky: in what relation do that particular number and colour stand to you, to your life's affairs, your own constitution, your stage of evolution. If they stand in harmony with your life then they are harmonious and lucky. If not, they are inharmonious and unlucky. This does not mean that a particular colour is inharmonious; it is just how it stands in your life that decides whether it is harmonious or not.

So it is with sounds. But the power of sound is greater than the power of colour. Why is this? It is because sound arises from the depth of one's being, and because sound can also touch the depth of one's being. The *mantrayoga* of the Hindus is based on this principle. The Sufi term for this is *dhikr* (zikar): that is the use of words for the unfoldment of the soul. But it is not merely for bringing about any desired result that words can be used in *dhikr*. People often make the mistake of using the word without any spiritual idea behind it, simply for the attainment of some magical power. The Sufis of all ages have warned against this mistake, and have constantly taught that there is only one object worth striving for, the essential object of life, namely God. It is only when the science of words is being used for the attainment of truth, that is: for the attainment of God, that it is being used in the right manner. To use it for any other purpose whatever, is just like paying out pearls to buy pebbles.

We must remember the teaching of Christ, how he says: 'Render to Caesar the things that are Caesar's and to God the things that belong to God'. In other words, give to the world what belongs to the world, and give to God what belongs to God, namely: love, worship, reverence, devotion, trust, confidence. All those are due to God, so give them to God. That which belongs to the world is: wealth, money, service, sympathy, kindness, tolerance, forgiveness. All these are due to the world, so give them to the world. We only make a mistake when we give to the world what is for God, and when we do for God what belongs to the world; for instance, when a man flatters another man, and when man depends upon a human being instead of depending upon God. All those things which belong to God and are due to God we fail to give Him, and give them to man instead.

When all things which we gain are used for a selfish purpose, we at once become confronted with difficulties, troubles and disappointments. That is why the same mystical science may be used as a means of attaining God, or may be abused by turning it into a way called black magic. It is not that there is something special called black magic, or that there is something else called white magic; magic is all one and the same. It is how we use it that makes the difference; it is the use of it which makes it right or wrong, good or bad.

A question may be asked regarding the mysticism of colour and sound: Can we get our individual colour or note? The answer is that in the first place it is not a matter of our own colour being good for us. It is whether a number or colour is in harmony with us or not that makes it good or not. In the second place, at every moment of our life our evolution changes. A person who was a thief yesterday is not a thief today. So also a given number or colour belonging to us at one moment does not belong to us at another moment; it changes every moment. Therefore, to restrict oneself to a certain number or colour is like tying one's feet with a chain, so that no more progress can take place. In the third place, were we to settle upon a particular number or colour, we might induce a tendency to superstition in our nature, and this we must always avoid. We would always be thinking: What is the number of the house we are going to live in? What is the colour of the room I shall occupy? What is the colour of the dress? And so on! What would it be then if the person was obliged to live in that particular house, or was obliged to occupy that room in the hotel? If the number was inharmonious, he would think everything would go wrong while staying there!

While it is always well to learn everything one can, it is not good to give in to superstition. Otherwise it would be better never to have known such things at all. The whole aim of the Sufi is to reach to reality, and anything savouring of superstition should be avoided. What is colour after all? It is an illusion. What is number? It is an illusion. What are forms? They are illusions too. It is interesting to a certain extent to know about these things and to distinguish them. It gives a certain knowledge. But since these are all illusions, how can it be worthwhile to give oneself absolutely to them and to neglect the unfolding of the self, besides at the same time neglecting the search for the reality, the only aim of the soul? Therefore all other knowledge and all other pursuits should be given a secondary place. Our main pursuit must be after Truth, believing as we do that in the Truth there is God.

CHAPTER VII

The Spiritual Significance of Colour and Sound

IT SEEMS that what science realizes in the end, mysticism
reaches from the beginning. This accords with the saying of
Christ: 'First seek ye the Kingdom of God and all will be
added'. When one hears of the present discoveries about sound
and colour on the scientific side, one begins by being surprised.
One says: 'What a new discovery! Something we have never
heard of. It is something quite new'. And yet, when you open
the Bible there it says: 'First was the word, and the word was
God'. And if you open still older scriptures of the Vedanta, you
read in their verses that in the Creator there was that word, or
that vibration. When we come to the Qur'an we read: that first
there was the word 'Be', and then there became.

The religions of the world, the prophets and mystics who
existed ages ago knew these things. Today a man comes with
a little photographic plate and says: 'Here I have a photograph
of sound; that shows how important is vibration and its action
upon the plate'. He does not know that this is something
which has always been known, and has been spoken of by
those who knew it – but in spiritual terms. Therefore man
does not think about what was spoken of in the past; he thinks
that what is being spoken of today is something new. But
when we realize that – as Solomon has said – there is nothing
new under the sun, we begin to enjoy life seeing how, time
after time, the same wisdom is revealed to man. The one who
seeks through science, the one who searches through religion,
the one who finds it through philosophy, the one who finds it
through mysticism – in whatever manner they seek the truth,
they find it in the end.

I was once introduced in New York to a scientist, a
philosopher. The first thing he said about his accomplish-
ments was: 'I have discovered the soul'. It amused me very
much! All the Scriptures have spoken about it, thinkers have
spoken about it, mystics have spoken about it, the prophets
have spoken about it, and this man comes and says: 'I have
discovered the soul!' I thought: 'Yes, that was the new

discovery that we were expecting – something that we never knew!' Such is the attitude of mind today, the childish attitude. When one looks into the past, the present and the future one sees that life is eternal, and what one can discover is that which has always been discovered by those who seek. Philosophy or science, mysticism or esotericism will all agree on one point if they touch the summit of their knowledge, and that point is that behind the whole of creation, behind the whole of manifestation – if there is any subtle trace of life that can be found, it is motion, it is movement, it is vibration.

This motion has its two aspects. There are two aspects because we have developed two principal faculties: sight and hearing. One aspect appeals to our hearing, the other to our sight. The aspect of movement or vibration which appeals to our hearing is what we call audible and what we term sound. The aspect which appeals to our sight we call light, we call it colour, and we call it visible. In point of fact, all that is visible, all that is audible – what is it in its origin? It is motion, it is movement, it is vibration, it is one and the same thing. Therefore, even in that which is audible, in that which is called sound, those who can see trace colour, and to those who can hear, even the sound of the colour is audible.

Is there anything that unites these two things? Yes, there is. And what is it? It is harmony. It is not a particular colour which is harmonious, or which lacks harmony. It is the blending of that colour; it is in what frame it is fixed; how the colour is arranged. In accordance with that it has its effect upon the one who sees. So it is with sound. There is not any sound which is harmonious or inharmonious in itself; it is the relation of one sound with another sound that creates harmony. Therefore harmony is not a thing that one can point out; one cannot say: 'This or that certain thing is harmony'. Harmony is a fact. Harmony is the result of the relation between colour and colour, the relation between sound and sound, and the relation between colour and sound.

The most interesting part of this knowledge is how to different persons different colours appeal, and how different people enjoy different sounds. The more one studies this, the more one finds its relation with the particular advancement of man's evolution; for one will find that at a certain time of one's evolution one loved a certain colour, and then one lost contact with that colour. With one's growth and evolution in life one begins to like some other colour. It also depends upon a person's condition, whether he is emotional, passionate, romantic, warm or cold, whether sympathetic or disagreeable. Whatever be his emotional condition, in accordance with that he has his likes or dislikes in colours. Therefore that makes it easy for the seer, for the knower, to read the character of a man – even before he has seen his face – only by seeing his clothes. His liking for a certain colour expresses what the person is like. His liking for a certain flower, for a certain gem or jewel, for a certain environment in his room, the colour on his wall – all that shows what a person is like, what is his fancy.

As man evolves spiritually through life, so his choice of colour changes. With each step forward he changes, his idea about colour becomes different. There are some to whom striking colours appeal, to others pale colours. The reason is that the striking colours have intense vibrations; the pale colours have smooth and harmonious vibrations, and it is according to the emotional condition of man that he enjoys different colours.

Now coming to sound, every person, whether he knows it or not, has a certain choice of sound. Although everyone does not study this subject, and man mostly remains ignorant of this idea, yet every person has a liking for a certain sound. It is therefore that there is a saying, a belief among people, that each person has his note. It is a fact that each person has his sound, a sound which is akin to his particular evolution. Besides the divisions that the singers have made, such as tenor, bass or baritone, each person has his particular pitch, and each person has his peculiar note in which he speaks, and that particular note is expressive of his life's evolution, expressive of his soul, of the condition of his feelings and of his thoughts.

It not only has an effect upon children to hear certain sounds and to see certain colours, but it also has an effect upon animals. Colours have a great effect and influence upon all living creatures: animals, birds and human beings. Without knowing it, the influence of colours works in their lives, turning them towards this or that inclination. Once when I was visiting a house which had been taken by a certain club, one of the members told me: 'It is a very great pity that since we have taken this house there is always disagreement in our committee'. I said: 'No wonder. I see it'. They asked: 'Why?' I said: 'The walls are red, they make you inclined to fight. A striking colour from all around gives you the inclination to disagree. The emotions are touched by it, and certainly those inclined to disagreement are helped by it'.

It is from this psychological point of view that one finds among the ancient customs of the East that a certain colour is chosen for the time of wedding, and certain colours for other times of different festivities. It all has its meaning, there is a psychological significance at the back of it.

Since both colour and sound are perceived differently and we have different senses through which to perceive them, we have distinguished between visible and audible things. But in reality those who meditate, who concentrate, those who go within themselves, who trace the origin of life – they begin to see that behind these outer five senses there is one sense hidden, and this sense is capable of doing all that which we seem to do or experience.

We distinguish five external senses because we know the five organs of sense. In reality there is one sense. It is that sense which, through these five different organs, experiences life and distinguishes life in five different forms. And so all that is audible and all that is visible is one and the same. It is this which is called in Sanskrit *Purusha* and *Prakriti*. In the terms of the Sufis this is known as *Dhat* (zat) and *Sifat*. The manifestation of this, the outer appearance, is called *Sifat*. It is in the manifestation of *Sifat* that one sees the distinction, or the difference between that which is visible and that which is audible. In their real aspect of being they are one and the same. That plane of existence where they are one and the same is called *Dhat* (zat), according to that knowledge of the inner existence of the Sufi mystics, in which one sees the source and goal of all things.

What I wish principally to explain is that colour and sound are a language which can be understood not only in the external life but also in the inner life. For the physician and

for the chemist colour has a great significance. The deeper
one goes into the science of medicine and into the science of
chemistry, the more one recognizes the value of colour. Each
element, the development of every object, or the change of
every object is distinguishable by the changing of its colour.
The physicians of old used to recognize diseases by the colour
of face and form, and even today there exist physicians whose
principal way of recognizing a man's complaint is from the
colour in his eyes, on his tongue, on his nails, on his skin.
In every condition it is colour which is expressive of man's
condition. Also in objects their condition and their change
are recognized by their change of colour.

Psychologists have recognized the condition of objects by
their sound and of persons by their voice. What kind of
person a man is, whether strong or weak, what his character
is, what his inclinations are, what his attitude is towards life,
his outlook on life – all this is known and understood by his
voice.

Colour and sound are not only the language in which one
communicates with the life without, but also the language
in which one communicates with the life within. One might
ask how it is done. We can see the answer in certain scientific
experiments. Special plates are made, and by speaking near
such a plate marks are made upon the plate with sound
and vibrations. Those marks make either harmonious or
inharmonious forms. If that is true, then every person, from
morning till evening, is making invisible forms in space by
what he says. He is creating invisible vibrations around him,
and so he is producing an atmosphere. Therefore it is that one
person may come into the house, and before he speaks you
are tired of him, you wish to get rid of him. Before he has
said or done anything you are finished with him, you would
like him to go away, for in his atmosphere he is creating a
sound; a sound is going on which is disagreeable. There is
another person with whom you feel sympathy, to whom you
feel drawn, whose friendship you value, whose presence you
long for; harmony is continually created through him. That
is sound too.

If that is true then it is not only the external signs, but also
the inner condition which is audible and visible. Though not

visible to the eyes and not audible to the ears, yet it is audible and visible in the soul. We say: 'I feel his vibrations. I feel the person's presence. I feel sympathy, or antipathy towards that person'. There is a feeling, and a person creates a feeling without having said anything or done anything. Therefore a person who is in a wrong vibration, without doing or saying anything wrong, creates the wrong atmosphere, and you find fault with him. It is most amusing and very funny to see how people may come to you with a complaint: 'I have said nothing, I have done nothing, and yet people dislike me and are against me'. That person does not know that it is not because of his saying or doing anything: it is because of his being. 'What you are speaks louder than what you say'. It is life itself which has its tone, its colour, its vibration. It speaks aloud.

One may think: 'Where is it? What is it? Where is it to be found?' The answer is: What little man knows about himself is only about his body. If you tell a man to point out where he is, he will point out: this arm, this hand, this body. He knows little further than that. There are many who, if asked: 'Where is it in your body that you think?', will say: 'Thinking? In my brain'. They limit themselves to that little physical region which is called body, thus making themselves smaller than what they really are. The reality is that man is one individual with two ends, just like one line with two ends. If you look at the ends, it is two; if you look at the line, it is one. One end of the line is limited, it is limitedness; the other end of the line is unlimited. One end is man, the other end is God. Man forgets this end, and knows only that end of which he is conscious, and it is the consciousness of limitedness which makes him more limited. Otherwise he would have a greater scope for approaching that Unlimited which is within himself, which is only the other end of the same line, the line which he calls, or which he considers to be, himself. When a mystic speaks of selfknowledge this does not mean knowing: how old I am, or how good I am, or how bad I am, or how right or wrong I am. It means knowing the other part of one's being, that deeper, subtler aspect of one's being. It is upon the knowledge of that being that the fulfilment of life depends.

One might ask: 'How can one draw closer to it?' The way
that has been found by those who searched after truth, those
who sought God, those who wished to analyse themselves,
those who wished to sympathize with life, is one way, and
that is the way of vibrations. It is the same way as of old; by
the help of sound they prepared themselves. They made these
physical atoms, which in time had become deadened, live
again with the help of sound. They worked with the power
of sound. As Zeb-un-Nissa says: 'Say continually that sacred
name which will make thee sacred'. The Hindus have called it
mantrayoga; the Sufis have termed it *wazifa*. It is the power of
the word which works upon each atom of the body, making
it sonorous, making it a medium of communication between
the external life and the inner life.

What one begins to realize as the first experience of
one's spiritual development is that one begins to feel in
communication with living beings, not only with human
beings, but with animals, with birds, with trees, with plants.
It is not an old tale that the saints used to speak with the trees
and the plants. You can speak with them today if you are in
communication. It was not only the ancient times which were
blessed; the blessing which was of old is there today. The old
blessing is not old today, it is new! It is the same old one that
was, that is, and that will be. No privilege was ever limited
to a period of the world's history. Man has the same privilege
today, if he will realize that he is privileged. When he himself
closes his heart, when he allows himself to be covered by the
life within and without, no doubt he becomes exclusive, no
doubt he becomes cut away from this whole manifestation
which is one whole and is not divided. It is man himself who
divides himself; if not, life is undivided, indivisible.

It is the opening of the communication with external
life which makes man wider. Then he does not say of
his friend: 'This is my friend, I love him', but he says:
'This is myself, I love him'. That is the time when he
can say that he has arrived at the realization of love. As
long as he says: 'I feel sympathy with him because he is
my friend', his sympathy has not yet fully awakened. The
real awakening of his sympathy is on that day when he sees
his friend and says 'this is myself'. Then the sympathy

is awakened, then there is the communication within one's self.

Man does not close himself only from the external life, but also from the inner part which is a still more important part of his life. That inner part is also sound, that inner part is light; and when one gets in touch with this sound and this light, then one knows that language which is the language of heaven, a language which is expressive of the past, the present and the future, a language which reveals the secret and character of nature, a language which is receiving and giving that divine message which the prophets have tried at times to reveal.

CHAPTER VIII

The Ancient Music

WHEN ONE looks at this subject from the Eastern point of view one finds that the Eastern idea of music originated from intuition. But the tradition of any art, or even of science, will tell the same thing. It is only later on that man begins to believe in the outer things and forgets the origin, which is intuition.

Music, according to the ancient people, was not a mechanical science or art: music was the first language. The proof of this can be found even now in the language of the animals and birds, who express their emotions and passions to one another without words, only in sounds. It is the combination of the different sounds of animals and birds which also has an effect upon the numberless multitudes of the lower creation. If music was the first expressive thing in the lower creation, so it was also in the human kind. And since it was the first expression of the emotions and passions of the heart, it is also the last expression of the emotions and passions; for what art cannot express, poetry explains, and what poetry cannot express is expressed by music. To a thinker, therefore, music in all ages will stand on the highest pedestal for the expression of what is deepest in oneself.

When the ancient music is compared with the modern, one will no doubt find that there is too vast a gulf between them. If there is anything which gives one some little idea of the music of the human race, it is Eastern music, which still has traces of ancient music in it. Had it been preserved in the East only as music, it would perhaps not have been kept intact as it has been. But it was kept as a part of the religion, and that is the reason why it has been continued through the tradition for thousands of years.

One might ask: How can the music of ancient times be kept pure, as there is always a tendency in human nature to alter things? It was always difficult for the human race to change religion; anything else might be changed, but there was one thing that was always kept, and that was religion. In the religion of the Hindus one aspect was music; it was called

Sama Veda. In the Western world there came a time when translations were made of the *Vedas*, but there is a part of them of which the translation is not to be found: it is of that *Veda*. The reason is that, being musical, this *Sama Veda* could not well be regarded as being language.

From a study of the music of the Hindus one can trace back in the traditions that thousands of years ago there was a time when musicians knew as fine a distance between tones as quarter tones. It was not only the degree of the sound that was considered in that way, but also the nature and character of the sound was analysed, just as in chemistry. We can find today in ancient traditions the different effects attached to the different notes, whether dryness or liquidity, whether cold or heat. No doubt it is difficult today to distinguish the sounds which express these different effects, because the distinguishing is now done from the instruments, and in those times it was done only from nature. Yet it is most interesting to know that we find today in Sanskrit scriptures the different pitch of sound distinguished in ancient times. In the absence of a piano or of a tuning fork the musicians had to determine the pitch by the sound of different animals and birds.

One might ask in what way the art developed among the ancient people, reference of which is to be found even now in the East. The idea was that they attached different themes of music to different seasons, and different strains of music to different times of the day and night. And as there is nothing in the world which is without reason, that also was not only an imagination or a fancy: there was a reason behind it, a logical reason for attributing certain melodies to certain times. Had it been a poetic fancy, it would have lasted for a short period, and would have influenced a little circle only. But it has lasted for ages, until now, and has influenced the whole country of India. It is a usage which was carried on for thousands of years, and today one finds in the East or the West, the North or the South, that the same *Raga* is sung in the same times. When sung out of these times, then it is not appealing.

When we look at it from the metaphysical point of view, we shall find that the realization and knowledge that science has today – and will ever have – that vibration is at the root of the whole creation, was a certainty to the ancient people;

it was the basis of their whole science. They knew that that which has created, and which is holding, and in which is held the whole manifestation and the whole cosmos, is one power, and that is vibration. It is because of this that astrological science, which had much to do with the way human beings and different countries were influenced, also arose out of that science of vibration. Thus music, as a science, was known by them to have a great deal to do with the influence of the planets. And the continual moving and working of the planets, and their action upon the earth, were the basis of the *Ragas* on which their music was founded.

In the Sanskrit tradition of ancient times there were verses to be found having relation to certain planets. The musicians therefore made their programme according to the influence of the planets of the cosmos, and that programme was carried out throughout the whole year. One might think that the influence of the planets is too vague to perceive, and that one could not make a programme upon it, but in all periods the whole of humanity has arranged its life according to the planetary influences just the same.

In order to keep their music akin to nature, it was necessary to give liberty to the singer and player to sing and play as he wished. Naturally, uniformity was lacking, and a standardized system could not be made. That is why this music always remained an individualistic art only – not an education. For this reason the music of the ancient people had its advantages and a great many disadvantages. The advantages were this: a musician – a singer or player – was never bound to sing in a particular way in order to execute properly the music he wanted to play before the public, but was always free to give the music according to his inspiration at the time. It gave him full liberty to express his emotions, his passions, without any outward restrictions which he should obey. When there were a number of singers or players, no doubt it was then necessary to set a certain standard – yet that standard did not restrict them very much. It is this order which was called music.[2]

The word music, or *sangita* in Sanskrit, has three aspects. One aspect is language, the other aspect is playing, and the third aspect is movement. Hindus have never separated the science of movement or dance from music; they have always combined the three aspects of what they called music. As the music of the Eastern people developed, each of these three aspects developed also. For instance, the way of singing of the more refined people was quite different from the way the peasants sang. The song of the temple was altogether different from the song of the stage. These differences were great. Not only were there particular rules and regulations to be followed, or more mechanical differences, but there was a natural difference.

The most important or valuable thing that the music of the ancient people produced, and which greatly benefited humanity, was that they distinguished the different aspects of music, and thereby came to realize that there was a certain way of expressing the tone and rhythm which brought about a greater emotion, or an inclination towards action. Together with it they found out that there was a certain use of time and rhythm which brought about a greater equilibrium, and a greater poise. This science, developing after many years of practice, formed in itself a special psychological science or art called *yoga*, and the special name for this science was *mantrayoga*.

The meaning of the word *yoga* is unity or connection, and *mantrayoga* means the sacred union between the outer life and the deeper life. For the Yogis found out that there are psychological inclinations: one of the tendencies of the breath is to go outward, the other inclination is to go inward. These two tendencies are to be found in nature also: in the ebb and the flow, in the sunset and sunrise. One sees this difference in oneself: the vibrations of one's own body and action are very different in the morning and in the evening. The Yogis therefore regulated the rhythm of the circulation, of the heart and of every action of the breath, with the help of vibration, of music, of both tone and rhythm. This brought them from the audible vibrations to the inward vibrations, which means: from sound to breath, which in the language of the Hindus are one and the same. It is *sura* which is a name for sound and for breath. The one blends into the other, because it is the same thing in the end. It is the breath of an object which may be called a sound, and it is the audibility of the breath which may be called voice. Therefore breath and voice are not two things. Even breath and sound are not two things, if one can understand that both have the same basis.

Is there an explanation of why man rejoices, or why he is impressed by the music played to him? Is it only an amusement, or a pastime? No, there is something else besides it. The principal reason is that in man there is a perpetual rhythm going on, which is the sign of life in him, a rhythm which is expressed in his pulsation and in his heart-beats, even in his heart. Upon this rhythm depends his health – not only his health, but his moods. Therefore, anywhere, a continued rhythm must have an effect upon every person, and upon every person its effect is distinct and different.

It is amusing and interesting to know that when the jazzband came into existence everyone said to his friends: 'Something crazy has come into society'. Yet one has not resisted it! It has come more and more into fashion and, however much a person hates it and is prejudiced against its name, he at least likes to stand and listen to it for five minutes. What is the reason? The reason is that, in whatever form the rhythm is emphasized upon the body and the mind of man, it has a psychological effect.

It is said of a very great Persian poet, who was also a mystic, that when he got into a certain mood he used to make circles around a pillar that stood in the middle of his house. He then began to speak. People would write down what he said, and it would be perfect poetry. And what is most amusing is that I have known of a lawyer who, when pleading at the bar and being unable to find an argument, would turn himself around. After that he would find the right argument.

But in order to find a mystery we need not go to such cases. A person who cannot find an idea beats or taps with his fingers on the table, and the idea comes. Many who cannot get hold of their thoughts, begin to walk about the room. When they have made two or three turns, their thoughts become clear. If this is true, we come to the realization that the human body is a kind of mechanism which must go on regularly. If it is stopped in some way, there is something stopped in the body or in the mind. This brings us to understand that upon the rhythm the mood, health and condition of man's mind depend – not only upon the rhythm which he gets from music, but also upon the rhythm of his own breath.

This rhythm has also a great deal to do with the rhythm of man's life. There are certain kinds of sound which irritate man and have a bad effect upon the nerves, and there are other kinds of rhythm which have a soothing, healing and comforting effect upon the mind. Music is sound and rhythm, and when sound and rhythm are understood in their nature and character, then music is not only something used as a pastime, but then music will become a source of healing and upliftment.

The Sufis of ancient times, the great mystics, used to develop this art in order to bring about poise in life after their everyday activity. They called this art *sam'a*, and *sam'a* has been the most sacred thing for the Sufis; it has been a meditation for them. They meditated by the help of music, by having a certain music played which had a certain effect upon the development of the individual. The great poets, such as Rumi of Persia, used to have music for their meditation, and by the help of music they used to repose and to control the activity of their body and mind.

We see today that there is a greater and greater tendency to nervousness. It is caused by too much activity in life. Life is becoming more and more artificial every day, and with each step forward man is missing that repose which has been as yeast to the human race. Therefore for the betterment and education of humanity today the art of repose, which seems to be lost, greatly needs to be found.

Many people in the Western world, who have read about the traditions of the ancient people, have often thought that there was an art that seemed to have been lost, and that they should go to the East in order to find it. So as to make it easy for those who are in search of that art and science which are most necessary in the evolution of mankind, the Sufi Movement has made a facility for those who wish to study and practise it, to do so here, instead of going so far to the East for it.

CHAPTER IX

The Divinity of Indian Music

IN INDIA life begins with the soul; therefore science, art, philosophy, mysticism – all were directed to one and the same goal. Not only arts and sciences, but even professions and commerce were not without a religious view. One can imagine how, in a country where even business and profession had a spiritual view, the musician's life was full of religious thought.

No part of the world, East or West, can deny the divinity of music. In the first place music is the language of the soul, and for two people of different nations or races to unite there is no better source than music. For music not only unites man to man, but man to God.

Now the question comes: When is it that music unites man with God, and how? Belief in God has two aspects. One belief in God is that a person thinks: 'Perhaps there is a God', or: 'As others believe, I believe too'. He does not know God by reason, nor does he see God before him. God for him is perhaps in heaven. Whether He exists or does not exist, he does not know. From one who has this kind of belief a little confusion or disappointment or injustice takes away his belief in God, and it is for this reason that thousands and thousands of men who worshipped God gave up their belief in God.

There is another aspect of belief, and that belief is the realization of God's presence, not only in the heavens, but in one's own surroundings. When a person arrives at this point his belief becomes a living entity. To him God is not only a judge or a sustainer, to him He is a friend – a friend who hears the cry of his soul in the solitude and knows the best and greatest secret he has in his heart, a friend upon whom he can always rely in good and bad experiences, and even in the hereafter. For a musician music is the best way to unite with God. A musician with a belief in God brings to God the beauty and the perfume and the colour of his soul.

From the metaphysical point of view there is nothing that can touch the Formless except that art of music which in itself is formless. There is another point of view: that the innermost being of man is the *akasha*, which means capacity. Therefore all that is directed within from the external world, can reach this realm, and music can reach it still more. A third point of view is that the creation has come from vibrations, which the Hindus have called *nada*. In the Bible we find it as the word which was first. On this point all the different religions unite. It is therefore that man loves music more than anything else. Music is his nature; it has come from vibrations, and he himself is vibration.

There are two aspects of life: the first is that man is tuned by his surroundings, and the second is that man can tune himself in spite of his surroundings. This latter is the work of the mystic. The Sufis in the East work for years together to tune themselves. By the help of music they tune themselves to the spheres where they wish to be. The Yogis do the same. Therefore the beginning of music in India was at the time of Shiva, Lord of the Yogis. This great Yogi teacher taught to the world the science of breath. Among the Sufis there was a great saint, Moin-ud-Din Chishti of Ajmer. At his grave music is played and Hindus and Moslems go there on pilgrimage. This shows that the religion of the knowers of truth is the religion of God, and the prayer of the greatest devotee rises from his heart in the realm of music. All different methods of bringing about calm and peace can be attained through the help of music.

CHAPTER X

The Use Made of Music by the Sufis of the Chishti Order

The Sufi especially loves music, calling it *ghiza-e-ruh* – food of the soul.

1

THE YOGIS and the Sufis, in their meditation, have always had music. Music is the greatest mystery in the world. The whole manifestation is made of vibrations, and vibrations contain all its secret. The vibrations of music free the soul and take from a person all the heaviness which keeps him bound. Music reaches the soul in a moment, as the telegraph reaches from London to New York.

There is one difference between the Sufis and the Yogis, and all the other mystics. Their ideas, their thoughts and their life are quite the same, but you will see the Sufis sometimes in tears and sometimes in joy. Worldly persons think: 'They are mad!', and mystics may think: 'They are on the surface; they are not on the same level'. To the Sufi self-pity, tears at what happens to the self, are *haram* – prohibited. But tears in the thought of the Beloved, in the realization of some truth, are allowable. Extreme joy for what happens to the self is not allowable, but joy in the thought of the Beloved, is allowable. The heart is touched, it is moved by the thought of God. It is then that the dervishes dance. Sometimes the dance expresses the action of the Beloved, sometimes it is the face of the Beloved.

The Sufis have used music not as an amusement, but as purification, as prayer to God. The Chishti Order of Sufis especially uses music. This Order exists chiefly in India, and has come from Russia. Chishti in Russian means pure, and Sufi – *safa* – means pure. There are different means of purification. It is according to our view that all seems good, or that all seems bad. The old Greek motto says: 'Evil is to him who thinks evil'. What may seem an amusement, something light, is prayer to God. There are different ways of praying to

God. In times when the world was most interested in music, art, science, and in amusement, these were used to bring before people the idea of something higher. Music and plays have been used, and the churches used some sort of show.

If you go among people of other occupations you will find them cold. They will pay little attention, they will speak just one word to you. But the heart of the musicians who have to do with sound is warmed by sound.

2

Once when I was sitting in the presence of Shakr Ali Ebah Ganj, a very great mystic, I asked him whether he knew the Sufis of Afghanistan. He had travelled very far. He said: 'They are Chishtis, but they do not like music'. This astonished me very much, because the Chishtis have a great devotion for music. He explained that the cold climate of Afghanistan does not allow music to have its effect.

The Chishti Order of the Sufis makes a great use of music to warm the heart, to produce feeling. When a person has understood that everything in the world is false, that every being is untrue – when this wisdom comes, then coldness comes. A little child is very magnetic because of its warmth. It is friendly to everyone. When its intelligence grows it distinguishes: 'This one favoured me; that one did not favour me. This one was kind; that one was not kind. This one gave; that one did not give'. Then coldness comes. Then we think: 'This one is my enemy; I should not speak with him. This man has written an article against me; therefore I should have nothing to do with him. This man's grandfather was my father's enemy; therefore I should avoid him'. The selfishness and coldness grow in us to such an extent. To stop this coldness, to produce feeling, the Chishtis use music. The vibrations of sound produce warmth.

When I was travelling through Russia I made this prayer: 'O God, do not let anyone who is poor come here. For anyone who is poor the cold is terrible. If he has no shoes, he has to bind bundles of rags round his feet. If he has no fire in the house, if he has no warm coat, if he has to go out to work or if she has to go out to work thinly clad – it is terrible!'

CHAPTER XI

The Use Made of Music by the Dancing Dervishes

DERVISHES ARE those among Sufis who adopt a certain method of progressing through the spiritual path, and who try to live a life as far away from the midst of the world as possible. Dervishes are also called *faqirs* and are most powerful. They have the power of wonder-working, and the power of insight. They are dreamers, and lovers of God. They worship God in nature, especially in human nature.

Among the many ways of spiritual development they have one way, called *sam'a*, which is listening to music. They listen to music in an assembly of initiates; no non-initiate is allowed to enter their assembly. They address one another saying: 'O king of kings, O sovereign of sovereigns', and they are mostly clad in robes or patches, or in rags.

They never think of tomorrow. Their thought is only for the moment: to quench the thirst of the moment, and to satisfy the hunger of the time. The care of tomorrow they leave to the morrow; it is with 'just now' that they are concerned – if they are at all concerned with life.

They are the ones who are really entitled to enjoy the beauty of music, whose spirit and soul are responsive with open centres, who make themselves as a medium of resonance of the music they hear. Therefore music touches them differently from any other person; music touches the depth of their being. Thus moved by music, they manifest different conditions, termed by Sufis *hal*, which means condition. Whoever among them is moved by spirit may manifest the ecstasy, which is called *wajad*, in the form of tears, sighs, or dance. It is therefore that those who do not understand the meaning of their dance call them howling dervishes, or dancing dervishes.

The gold of heaven is dust to the worldly man, and the gold of the earth is as dust to the heavenly man. To either the gold of the other means nothing but dust: their coins are not interchangeable. Therefore, the bliss of the dervish is understood by very few.

What one can learn from this is the theory of the whole process of their spiritual development. By making God their Beloved, and by seeing God in the sublimity of nature, they create the presence of God. As the whole day's affairs in life consist of both joy and pain, so the life of the dervish is also filled with both joy and pain in the presence of God. By the help of concentration, of poetry and music, both joy and pain are felt more deeply. Therefore God becomes living to the dervish. His presence is before him in all his moods. When once his pain has had an outlet in some form or other in the *sam'a*, the musical ceremony, the condition that follows is that of deeper insight into life. Upon whatever object or person he may cast his glance, these reveal to his soul their deepest nature, character and secret, thus making the whole of life clear to his vision in the light of God.

Question: What do you mean by 'joy and pain in the presence of God'? Why should there be pain?
Answer: If there were no pain, one would not enjoy the experience of joy. It is pain which helps one to experience joy. Everything is distinguished by its opposite. The one who feels pain deeply is more capable of experiencing joy. If you would ask me personally, I would say: if there were no pain, life would be most uninteresting to me, for it is by pain that the heart is penetrated, and the sensation of pain is a deeper joy. Without pain the great ones, the great musicians, poets, dreamers, and thinkers would not have reached that stage which they reached, and would not have moved the world. If they had always had joy, they would not have touched the depth of life.

What is pain? Pain, in the real sense of the word, is the deepest joy. If one has imagination one can enjoy tragedy more than comedy. Comedy is for children, tragedy is for the grown-up. It is through pain that a person becomes an old soul. A person may be young in age, but deep in thought.

Question: Not thinking of tomorrow, living in the thought of the moment is also taught by Christ. But can it be the ideal for a nation whose life must be built upon organization?

Answer: The path of spiritual attainment is not to be journeyed by nations. Spiritual progress is individual progress: every individual in his own direction. The teaching of Christ in this respect also was individualistic.

CHAPTER XII

The Science and Art of Hindu Music

MUSIC, LITERATURE and philosophy are akin to our souls, whatever be our faith or belief, or our way of looking at life. India, in the history of the world, represents a country and a people which engaged themselves in the search for truth through the realm of music, philosophy and poetry at a time when the rest of the world had not yet begun its search for truth. It is therefore necessary to study Indian music, philosophy and poetry in order to see the foundation of words. Some linguists today state that the Sanskrit language was the origin of all language. The origin of the science of music is to be found in Sanskrit.

It is a fact that not only art, but even science has its origin in intuition. This seems to have been forgotten lately, now that man is so busy with his search through matter. Undoubtedly, even the scientist is helped by intuition, although he may not recognize the fact. Scientists, who have touched the depths, will admit that science has its source in intuition. Intuition, working in answer to the need of the mind and the body, inventing through matter things of use, and gaining a knowledge of the nature and character of things, is called science. And intuition working through the beauty that is produced in the form of line and colour and in the form of rhythm, is called art. Therefore the source of both science and art is intuition.

Realizing this source, the Hindus based their music on intuition, and the practice of Indian music has been a culture of stimulating intuition and awakening the faculty of appreciating beauty, and then expressing itself in beautiful forms.

The science of Indian music has come from three sources: astrology, psychology and mathematics. We also find in Western music that the entire science of harmony and counterpoint is derived from mathematics, and so the science of Hindu music is called by the Sanskrit word *prastara*, which means mathematical arrangement of rhythms and modes.

In the Indian system of music there are about 500 modes

and 300 different rhythms which are used in everyday music. The modes are called *Ragas*. There are four classes of *Ragas*. One class has seven notes, as in the natural scale of Western music. Then there are the modes of six notes, omitting one note from the seven-note *Raga*. That gives quite another effect to the octave, and has a different influence on the human mind. Then there are the *Ragas* of five notes, omitting two notes from the scale – any two notes. In China they use a scale of four notes, but not in India.

Some say that the origin of the scale of four notes or five notes lies in the natural instinct that man shows in his discovery of instruments. The first instrument was the flute, symbolical of the human voice. It seems natural that man took a piece of reed from the forest and made in the heart of that reed four holes in places where he could easily put the tips of his fingers – the distances of the holes corresponding to the distances between the finger tips – and then one hole below. That made the *Raga* of five notes.

It was only later that scientists followed with the knowledge of different vibrations, but this scale of five notes comes naturally when a man places his hand on the reed, and a great psychological power seems to be attached to it. It has a great influence on the human nature, and this shows that the power of all things that have been derived directly from nature is much greater than when man has changed, turned and altered them so as to make a new form of art.

The science of astrology was based on the science of cosmic vibration. Everything depends on vibratory conditions, including the position of the stars and planets, individuals, nations, races, and all objects. A great deal of the secret power, which the Hindus have found in the science of music, has been derived from the science of astrology. Every note of Indian music corresponds with a certain planet; every note has a certain colour; every note denotes a certain pitch of nature, a certain pitch of the animal world.

The science which existed in the ancient *Vedas* was the science of the elements: fire, earth, water, air, ether. But these words should not be taken as meaning the same as in everyday language. The element of water, for instance, signifies the liquid state, fire signifies heat or warmth. Through this science the Hindus were able to construct *Ragas* or modes to be sung or played at a certain time of the day or night, or at a certain season. After these songs have been sung for thousands of years, the race has developed such a sense of appreciation of these *Ragas*, that even an ordinary man in the street cannot bear to hear a *Raga* of the morning sung in the evening. He may not know the form or the notes, but to his ears it sounds disagreeable; he cannot stand it. We may say it is a matter of habit – and that is true – but I have made experiments with different *Ragas*, and found that a mode that should be sung in the middle of the night loses its beautiful influence if we sing it at noon.[3]

Every planet has a certain influence, and there must be a certain mode to answer it. If it is not so, then music may become a pastime, but it does not do the work for which music is designed.

To an Indian, music is not an amusement or only for entertainment. It is something more than that. Music, for the Indian, is the food of his soul. It answers the deepest demand of his soul. Man is not only a physical body. Man has a mind, and behind the mind there is the soul. It is not only the body that hungers for food, the mind hungers for food, and the soul hungers for food. What generally happens is that man only ministers to his bodily needs and gives no attention to his inner existence and its demands. He experiences momentary satisfaction, then hungers again, not knowing that the soul is the fineness of man's being. And so that unconscious craving of the soul remains.

In the undeveloped person that silent craving of the soul causes him to be disagreeable, restless, irritated. He does not feel contented with anything in life, he feels like quarrelling and fighting. In the person of fine feeling this hunger of the soul expresses itself in depression or despair. He finds some satisfaction in love of reading, love of art. The soul feels buried in the outer, material world, and the soul feels satisfied and living when it is touched with fine vibrations. The finest matter is spirit, and the grossest spirit is matter.* Music, being the finest of arts, helps the soul to rise above differences.

* For a complete explanation about spirit and matter see Volume XI.

It unites souls, because even words are not necessary. Music stands beyond words.

The art of Hindu music is unique in its character, for every player or singer is given perfect freedom in expressing his soul through his art. The character of the Indian nation can be understood through its spirit of individualism. The whole education tends to individualism: to express oneself in whatever form one is capable of. Therefore, in some ways to their disadvantage, in many ways to their advantage, the Indians have expressed this freedom. Uniformity has its advantages, but it very often paralyses progress in art. There are two ways of life: uniformity and individualism. Uniformity has its strength, but individualism has its beauty.

When one hears an artist, a singer of Hindu music, the first thing he does is to tune his *tàmpura* to give one chord, and while he tunes his *tàmpura* he tunes his own soul. This has such an influence on his hearers that they can wait patiently for fifteen minutes. Once he finds that he is in tune with his instrument, with that note, his soul, mind and body all seem to be one with the instrument. A person with a sensitive heart listening to his song, even a foreigner, will perceive the way the artist sings into that chord, the way he tunes his spirit to that chord. By that time he has concentrated; by that time he has attuned himself to all who are there. Not only has he tuned the instrument, but he has felt the need of every soul in the audience, and the demands of their souls – what they want at that time. Perhaps not every musician can do this, but the best can. Then he synthesizes and it all comes automatically. As he begins his song, it seems that it touches every person in the audience, for it is all an answer to the demands of the souls who are sitting there. He has not made a programme for the music beforehand; he does not know what he will sing next. But every moment he is inspired to sing a certain song, or to play a certain mode, he becomes an instrument of the whole cosmic system, open to all inspiration that comes, at one with his audience, in tune with the chord of the *tàmpura*. And it is not only music that he gives to the people, but a phenomenon in itself.

The ancient traditional songs of India, and those composed by great masters have been handed down through the ages from father to son. The way music is taught is different from the Western way. Music is not always written, it is taught by imitation. The teacher sings, and the pupil imitates; so all the intricacies and subtleties are learned by imitation.

It is the mystical part which has been the secret of all religions. The great ones of this world, such as Christ, Buddha and others, have come from time to time to be examples for the people and to express that perfection which is the object of every soul. The secret, which was hidden behind all these great religions and in the work of these great teachers, was that man should reach to that utmost height which is called perfection, and it is this principle which is taught from the first lesson the musician gives to his pupil. The pupil not only imitates the teacher, but he focuses his spirit upon the spirit of the teacher, and he not only learns, but he inherits from this spirit.

The lack we find today, in spite of all spiritual awakening, the reason why so many seekers after truth do not come to a satisfactory result, is that they always pursue outwardly; they take it from a book, or they learn it from a teacher. There was a time in the East – and this exists even now – when a little boy who went to learn from a teacher had a great regard for the teacher; his respect, his attitude towards his teacher was as towards his priest. Therefore in this manner he learned to value and appreciate and respect knowledge. Not only did he learn, but he inherited knowledge from the teacher. It is most wonderful to read about the lives of the great singers of India: how they imitated their teachers, and how they sometimes became even greater than their teachers.

The object of Indian music is the training of mind and soul, for music is the best way of concentration. When you tell a person to concentrate on a certain object, the very act of trying to concentrate makes his mind more disturbed. But music, which attracts the soul, keeps the mind concentrated. If only one knows how to appreciate it and to give one's mind to it, keeping all other things away, one naturally develops the power of concentration.

Besides the beauty of music, there is that tenderness which brings life to the heart. For a person of fine feelings, for a person of kindly thought, life in the world is very trying. It is jarring and sometimes it has a freezing effect. It makes the heart, so to speak, frozen. In that condition one experiences depression and the whole life becomes distasteful. The very life which is meant to be heaven becomes a place of suffering.

If one can focus one's heart on music, it is just like heating something which was frozen. The heart comes to its natural condition, and the rhythm regulates the beating of the heart, which helps to restore health of body, mind and soul, and brings them to their proper tone. The joy of life depends upon the perfect tuning of mind and soul.

CHAPTER XIII

The Connection Between Dance and Music

1

INDIAN MUSIC, which is called *sangita*, is divided into three sections, *gayan* – singing, *vadan* – playing, and *nirtan* – dancing; for the vibration takes three forms of expression: in the voice in singing, in sound in playing, and in movements in dancing. Singing, however, is considered to be the principal part in *sangita*.

Sangita in these three sections forms part of Hindu worship, and even the paradise of the Hindus contains players, singers and dancers. Musicians and dancers are used to playing, singing and dancing in the temples of India. It may be surprising that a dancer should be dancing in the temple, but travellers in the East will know that in the Hindu temples musicians and dancers dance and play in praise of God. According to our view, all things may seem to us high or low, praiseworthy, or not. So-called religious people who condemn all enjoyable occupations have always called dancing sin. The whole world is the manifestation of God, and we may see God in all. The musician praises God in his music; the painter and sculptor see the praise of God in their paintings and statues, and the dancers too may devote their dancing to the praise of God.

2

The word dance has been much debased because the dance has been taken up mainly by entertainers who have made of it an amusement, and we see that, when a thing is made into an amusement, it always degenerates.

The voice that comes from the lungs and the abdomen cannot express itself fully without the bones of the head, the lips, the teeth, the tongue, the palate. So we see that this body is an instrument of sound. When the tree swings in the wind, each leaf gives a sound. The breeze alone cannot produce the full sound. The leaves of the tree rustle and become the instrument for the air. This shows us that the whole framework of this world is the instrument of sound.

If, while speaking to you, I remained as still as a statue, my words would have much less effect than when accompanied by gesture. If a person says: 'Go away from here!', and does not move, his words will not have much expression. If he moves his arm, they will have more expression.

In India the pupil is taught to sing with gestures; these take the place of notation and guide him. A person might think: 'Notation would be a much surer method', but Indian music is so complicated that no notation can render it exactly. Then, too, the intervals are all filled up, and the movements of the hand and arm can express and guide more easily than any written signs.

The third part of music, dancing, is not the made-up dance, but the expression through movement. Mahadeva, the greatest *Avatar*, himself danced. If you sing or play to a dervish he may begin to move his head and to move his hands.

A great Indian poet, when speaking of what a singer should be, says: 'He must have a good voice. He must know the *Ragas*, and be able to sing them. He must be a master of graceful movements. He must be calm, unaffected by the audience. He must impress the audience'.

Our life is so full of occupations that we have little time to observe animals. If we did, we should see that most of their language is movement. They speak little with one another, mostly they express through their motions. If you call a dog, the dog will at once begin to wag its tail; it will move its whole body to show its joy and affection. If you speak roughly to the dog, its whole body shows that it feels sorry. If the cat is pleased or becomes angry, it shows its feelings at once by its movements.

We waste much energy in useless speech. Among the old races we see that a motion of the hands, an inclination of the head, takes the place of words for many things.

As soon as a person comes into the room we see by his movements, by his manner of walking, what he is, how much refinement he has. If we compare the horse whose price is five thousand guineas with the horse whose price is fifty guineas, we see what a difference there is in their movements. The horse of five thousand guineas has not been taught to move as he moves, but in every movement he is graceful. We see also that the beauty given to the peacock has inspired its graceful movements.

3

Dance is a very wonderful thing, and is in itself a great proof of mysticism. We have each of us in us the nature of the bird, and the nature of the animal. The nature of the bird is to fly, the nature of the animal is to jump. The tiger will jump from here to the top of the wall. If we cannot do this, it is because by eating, drinking, sleeping, we have lost the power to do it. If a man sits in an armchair, and to get up he pulls himself up by the arms, and then by eating, drinking and sleeping has become so heavy, he is not what he should be. That government is proper which knows what each of the governed is doing. Our mind governs the body; our mind should have every muscle, each atom of the body, under its command. When we move upward, all must come up; when we turn to the right, all must turn to the right; when we turn to the left, all must turn to the left.

CHAPTER XIV

Rhythm

1

IN THE *fikr** – in what rhythm you began, you should continue to breathe. By losing the rhythm much is lost. Music is the miniature of life's harmony in sound in a concentrated sense. The person who has no rhythm physically cannot walk well; he often stumbles. The breath, the speech, the step, all have rhythm. The person who has no rhythm in his emotions falls easily into a spell, such as laughter, or crying, or anger, or fear. We should practise rhythm in our lives, so that we may not be so patient and yielding that everybody takes the best of us, nor so carried away by our enthusiasm and frankness that we say things that are undesirable in the world, nor so meek and mild that we fall into flattery, timidity and cowardice. Then, by and by, we may understand the rhythm of emotions, the rhythm of thoughts, then the rhythm of feeling. Then a person comes into relation with the inner rhythm which is the true meaning of the world.

2

Everything in the world has two movements: the moon has its waxing and waning; the sun has its rising and setting; the tide has its flow and ebb; man has his rise and decline. This shows us that time is not in the watches and the clocks that we have made, but time is the rhythm that is in the whole universe.

* A mystical breathing exercise.

CHAPTER XV

The Vina

1

THE *Vina* is the oldest instrument in the world – not, of course, in its present form, but in its original form. It is the mother instrument of all instruments in the East, and it is chiefly used for concentration and meditation.

The first *vina*, an invention of Mahadeva, was a bamboo with gourds attached to it. Guts were used, veins of animals, and all things that could be found in the jungle. When the *Rishis* went into the jungle for their *yoga* practices, the wish for companionship led them to take first a bamboo and a piece of gut, then to fasten two gourds to the bamboo. This was called the *rudra vina*, and on this the *Rishis* played.

The birds and deer in the jungle gathered to listen. One of the *Rishis* listened to what the deer said to him and, as he was a mystic, he understood the deer's language. He told this in a poem:

> 'The deer said:
> Make a string of my veins,
> make a carpet of my skin –
> but, whilst there is breath in this body,
> play!'

There was no carpenter's work on the first *vina*, there were no wires. It had only one string, because the *Rishis* thought that the one sound – and not a variety – could help their concentration. Later there were seven strings. The *vina* is considered to be the perfect instrument, and seven is the number of perfection. The gourd is there to lessen the sound, not to augment it, to make it more solid than a sound that goes out more; to make it fuller and less sonorous.

Every century has altered the form of the *vina*. It is very artificial now. Still it has kept something of what it was first. When the *vina* was taken to the palaces, it was made more elaborate: as you see it.* You may say: 'Why make such a head which is like nothing?' There is a great philosophy in it. It has the trunk of the elephant, the jaw of the tiger, it has horns and wings, the neck of a fish, while the eyes, the nose and the moustache have something of man. This shows that all faces are God's, and God appears in all forms.

2

You wish to hear from me the praise of the *vina*; therefore I shall quote the words of a great Indian poet who wrote a praise of the *vina* in Sanskrit. Please do not be surprised to hear the interpretation of it: 'An instrument of gut strings that we produce – by looking at it, by touching it, by hearing it, you can be made free, even if you kill a Brahmin' – which is considered the greatest sin!

This instrument was invented by the Lord of Yogis, Shiva, whose name is also Mahadeva. He gave to the world his life-long experiences in the practice of *yoga*. He is worshipped in India as a godhead, and his literature is considered holy scripture. He was a very great master of breathing, and an ascetic. He lived in the mountains, where he sat and breathed the fresh air of the wide horizons of the East, and practised *mantras*: words or phrases which change the whole being of man.

There he wanted to make some experiments on himself of higher exaltation by the help of music. What he could do in the forest was to cut a piece of bamboo. He then took two pumpkins, hollowed them out, dried them and fastened them on to the bamboo. Gut strings he got from animals, and these he tied on to the instrument. In this way he made his first *vina*, and he practised upon it in the solitude.

Mahadeva made experiments with the human body and with the mind, considering their condition in the morning, in the midst of the day, in the afternoon, in the night, and when waking at dawn. He found that at every time of the day and night a particular effect was made upon the human body and spirit, and that the rhythm akin to that particular time should be prescribed psychologically and mystically in order

---

* This remark shows that a musical performance had taken place.

to elevate the soul. So a psychological science of music was made by Mahadeva, a science of *Raga*, which means emotion; emotion controlled and utilized to the best purpose.

When Parvati, Mahadeva's consort, saw this instrument, she said: 'I must invent *my* vina'. So she cut a pumpkin in halves, made a body on them, and produced another kind of *vina*, the *saraswati vina*. So there are two *vinas*: one is played by men, the other by women. On this latter instrument not only sharp and flat notes are produced, but also micro-tones, and in this way the music becomes rich. But to master the science of micro-tones is so difficult, that it takes a lifetime. The musicians of India devote twelve hours of the day to the practice of the different rhythms, improvising upon them. In the end they produce a psychological effect which is not music but magic; a music that can thrill a person and that can penetrate the heart of man. It is a dream, a meditation, it is paradise. By hearing it one feels in a different world. Yet their music is hardly audible. Instead of being played before thousands of people, only one or two or three persons of the same quality and nature should be together to enjoy that music thoroughly. If a foreign element is present the musician does not feel inspired.

You will be amused to hear of a musician who was once invited to play the *vina*. The musician came and was welcomed. He uncovered his instrument; then he looked here and there, and found some discomfort, some discord, so he covered his *vina*, saluted, and went out. Those present felt disappointed and begged him to play, but his answer was: 'No matter what you give me, I do not feel like playing'. This is quite a different thing from making a programme months ahead. The musician in the West is bound six months beforehand to play a certain programme; he is helpless. But in this way it is not music, it is labour, it is done mechanically. Would you believe that a singer in the East never knows what he is going to sing before he starts singing? He feels the atmosphere of the place and the time, and he begins to sing or to play whatever comes to his mind. I do not mean to say that music of this kind can be universal music. Those musicians have always been rare, and found only in some remote parts of India. They are now dying out because of lack of appreciation. Those potentates, those gurus, those teachers of high inspiration who lived in the past – they appreciated this music. Even in India people are becoming 'civilized', and therefore music is dying away. Now there are no more those musicians of former times who could make all those who listened spellbound; they do not exist any longer. Among a million there are perhaps three or four, and they will have vanished in a few years.

Maybe one day the Western world will awaken to India's music, as now the West is awakening to the poetry of the East, and beginning to appreciate such works as those of Rabindranath Tagore. There will come a time when they will ask for music of that kind, and then it will not be found; it will be too late. But there is no doubt that, if that music, which is magic, which is built upon a psychological basis, is introduced in the West, it will root out all such things as jazz.

People seem to spoil their senses; this jazz music is destroying people's delicacy of sense. Thousands every day are dancing to jazz music, and they forget the effect it has upon their spirit, upon their mind, upon their delicate senses.

I know of a prince of Rampur who wanted to study music with a great teacher. The teacher said: 'I can only teach you on one condition. You are a prince fond of music; many musicians will want to show you their talent. I do not want you to hear any musician who is not an accomplished artist, because your sense of music must not be destroyed. It must be preserved for delicate music, it must be able to appreciate its finer intricacies'. If that sense is spoiled, instead of going forward one goes backward, and if music, which is the central theme of the whole human culture, is not helping people to go forward, it is a great pity.

Vina music has a likeness to the human voice. If you hear the *vina* played you will never think that it is an instrument, you cannot imagine that it is an instrument. *Vina* music is not as magnetic as the music of the human voice, but it is more attractive, more impressive, and all the delicacies of the human voice and the silky structure of it are finished in the sound of the *vina*.

3

Music has an effect upon animals. I have made experiments with cows and found that they very much liked to listen to music. There was an old ox in particular which, when it heard an instrument played, would leave its fodder and come to listen.

Birds are very fond of music. I have seen a peacock which, when I played the *vina* before it, would listen and spread out its wings and begin to dance. Then it would follow me and each day it would come a little nearer. It took such a delight in music that it danced and quite forgot everything else. When I stopped playing, it would come and tap the *vina* with its beak to get me to come back and play again.

Snakes too are easily attracted by music – by the Indian flute, a piece of bamboo, or by the *vina* if they hear it. A special *Raga* is used for charming snakes. But *vina* players are serious people, and would rather charm human beings than snakes!

CHAPTER XVI

The Manifestation of Sound on the Physical Sphere

MODERN SCIENCE has discovered recently that on certain plates one can see clearly the impression of sound. It is made visible. But in reality on all objects the impression of sound falls clearly, only it is not always visible. It remains for a certain time on any object and then it disappears. Those who have discovered scientifically the different impressions that are made by sound, have found the clear forms of leaves and of flowers and of other things of nature, which is the proof of the belief that the ancient people held, and which is expressed in the Vedanta in the wellknown phrase: *Nada Brahma,* meaning Sound, the Creator. And we read in the Bible that first was the word, and the word was God, and that first was sound (the word), and then was the light. This only means that the source of creation was sound. In other words, the creative source in its first step towards manifestation was audible, and in its next step it was visible. It also shows that all we see in this objective world – every form – has been constructed by sound: it is the phenomenon of sound.

When we go further into this subject we see that from a mystical point of view every syllable has a certain effect. As the form of every sound is different, so every syllable has a certain effect, and therefore every sound made, or word spoken before an object, has charged that object with a certain magnetism. This explains to us the method of the healers, teachers and mystics who, by the power of sound, charged an object with their healing power, with their power of thought. And when that object was given, as water or as food, that object brought about a desired result.

Besides that, many masters of occult sciences who have communicated with the unseen beings, by the power of sound have done still greater things: they have created beings. In other words, they have given a body – by the power of sound – to a soul, to a spirit, making it into a certain being, which is not yet a physical being, but a being of a higher kind. They called such being *Muwakkuls*, and they worked through these beings, using them in any direction of life towards a certain purpose.

The physical effect of sound has also a great influence upon the human body. The whole mechanism, the muscles, the blood circulation, the nerves, are all moved by the power of vibration. As there is a resonance for every sound, so the human body is a living resonator for sound. Although by one sound one can produce a resonance in all substances, such as brass and copper, yet there is no greater and more living resonator of sound than the human body. The effect of sound is upon each atom of the body, for each atom resounds; on all glands, on the circulation of the blood and on the pulsation sound has its effect.

In India there is a feast every year at which the people think of the great heroes of the past and mourn over their life's tragedy. Certain instruments are played, certain drums; sometimes very badly, sometimes by one who knows better. There are some people who, on hearing those drums, instantly enter into ecstasy, because the sound of the drum goes directly into their whole system, bringing it to a certain pitch where they feel ecstasy. And when they are in ecstasy they can jump into the fire and come out without being burned; they can cut themselves with a sword and they are instantly healed; they can eat fire and they are not burned by it. One sees it every year at that particular time.

They call such a condition *hal*. *Hal* means condition, which is an appropriate term for it, because on hearing the drum they think of that condition and they enter into it. In order to go into that trance they need not be very educated or very evolved. Sometimes they are very ordinary people, but the sound can have such effect upon them that they are moved to a higher ecstasy.

Now coming to the question of music: why music has an effect upon a person, why a person – by nature – likes music. It is not because he is trained in it or because it is a habit, but because it is a natural effect of sound that it attracts. First it touches the physical plane. The snake charmers in the East have proved many times that by playing their simple instrument called *pungi* they can attract the serpents of the vicinity. The sound has this effect upon the physical body of the serpent, and it begins to feel quite different; through that effect it is attracted to the sound, even to sacrifice its life, for then it is caught by the snake charmer.

It is for this reason that the wise considered the science of sound to be the most important science to use in every condition of life: in healing, in teaching, in evolving, in accomplishing all things in life. It is on this foundation that the science of *dhikr* (zikar) was developed by the Sufis, and that the Yogis made *mantrashastra*. By *dhikr* is not meant one particular phrase: by *dhikr* is meant a science of words.

Apart from the meaning a word has, even syllables of sound can bring a good result or a disastrous result. Those who know about this can recall several instances in history where, through the mistake of a poet who did not use the proper words in the praise of a king, the kingdom was destroyed. And yet, how little one thinks about it if one says: 'Well, I have said it, but I did not mean it'. People think that by saying something they have done nothing, as long as they did not mean it. But even saying something without meaning to, has a great effect upon life.

The science of sound can be used in education, in business, in industry, in commerce, in politics, in order to bring about desired results. But the best use of this science is made in spiritual evolution. By the power of sound or word one can evolve spiritually and experience all the different stages of spiritual perfection.

Question: Can one use music to awaken the soul to mysticism?
Answer: Music is the best medium, nothing is better. Music is the closest, the nearest way to God – that is, if one knows which music and how to use it.

Question: How do you explain that some people have no feeling for music?
Answer: I only explain that feeling is not yet created in them. The day when they begin to feel life, they will begin to enjoy music also.

Question: How is the sudden healing brought about of the sword-cut made while in ecstasy?

Answer: This point was touched upon by a physician in San Francisco, Dr. Albert Abrams.[4] Although all the doctors were against him, he intuitively thought that illnesses could be cured with the help of vibrations. But instead of finding the power of vibration in the word, he wanted to find the power of vibration in electricity. Yet the principle is the same. He took the rate of vibrations of the body, and with the same rate of vibrations of electricity he treated the elements of the body. He began to get some good results, but it is a subject which will need at least a century to develop fully.

He still has representatives. I went to the Institute of Dr. Abrams in San Francisco to see how far they had developed and I saw that they were using a person as a medium. That person feels the vibrations of the drop of blood which is put in his hand. The vibrations of that drop of blood go through his body and he feels them in a certain part of his body. In that way they find out the rate of vibrations of the blood. No doubt it is a vast subject, and this is just the beginning. Therefore there is still no end to the errors. At the same time, if people could bear with it, something might come out of it in many years' time which could be of great use in the medical world.

This example shows that, when a man can cut himself and at the same time be healed, it only means that he creates by sound such a condition in his body that the vibrations of the body are in such a condition that any wound can be healed immediately. But if the same person is not in that condition, then – if there is a cut at that time – he cannot be healed. He must be in that particular condition; the vibrations of his body must be working at a particular rate. If they are not vibrating at that rate, then he will not be healed.

There is a school of Sufis in the East called the Rifai school. The main object of this school is to increase the power of spirit over matter, and such experiments as eating fire, or jumping into the fire, or cutting the body are made in order to get power and control over matter. The secret of the whole phenomenon is that by the power of words they try to tune their body to that pitch of vibration where no fire, no cut, nothing can touch it. Because the vibrations of their body are equal to those of the fire, therefore the fire has no effect.

Question: In human life is it possible to hear the soundless sound?
Answer: Yes. It is by hearing the soundless sound that souls have reached the highest point and have discovered that there is a soundless sound.

Question: What do you mean by the soundless sound?
Answer: Sound is that which is heard by the ears, and soundless sound is audible without the help of the ears.

Question: Those who hear the soundless sound, are they clear-sighted?
Answer: It is not necessary for a person to be born with clear-sight or with the hearing of the soundless sound. If a person is born with that tendency then it is no credit to him. I think that the best thing is to be like everybody else and at the same time to evolve so that one experiences all that is possible, all that is latent in man, giving others the proof that we are not different from everybody else: we are the same, but this is latent in man.

Question: By evolving you get it?
Answer: Yes.

Question: Is it possible for a person who is born with a gross nature to become fine?
Answer: Certainly. Other things apart, even those who have done the *dhikr* (zikar) in the right way – in six weeks' time the vibrations of their body change; in six weeks' time those who do it properly become finer. Take the grossest person, make him do the *dhikr*, in six weeks' time his vibrations will change.

Question: In the spoken words are there vibrations of air, as science teaches, or are there still more inner, finer vibrations?

Answer: They are finer vibrations. The vibrations of the air are nothing. Every word has a breath behind it, and breath has a spiritual vibration. So the action of the breath vibrates physically, yet at the same time breath itself is an electric current. Breath is not only the air, but an electric current also: therefore it is an inner vibration.

CHAPTER XVII

The Effect of Sound on the Physical Body

WIND INSTRUMENTS, instruments with gut strings and with steel wire and the two instruments of percussion, drums and cymbals, have each a distinct, different, and particular effect on the physical body. There was a time when thinkers knew this and used sound for healing and for spiritual purposes. It was on that principle that the music of India was based. The different *Ragas* and the modes which these *Ragas* contain were supposed to produce a certain healing and elevating effect.

When we consider single notes or sounds – their effect upon the physical body leads us to think deeply on the subject. There are snake charmers, mostly to be found in India, who by playing their instrument, a wind instrument called *pungi*, attract cobras and other snakes from their vicinity. Often and often this experiment has been made, and one has always found that all kinds of snakes, or cobras, are attracted on hearing the sound of the *pungi*. First they come out of the holes in which they live and there is a certain effect on their nervous system which draws them closer and closer to the sound of the *pungi*. They forget that instinct which is seen in every creature to protect itself from the attack of man or of other creatures. At that time they absolutely forget, they do not see anyone or anything. Then they are aroused to ecstasy: a cobra begins to raise its head and to move it right and left, and as long as this instrument is played the cobra continues to move in ecstasy. This shows us that, apart from the psychical effect and apart from the spiritual effect that sound has on mankind, there is a physical effect also.

From a metaphysical point of view breath is the life current, *prana*. This life current exists also in things, such as the gut or the string or the skin of the drums. There is also a part of life in these things, and it is to that extent that their life current becomes audible, and that it touches the life current of the living creatures and gives it an added life. It is for this reason that the most primitive tribes who have only a drum to play, or an instrument to blow, get into such a condition by that continual playing of the drum that they enjoy the state of ecstasy.

Apart from this, how does the great success of jazz come about? It comes from the same principle. It does not give the brain much to think about in the technicality of music, it does not trouble the soul to think of spiritual things, it does not trouble the heart to feel deeply. Without troubling the heart or the soul it touches the physical body. It gives a renewed strength by the continuity of a particular rhythm and a particular sound that give people – I mean the generality – a greater strength and vigour and interest than music that strains the mind making it think. Those who do not wish to be spiritually elevated, who do not believe in spiritual things and do not wish to trouble, the jazz-band leaves alone, yet touching everyone who hears it.

When one compares the voice with the instrument, there is no real comparison, because the voice is life itself. The movement, the glance, the touch, even the breath that comes from the nostrils do not reach so far, not as far as the voice reaches.

There are three degrees of breath current. One degree is the simple breath that is inhaled and exhaled by the nostrils. This current reaches outside and has a certain effect. A greater degree of it is blowing. When a person blows from his lips, then that breath current is more intensely directed; therefore healers who have understood this principle make use of it. The third degree – in which the breath is most intense – is sound, because in that degree the breath, coming in the form of sound, is vitalized.

In the Near East, among Orthodox Christians and among Armenians, there is a custom not to use an organ in the church; they use a chord or sound made by ten or twelve persons sitting there with closed lips. Anyone who has heard it, will say that they are right. The sound of the organ is most artificial in comparison with the sound that the voices of ten or twelve persons produce with closed lips. This has such a wonderfully magic effect, it reaches so far and so deeply into the heart of man, and it produces such a religious atmosphere among them, that one feels that there is no necessity for an organ: this is a natural organ which God has made.

Brahmins, when they study the *Vedas*, even now do not study only what is written there or the meaning of it: they study the pronunciation of each syllable, of each word, of each sound, and they study for years and years. It is not that the Brahmin hears the sound once with the ears and thinks: 'I have learned it'. No. He thinks that a thousand repetitions of the word will one day produce that magnetism, that electricity, that life current which is necessary, and which only comes by repetition.

Now this life current that comes through the breath and manifests through the voice and touches another person – what action does it take? It touches the five senses: the sense of sight, the sense of hearing, the sense of smell, the sense of taste, and the sense of touch, although it comes directly through the sense of hearing. It is not true that a person hears sound only through his ears; he hears sound through every little pore of his body. It permeates through his whole being, and according to its particular influence it either slows the rhythm or it quickens the rhythm of the blood circulation; it either wakens the nervous system or it soothes it; it arouses a person to higher passions or it calms him by bringing him peace. In accordance with the sound and its influence a certain effect is produced.

Therefore the knowledge of sound can place in the hand of a person a magical instrument with which to wind, tune, control and utilize the life of another person to the best advantage. The ancient singers used to experience the effect of their spiritual practices upon themselves first. They used to sing one note for about half an hour and observe the effect of the same note upon all the different centres of their own body, noting what life current it produced, how it opened the intuitive faculties, how it created enthusiasm, how it gave added energy, how it soothed and how it healed. So for them it was not a theory, it was an experience.

When this is not understood and when people only know that sound has something to do with the body, they think that they must make some use of it, and instead of making the right use of it they make the wrong use! The Maharaja of Baroda, hearing of this science, thought that he should introduce music into the hospitals. Singers were sent there who had never learned what effect sound or song has. When the singers began their technical traditional songs while the patients were suffering pains and tortures, the patients said: 'Oh, take them away, take them away! Throw them into the river!' But it was the Maharaja's order that the singers were to sing. After a week the patients were far more ill, and the Maharaja had to send another order: 'No more music is wanted'.

In my travels I have seen now the same thing. There are some people here and there who think that music has a great effect upon patients, on health, but instead of using the right music, they use the wrong music, and its effect is to make people more ill.

Sound becomes visible in the form of radiance. This shows that the same energy which goes into the form of sound, before it becomes visible is absorbed by the physical body. In that way the physical body recuperates and becomes charged with new magnetism. By a keen study of psychology you will find that singers have a greater magnetism than the average person: because of their own practising their voice makes an effect upon themselves and they produce electricity in themselves. In that way they are charged with a new magnetism every time they practise. This is the secret of the singer's magnetism.

As to the question which is the wrong and which is the right use of sound, it all depends upon the particular case. In one case a certain sound may be rightly used, in another case the same sound may be wrongly used, but whether it was right or wrong will be seen by the harmonious and inharmonious effects it produces. When a pitch is a natural pitch of the voice; and a person sings a note in that pitch – in any pitch which is quite natural to him – that will be a source of that person's own healing as well as that of others. But the person who has found out the key note of his own voice, has the key to his whole life. That person, through the key note of his own voice, can then wind his own being and can help others. There are, however, many occasions when this much knowledge is not enough, because this knowledge only concerns oneself: one knows what is one's own note and the natural pitch of one's voice.

The great drawback today in the world of song is that people are going far away from what is called the natural voice, and this is brought about by commercialism. They have made a hall for one hundred persons, then for five hundred, and then for five thousand persons. A man must shout in order to make five thousand people hear him, in order to have a success – a success that can be had at the ticket office! But that magic charm of the voice is in the natural voice.

Every person is gifted. God has given him a certain pitch, a natural note, and if that pitch develops and he develops that natural note, it is a magic, he can perform a miracle. But he must think about the hall where he has to sing, and of how loud he must shout!

There was a man from India visiting Paris. For the first time in his life he went to the opera to hear the music and he was trying hard to enjoy it. The first thing he heard was a soprano who was doing her best, and then came the tenor, or the baritone, and he had to sing with her. So this man became very annoyed and said: 'Now look, he has come to spoil it!'

When we come to the essence and the inner principle of sound, the closer to nature we keep it, the more powerful, the more magical it becomes. Every man and woman has a certain pitch of voice. Then the voice producer says: 'No, this is alto, soprano, tenor, baritone, or bass'. He limits that which cannot be limited.

How can there be so many voices? There are as many voices as there are souls; they cannot be classified. As soon as he is classified, that person is obliged to sing in that pitch. If his pitch is different, he does not know it; if his voice is higher, he does not sing in that pitch. Because the voice producer says: 'This is a soprano', that person cannot be anything else. Besides that, a person has to depend upon what the composer has written. The composer never knew the voice of that particular person, the composer wrote only for a distinct pitch, either this one or that one. When a person has to sing in the pitch that is prescribed, then he loses the natural pitch he had.

Apart from singing, even in speaking, among one hundred persons you will find one who speaks in his natural voice, and ninety-nine who imitate. They imitate someone else; they do not know it. The same thing that you find in grown-up people you will find in little children. The tendency in a little child is to change and to imitate. Every five or ten days, every month a child changes his way of speaking; his voice, his words, many things he changes. And where does he learn it? From the children in school. He sees a child walking in some way, or making gestures, or frowning, or he hears it speaking in a certain way. He does not realize it, but he has heard it and he does the same thing; so he goes on changing.

In the same way every person – also without knowing it – changes his voice, and so the natural voice is lost. To retain one's natural voice is a great power in itself, but one cannot always retain it. In order to have a great, a good, a powerful effect with one's voice and sound, one does not have to be a singer. What one has to do is to practise the breath in different ways. One must first know how to breathe; one must then know how to blow; one must then learn how to make a sound, how to say a word. If one practises in these three ways, one will attain that power which is latent in every soul.

One need not be a singer, but for every person it is necessary that he should give some part of the day – even the shortest time he can give: five, ten, or fifteen minutes – to his voice, to the development of his voice.

Question: How does one find one's key note once it is lost?
Answer: But where is it lost? It is only lost from one's view. It is not altogether lost. It is just the same when people say that a person has lost his soul. But the person himself is the soul! How can the soul be lost? The key note is there, one must discover it, one must find it. Just as the soul is there – but hardly one person among so many finds it.

Question: How can one find one's key note?
Answer: By trying to find it.

Question: How can one be sure that the note one believes to be the key note of one's being is really the key note?
Answer: Belief is the first truth, and faith is the last truth. You must begin from the first, and end with the last.

Question: Has not every nerve its own sound?
Answer: Yes, it has its own vibration. You may call it sound.

Question: Does the sound we hear on the radio produce the same effect as the natural sound?
Answer: Yes. It is the natural sound just the same. Coming through a medium, coming through an instrument, that much is lost from it, but it is a natural sound just the same.

Question: How can one best check the tendency to imitate?
Answer: The tendency to imitate has some use also. If we did not imitate, we should not know the language; if we did not imitate, we should not be what we are. Therefore imitating is not a bad thing as long as we do not imitate too much. One must know what to imitate and what not to imitate. If one went blindly imitating anything one saw, then one would imitate both right and wrong.

Question: If a singer strains his voice it is heard easily and it spoils everything.
Answer: That is quite true. But to strain the voice is one thing, and to develop the voice – if it can be called a development to make an unnatural voice out of a natural voice – is a different thing. It is not a question of straining the voice, it is making the voice quite different from what was given by nature. Then the magic is lost. Nature has given a certain kind of voice; that voice represents the spirit, the soul, the heart, the intellect, everything that is in man. Evolution in man is to be seen in his voice, and when that voice is changed, then it is different. One need not strain one's voice in order to become unnatural; it is very easy to become unnatural!

Question: Is not the voice developed by *dhikr* (zikar)?
Answer: Well, that is the best way one can do it.

CHAPTER XVIII

The Voice

THE VOICE is not only indicative of man's character, but it is the expression of his spirit. The voice is not only audible, but also visible to those who can see it. The voice makes impressions on the ethereal sphere, impressions which can be called audible; at the same time they are visible. Those scientists who have made experiments with sound and who have taken impressions of the sound on certain plates – which impressions appear like forms – will find one day that the impression of the voice is more living, more deep, and has a greater effect. Sound can be louder than the voice, but sound cannot be more living than the voice.

Knowing this the Hindus of ancient times said that singing is the first art, playing the second art, and dancing the third art which make music. The Hindus who have found that by these three different aspects of music one attains to spirituality much sooner that by any other way, have discovered that the shortest way to attain spiritual heights is by singing. Therefore the greatest prophets of the Hindus were singers: Narada and Tumbara. Narada inspired Valmiki who wrote the Ramayana and the Mahabharata, the great Hindu scriptures.

There are three principal kinds of voices: the *jelal* voice, the *jemal* voice, and the *kemal* voice. The *jelal* voice indicates power; the *jemal* voice indicates beauty; the *kemal* voice indicates wisdom.

If you take careful notice in everyday life, you will find that sometimes before a person has finished his sentence you have become annoyed. It is not because of what he has said, but it is his voice. And you will also notice – perhaps not every day in your life, but sometimes – that you once heard someone say something that has always remained with you: it gives always a beautiful feeling, it is always soothing, it is healing, it is uplifting, it is inspiring.

A doctor coming to see a patient may, by his voice, frighten the patient and make him more ill if his voice is not harmonious. And another doctor may, by his voice, treat the patient so that before the medicine is brought he is already feeling better. The doctor gives the medicine, but it is the voice with which he comes to the patient that counts.

In the history of the world have not men marched hundreds of miles with strength and vigour, not knowing what they were going to face, on hearing the voice of their commander: 'Quick march!'? It seemed that all fear, all anxiety were taken away, and all vigour and courage were given to them, as they were going to march. And again have you not heard of commanders who said: 'Fire!', and the soldiers turned back and fired at them? That is the voice too.

The voice, therefore, is a wine. It may be the best wine, and it may be the worst liquor. It may make a person ill, or it may uplift him.

There are five different qualities of the voice, which are connected with the peculiar character of the person. The earth quality of the voice is hope giving, encouraging, tempting. The water quality is intoxicating, soothing, healing, uplifting. The fire quality is impressive, arousing, exciting, horrifying; at the same time it is awakening, because very often warning is given in the voice of the fire quality. The use of the words 'tongues of flame' in the Old Testament is narrative of that voice and word which were warning of coming dangers. It was alarming for the people to awaken from their sleep, to awaken to a greater consciousness, to a higher consciousness.

Then there is the air quality of the voice. It is uplifting, raising a person, taking him far, far away from the plane of the earth. And the ether quality of the voice is inspiring, healing, peace giving, harmonizing, convincing, appealing; at the same time it is most intoxicating.

Every *jelal* voice, *jemal* voice, or *kemal* voice has one or another of these five qualities predominant in it, and according to that it creates an effect.

The most wonderful part in the study of voice is that from the voice you can find out a man's particular evolution, his stage of evolution. You do not need to see the person, just his voice will tell you where he is, how far he has evolved. There is no doubt that the character of the person is apparent, is evident in his voice. There is another most wonderful thing to be found in the science of the voice: that the fortunate person has a different voice from the one who is not so fortunate. If you gather five persons who have really proved to be most fortunate, and you hear their voices, you will find what great difference there is between their voice and the ordinary voice. When you compare the voice of great people – no matter what their line may be – with the voice of others, you will find that there is a difference.

But what is meant here is the speaking voice. When we come to singing it is quite different, because today the art of singing has become as artificial as can be. The whole idea is to train the voice and make it different from what it is naturally. The training of the voice does not develop what is natural in it, it mostly brings into it something which is not natural to it. Therefore when a person sings according to the method of the day he has a different voice. It is not his voice, it is not his character. He may have a great success, he may be audible to thousands of people, but at the same time he is not singing in his natural voice. You cannot see his stage of evolution in his voice. Therefore the real character of the person is to be seen in his speaking voice.

Then there is another thing to be understood: that is the softness and the loudness of the voice; that there are times when the voice is softer, and there are other times when the voice is louder. Naturally that shows the condition of the spirit at that particular time, because sometimes the spirit is tender, and with the tenderness of the spirit the voice becomes softened. Sometimes the spirit is harder, and with the hardness of the spirit the voice becomes hardened. In order to scold a person you do not need to put on a hard voice; the voice becomes hard naturally. In order to sympathize with a person, in order to express your gratitude, your love, your devotion, your affection to someone, you do not need to soften your voice; your voice is soft before you can feel it, before you can think about it. This shows that the voice is an expression of the spirit. If the spirit is soft, the voice is soft; if the spirit is hard, the voice is hard; if the spirit is powerful, then the voice has power; if the spirit has lost its vigour, then the voice loses its power.

Furthermore I should like to tell you an amusing thing on this subject. Sometimes a person comes to you and begins to speak about something; and then he says: 'Hm, hm'; next he says another word and then continues to say: 'Hm, hm'. It may be that he has a cold, but it may be that he has not. Yet at that time he is doing this. Why? Because there is something that he is bringing forth from his mind, and it does not come quickly. The same condition that is going on in the spirit is manifesting in the voice. He wants to say something, but he cannot say it: the voice does not operate, because the mind is not operating. If in the mind there is some obstacle, some hindrance, then in the voice there is also something hindering.

Inspiration chooses its own voice, and when a speaker has to change his voice in accordance with the hall where he is going to speak, then inspiration is lost. Because the inspiration begins to feel: 'It is not my voice', it does not come. Then the speaker has to struggle twice: one struggle is that he must speak without inspiration, and the other struggle is that he must be audible to the number of people present. That cannot be done!

Nowadays* people have adopted a new method of elocution. A person who has learned elocution can shout as loudly as ten people shouting at the same time, and everyone will think: 'How wonderful!' But what impression has it made? None!

Nowadays radio technicians have made a kind of horn which they use at stations in the United States. A person takes that horn and on speaking into it his voice becomes twenty times louder. It is all right for trade and business purposes, but when you come to life itself, and when you come to conversation, to speaking to your friends, it is different. It is a most psychological occasion when you speak to one person or to many persons, because something is taking place which has its echo in the cosmos. No word ever spoken is lost; it remains, and it vibrates according to the spirit put into it. If a person makes his voice artificial in order to convince people, in order to be more audible, and in order to impress people, it only means he is not true to his spirit. It cannot

* i.e. in 1926.

be. It is better for a person to be natural in his speech with individuals and with the multitude, rather than that he should become different.

Now coming to the subject of singing: there are certain things which must be retained in the voice. However much the voice may be developed, however great its volume, however far reaching it may be and should be made by practice, at the same time one must feel responsible for keeping one's natural voice through every stage of development – that the natural voice is not hurt by it. It does not mean that one should not have a far reaching voice, it does not mean that one should not have a voice of a larger volume, that one should not have a voice that is vigorous and flexible. Everything that enriches the voice is necessary and must be developed by practice, but all the time keeping in view: 'I must not sacrifice the natural quality of my voice'. For every person, every soul must know that there is no other voice like his. And if that particularity of its own voice which each soul has is lost, then nothing is left with it.

Besides this, every person is an instrument in this orchestra which is the whole universe, and his voice is the music that comes from each instrument. Each instrument is made distinct and particular and peculiar, so that no other voice can take the place of that particular voice. If then – with the instrument that God has made and the music that God has intended to be played in the world – one does not allow that music to be played and one develops a voice which is not one's own, naturally that is a great cruelty to oneself and to others.

For those on the spiritual path, thinkers, students and meditative souls, it is of the greatest importance to know the condition of their spirit from time to time by consulting their voice. That is their barometer. From morning till evening one can see the weather – the weather created by oneself: whether it is warm or cold, or whether it is spring or winter. One's voice is that barometer that shows to us what is coming, because what will come is the reaction, the result of what is created, and the voice is indicative of it.

Those who think still more deeply on this subject will be able to see how, step by step, they are progressing in the spiritual path, if only they consult their voice. Every step in the spiritual path brings about a little change. By a distinct study of the voice you will find that it is so. When you go back, you will find by the change: 'I had gone so much further, and I have gone back again'. The voice will tell you.

There is another point which is most wonderful about the voice: that once you have worked with the voice and have cultivated it, deepened it, widened it, and it has become invigorated, and then you have left it, you may leave it for months and years, and the voice may take a different shape and a different appearance, but at the same time what you have once developed remains with you somewhere. It is just like a kind of deposit kept in a bank. You do not know of it, you have forgotten it perhaps, yet it is there. The day when you will touch it again, it will come back in the same way and it will take very little to complete it.

If the voice has developed a spiritual quality and one finds later that it has lost that spiritual quality, one must not be discouraged or disappointed. One has not lost it. One must correct oneself and want to go forward again, and be sorry for having gone backward, but never be discouraged, never be hopeless, because it is there; it only wants a little touch. It is just like a little candle which has gone out, but once you strike a match it is lighted again; it is a candle just the same. The voice is light itself. If the light has become dim, it has not gone out, it is there. It is the same with the voice. If it does not shine, it only means that it has not been cultivated. You must cultivate it again, and it will begin to shine again.

Question: Is it advisable to train one's voice, if one has not much of it?
Answer: One might ask: Is it advisable to do physical exercises when one is very thin? If one is thin, it is even more necessary to do physical exercises. So if there is no voice, it is more necessary that one should develop it.

Question: Does the voice change through the different ages?
Answer: Yes. Every age, infancy, childhood, youth, and more advanced age changes the pitch of the voice. The advanced

age is an expression of what a person has gained, and so the voice is also indicative of his attainment. No doubt, as with every step in the age of a person, so with every step forward in spiritual evolution, there is also a difference in the voice. Every experience in life is an initiation. Even in the worldly life it is a step forward, and that experience changes the voice.

Question: Do the words one has spoken in the past continue to affect one's life?
Answer: Certainly, certainly.

Question: Which is more powerful: to say something mentally or to say it aloud?
Answer: If you say it mentally and do not speak, it is powerful. If you speak and do not say it mentally, it is powerless. If you say it mentally and speak it at the same time, it is most powerful.

Question: Would you say a few words about the modern art of declamation or recitation?
Answer: There is little to be said about it. Very often people think that, when they have to recite, they must have a different voice, they must become a different being. A person does not want to remain what he is, he wants to be different. There is nothing more beautiful, nothing more convincing and appealing and impressive than reciting in one's own natural voice.

Question: Would you tell us how it was that Tansen kindled candles by singing?
Answer: It is told that Tansen, the great singer, performed wonders by singing. Tansen was a Yogi. He was a singer, but the Yogi of singing. He had mastered sound, and therefore the sound of his voice became living, and by his making the voice live everything that he wanted happened.

Very few in this world know to what extent phenomena can be produced by the power of the voice. If there is any real trace of miracle, of phenomena, of wonder, it is the voice.

CHAPTER XIX

The Influence of Music upon the Character of Man

ONE OF the reasons why music is called a celestial art is that it develops music in the personality of its lover.

Tone and rhythm, the principal elements which constitute music, are the only principles of this creation, and may be traced in its beginnings, in its continuity, and in its end. People of lofty and of low ideals, of amiable or unamiable disposition, show the difference of pitch in them. Balance in man, in his thought, speech and deed, in time show rhythm in him. The winning personalities of the world show music in their voice and words. And even before he utters a word, a person shows stupidity in the movements of his body, for they are unrhythmic.

Upon the rhythm of the breath health depends. This at once shows that both mind and body are sound when musical, and disorderly when unmusical.

All beauty in the realm of nature, art, or personality is silent music. Every soul has been born on earth to love what is beautiful, and beauty is its only sustenance.

'God is beautiful and He loves beauty'. (Hadith)

CHAPTER XX

The Psychological Influence of Music

IN THE the field of music there is much to be explored, and the psychological influence of music seems little known to modern science. According to modern science we are taught that the influence of music, or of sound and vibration, comes to us and touches the senses from without. But there is one question which remains: What is the source of the influence that comes from within? The real secret of the psychological influence of music is hidden in its source, the source where sound comes from.

It is more plain and easier to understand that the voice has a certain psychological value, that one voice differs from another, and that every voice expresses its psychological value and has its psychological power. Often one feels the personality of the one who is talking at a distance over the telephone. A sensitive person can feel the effect of the voice alone, without seeing the speaker. Many do not depend so much upon the words as upon the voice that is speaking the words. This shows that one's psychological development is expressed in speaking, and more especially in singing.

In Sanskrit breath is called *prana*, the very life. And what is voice? Voice is breath. If there is anything in life, in man's constitution, which may be called life, it is the breath. Breath manifested outwardly – the sound of the voice – is called *prana*. Therefore a person can best express himself in song, or in what he says. If there is anything in the world that can give expression to the mind and the feelings it is the voice. Often it happens that a person talks on a subject with a thousand words, and it has no influence. Another person expresses a thought in three words, and makes a deep impression. This shows that the power is not in the words, but in what is behind the words; that is: in the psychological power in the voice which comes from *prana*. According to the strength it has, it impresses the listener.

The same thing is found in the fingertips of the violinist, and comes from the lips of the flute player. According to the

influence coming from his thought the musician produces
that influence through his instrument. He may be very skilful,
but if his fingertips do not produce a feeling of life, he cannot
be successful. Apart from the music he plays, there is the value
of the *prana*, or psychological power that he gives to what he
plays.

In India there are *vina* players who do not need to play a
symphony in order to have influence, in order to produce a
phenomenon. They only have to take the *vina* in their hands
and strike one note. As soon as they strike one note it goes
through and through. In striking one or two notes they have
tuned the audience. It works on all the nerves; it is like playing
the lute that is in every heart. Their instrument becomes only
a source, the response to which is found in the heart of
every person, friend and foe alike. Let the most antagonistic
person come before a real *vina* player, and he cannot keep
his antagonism. As soon as the notes have touched him, he
cannot prevent the vibrations which are created in him, he
cannot help turning into a friend. In India, therefore, such
players are often called *vina* magicians, instead of musicians.
Their music is magic.

No doubt the power of the music depends upon the grade
of spiritual evolution that a person has touched. There is a
story of a Hindu musician, Tansen, who was at the court of
the great emperor Akbar. The emperor asked him: 'Tell me,
o great musician, who was your teacher?' Tansen replied: 'My
teacher is a very great musician – but more than that. I cannot
call him musician, I must call him music'.
Said the emperor: 'Can I hear him sing?' The musician
answered: 'Perhaps. I may try. But you cannot think of
calling him here to the court'.
'Shall I go where he is?'
'His pride may be revolted even there, thinking that he is to
sing before a king'.
'Shall I go as your servant?'
'Yes, there is hope then'.
So both of them went up into the Himalayas, into the
high mountains where the sage had his temple of music in a
cave, living with nature, in tune with the Infinite. When they
arrived the musician was on horseback, the emperor walking.

The sage saw that the emperor had humbled himself to come to hear the music, and he was willing to sing for him. When he felt in the mood for singing he sang. His singing was so great – it was a psychic phenomenon and nothing else. It seemed as if all the trees and plants of the forest were vibrating. It was a song of the universe. The deep impression made upon the emperor and the musician was more than they could stand, they went into a state of trance, of rest, of peace. And while they were in that state the Master left the cave. When they opened their eyes he was not there. The emperor said: 'O, what a phenomenon! But where has the Master gone?' Tansen replied: 'You will never see him in this cave again, for once man has got a taste of this, he will pursue it, even at the cost of life itself. It is greater than anything in life'.

When they were home again, the emperor asked the musician one day: 'Tell me what *Raga*, what mode did your Master sing?' Tansen told him the name of the *Raga*, and sang it for him, but the emperor was not content, saying: 'Yes, it is the same music, but it has not the same life. Why is this?' 'The reason is this: while I sing before you, the king of this country, my Master sings before God. That is the difference'.[5]

If we study life today – in spite of the great progress of science, radio, telephone, phonograph, and all the wonders of this age – we find that the psychological aspect of music, poetry and art does not seem to develop as it should. On the contrary, it is going backward. And if we ask what is the reason, the answer will be that the whole progress of humanity today is in the first place a mechanical progress. This hinders in a way the progress of individualism.

A musician has to submit to the laws of harmony and counterpoint; if he takes one step different from the others, his music is questioned. When I was in Russia I asked Taneiev, a very great musician who was the teacher of Scriabin, what he thought of Debussy's music. He said: 'I cannot understand it'. It seems that we are restricted by uniformity, that there is no scope, you will find the same thing in the medical and scientific worlds. But in art especially, where the greatest freedom is necessary, one is restricted by uniformity, painters and musicians cannot get their work recognized. They must follow the crowd instead of following the great souls. All that is general is ordinary, because the great mass of people is not highly cultured. Things of beauty and good taste are understood, enjoyed and appreciated by few, and there is no way for the artist to reach those few. In this way, what is called uniformity has become a hindrance to individual development.

What is necessary today is that in the education given to children the psychological value of music should be taught. That is the only hope, the only way in which, after some time, we can expect better results. Children learning music should not only know the music, but they should know what is behind it and how it is presented.

Of course there are two sides to this question: outward conditions, and the presentation of the art. Outward conditions may be more or less helpful. I myself have seen in my musical life that music, or a song, performed before two or three persons who are congenial, sympathetic, harmonious, understanding and responsive, brought quite a different vibration, created a different effect from the same music played before five hundred people. What does this mean? It means that some persons are like instruments. When good music is presented to them, they respond, they become attuned to it, they are all music, they take a share in the music, and so a phenomenon is created. This phenomenon can reach even that highest ideal that is to be expected of music, and that is the realization of the soul's freedom: what is called *nirvana* or *mukti* in the East, and salvation in the Christian world.

There is nothing in this world that can help one spiritually more than music. Meditation prepares, but music is the highest for touching perfection. I have seen wonders happen through the psychological power of music, but only when there were congenial surroundings. Five or six persons, no more, a moonlight night, or dawn, or sunset. It seems that nature gives its help to make the music complete, and music and nature both work together, for they are one.

If a great opera singer, or a violin soloist has to play before ten thousand people he cannot, with all his ability, touch every soul there. Of course it depends upon the greatness of the artist. The greater the artist, the more he will reach. But he has to consider what will please his audience, not what will be pleasing to God. When music has become commercial, its beauty is lost; it has lost much of its value.

There was a time in the East when every effort was made by the aristocracy of India to keep the art of music from being commercialized. They were successful for some time in doing so. Musicians were not paid a certain sum of money; their needs were supplied, even though they were extravagant. Musicians felt that they should have surroundings of harmony and beauty; they were generous; their doors were always open to others. They were always in debt, but their debts were paid by the kings.

Besides this, the musician was not restricted by his programme. He was left to feel by his intuition what the people wanted. He had to decide at the moment he saw them, and as he went on playing or singing he knew more. The chemical effect of the minds of the listeners told him what they wanted. So at the end it was a spiritual treat.

The secret of all magnetism, whether expressed through personality or through music, is life. It is life which charms, which is attractive. What we are always seeking for is life, and it is the lack of life which may be called lack of magnetism. If musical teaching is given on this principle it will be most successful in bringing about psychological results. It is on the health of the physical body, on thought, on imagination, and on the heart – which is often cold and frozen! – that the psychological power of music depends. It is this life which the musician puts through his fingertips when playing the violin, or through his voice when singing.

What the world is seeking, what human souls yearn for, is that life – whether it comes through music, colour and line, or through words. It is that life which everyone desires. It is life which is the real source of healing. Music can heal, if life is put into it. There is no great secret about it, if a person is able to understand the truth in its simplicity. When a person plays mechanically, the fingers running about the piano or violin almost automatically, it may create a temporary effect, but it soon passes.

Often one hears disagreeable music. At the time it does not seem so disagreeable, but afterwards one realizes the bad effect. It is exciting, it is harsh. The music that heals the soul is music with a soothing effect. One can have the soothing effect, or one can have the harsh effect. This depends not only upon the musician, but upon the composer also – upon the mood that has inspired him. A person awakened to the psychological effect of music will find it easy to understand what mood the composer was in when he wrote it. Every page shows his mood and his development at the time when he was writing. He can put life and beauty into his music, and after a thousand years it will still prove to be beautiful and life giving. No doubt, study and qualification help him to express himself better, but what is really needed is life behind it, which comes from the expanded consciousness, from the realization of the divine light which is the secret of all true art, and which is the soul of all mysticism.

Composition is an art rather than a mechanical arrangement of notes. A composer of music performs his small part in the scheme of nature as a creator. Music being the most exalted of arts, the work of the composer of music is no less than the work of a saint. It is not only the knowledge of technicality, of harmony, of theory that is sufficient: the composer needs tenderness of heart, open eyes to all beauty, the conception of what is beautiful, the true perception of sound and rhythm, and its expression in human nature.

By composing music a composer must create his own world in sound and rhythm. His work, therefore, is not a labour, it is a joy, a joy of the highest order. If the composer writes music because he is obliged to write something, that is not the thing to do. The composer should write when his heart feels like writing, when his heart is singing, when his soul is dancing, when his whole being is vibrating harmony. That is the time that he should write music*.

Question: Could you please explain what you mean by listening to music spiritually? Can one listen to common music spiritually, such as tunes played on a street organ?
Answer: But we do not sit and meditate in the street! Do we? Besides, there is a technical stage. As a person develops in

* This text is taken from the lecture "Art and Music"

technique and in appreciation of better music, so he feels disturbed by a lower grade of music. But then there is a spiritual way which has nothing to do with technique: it is to tune oneself to the music, and therefore the spiritual person does not care about its grade. No doubt, the better the music the more helpful it is, the higher the music the better. At the same time you must remember that there are Lamas in Tibet who do their concentration and meditation by moving a kind of rattle, the sound of which is not especially melodious. They cultivate thereby that sense of perception which raises a person by the help of vibrations to the higher spheres. There is nothing better to use than music as a means for the upliftment of the soul.

Question: Is it a distinct disadvantage for a human being to be born without a good ear?
Answer: It is, because what is received through the ears goes deeper into the soul than what is received through any other way. Neither by smelling, or tasting, or seeing does beauty enter so deeply into oneself as by hearing.

Question: As music is the means to perfection, are unmusical persons imperfect?
Answer: To play or sing oneself, and to listen to music are two different things. A person may become a musician by learning music theoretically and mechanically. But only he is really a musician who lives in music and loses himself in music.

All people have music in them, in the rhythm and harmony of their actions and life. If a musician has the desire for spiritual perfection, I think that he can perfect himself much more easily and quickly than another person.

Question: Why is it – if music is rhythm – that so often musicians are temperamental and easily disturbed?
Answer: But is it not beautiful to have a little temperament? Life is unmusical when there is no temperament. A person who does not get angry once in a while does not live! It is human nature to have all kinds of minor faults. The joy is in overcoming these faults. Music is not all sadness. There are higher octaves and lower octaves. Music is all. That is why music is even greater than heavens.

CHAPTER XXI

The Healing Power of Music

HEALING THROUGH music is in reality the beginning of development through the art of music, the end of which is attaining that which in the words of the Vedanta is called *samadhi*.

In the first place, if we see what is at the back of all medicines that are used for healing purposes, and if we ask what it is in them that heals, we shall find that it is the different elements which constitute our physical existence. The same elements are present in these medicines, and that which is lacking in us is taken from them, or that effect which should be produced in our body is produced by them. That vibration which is to be created in the body is created by their power, and that rhythm which is necessary for our cure is brought about by putting the circulation of the blood into a certain rhythm and speed. The intensity of vibration which may be necessary for our health is brought about by the medicines.

From this we learn that health is a perfect condition of rhythm and tone. And what is music? Music is rhythm and tone. When the health is out of order it means that the music is out of order, that the music in ourselves is not right. Therefore, in order to put ourselves into a state of harmony and rhythm, what is most necessary is the help of harmony and rhythm. This way of healing can be studied and understood by studying the music of our own life, by studying the rhythm of the pulse, the rhythm of the beating of the heart and of the head. Physicians who are sensitive to rhythm determine the condition of the patient by examining the rhythm of the pulse, the beating of the heart, the rhythm of the circulation of the blood. To find the real complaint a physician, with all his material knowledge must depend upon his intuition and the use of his musical qualities.

In ancient times, and even now in the East, we find two principal schools of medicine: one which comes from the ancient Greek school through Persia, the other which comes from the *Vedic* medicine, and is founded on mysticism. What mysticism? It is the law of vibration: it is the understanding of the nature of complaint by the rhythm and tone that can be perceived in the human body, and it is regulation through rhythm and tone, according to one's understanding of the proportions of the rhythm and tone that make for proper health.

Besides this there is another way of looking at this question. Every illness apparently has its peculiar reason, but in reality all illnesses come from one reason; from one reason, or cause, or condition, which is absence of life, the lack of life. Life is health; its absence is illness, which culminates in what we call death.

Life in its physical form, as perceived throughout the physical spheres, is called *prana* in Sanskrit. This life is given by food or medicine – or the body is prepared by a certain food or medicine to be able to breathe in this life itself, in order that it may be in better health, that it may experience perfect health. But this *prana*, which means breath – the central breath – attracts from space all the different elements which are there, as the herbs, plants, flowers, and fruits all attract from space the same element which they represent. All these elements are attracted by the breath. Therefore the great mystics, whether from Greece, Persia, or India, always had the culture of breath, the science of breath as their basis of spiritual evolution, and the source of all healing was the science of breath. Even now you will see in the East healers who magnetize water, or food, or the atmosphere. Where lies the secret of this magnetism? It is in their breath. It is the influence of their breath which is in the water or the food.

The religious people of India have a ceremony where something like a sacrament is given by a holy person to someone who is suffering, and it helps him. It is the holy person's power of breath which is so balanced, so purified and developed, that it attracts all elements, all that one can get from herb, flower, or fruit – and even more. Therefore his breath can do a thousand times more than what medicine can do. There are healers in the East who whisper some spiritual words. What is whispering? It is breath again – breath with words directed through it.

There was a physician in Delhi who mostly used his healing power with his patients. One day a sceptical friend came to consult him. The physician whispered a few sacred words before the patient and said: 'Now you may go'. This sceptical man said he could not understand how such a method could have any effect upon his health. The physician then did something quite unusual for him: he offended the man by speaking harshly to him. The man became very angry, and said: 'How can you, a physician, say such words to me!' The physician replied: 'Usually I never do such a thing, and I only did it to prove something to you. If my words can make you angry and ill, they can also make someone well'. If words can make one ill and upset, they also have the power behind them to harmonize the patient, and to put him into a good condition.

Now what is music? According to the Sanskrit thinkers there are three aspects of music: singing, playing and dancing. All three represent rhythm, and all three represent tone in some form or other. And what is the effect of music? The effect of music is to regularize the rhythm and to tune a person to the music that is being performed.

What secret is there in music which attracts all those who listen to it? It is the rhythm which is created. It is the tone of that music which tunes the soul, and raises it above the depression and despair of everyday life in this world. If one knew what rhythm is needed for a particular individual in his trouble and despair, what tone is needed, and to what tone that person's soul should be raised, then one could heal a person with music.

There was a time in India when music was used for healing. It was healing for the mind, for the character, and healing for the soul. For it is health of the soul that brings health to the physical body, but healing of the physical body does not always help the soul. That is why the material science of medicine can do good for some time, but does not entirely suffice the need of the patient. I do not mean by this that outward treatment is absolutely useless. There is nothing in this world which is useless, if we only know how to make use of it. All things in this world are needed, all things have their benefit and use, if we only know how to use them properly.

But if a cure is brought about outwardly, while inwardly the illness remains, sooner or later the illness which is buried in the body must come out and show itself.

Once I met a person who said she had been to many physicians for a complaint of neuritis. She was temporarily cured, but it always came back. She said: 'Can you tell me something that will help me?' I asked her a question: 'Is there any person in the world whom you dislike, whom you hate, or whose action is troubling your mind?' 'Yes', she said, 'there are many people whom I dislike, and especially there is one person whom I cannot forgive'. 'Well', I said, 'that is the neuritis; that is the root of the disease. Outwardly it is a pain of the body, inwardly it is rooted in the heart'.

Often the cause of illness is within, though no doubt many things are caused outwardly. No single rule will cover everything. No doubt as things have changed, and materialism has spread throughout the world, this has influenced things not only in the West, but in the East also. The use of music for spiritual attainment and healing of the soul, which was prevalent in ancient times, is not found to the same extent now. Music has been made a pastime, the means of forgetting God instead of realizing God. It is the use one makes of things which constitutes their fault or their virtue.

Still the remembrance of the ancient use of music remains among the poor in India, where there are healers who have their particular instrument of healing on which they play, and the people go to them for healing. By playing this instrument they arouse that certain feeling in the patient which has become cold, and that deep feeling which was buried begins to come out. It is really the old way of psychoanalysis. Music helps the patient to express in full the hidden influence which was there, and in this way many people are helped without going to a physician. But this is no doubt a crude and ordinary form of healing.

The Maharaja of Baroda, knowing that healing could be accomplished through music, introduced concerts in certain hospitals. The amazing result was that all those who were suffering began to cry out: 'For God's sake, keep quiet! Go away!' That was not the music to soothe them; it only made them suffer more. It was like giving a stone for bread.

In order to give healing through music, one must study
what is needed, what is wanted. In the first place one must
study what the complaint is: what elements are lacking, what
is the symbolical meaning, what mental attitude is behind the
illness. Then, by a close study, one can do great good to the
patient with the help of music.

Even if music were not used as a prescription particularly
intended for a certain illness, still the power of illness, which
has its abode in the heart of man, can be reduced by lifting up
his heart, by changing his thought. What brings illness is the
thought of illness rather than the illness itself. The existence
of illness in the body may no doubt be called a shadow of the
true illness which is held by man in his mind. By the power
of music the mind may become so exalted that it rises above
the thought of illness; then the illness is forgotten.

You may ask: 'What kind of music can heal man? Is it
singing, or playing, or something in the way of dance?'
Singing is the most powerful, for singing is living. It is
prana, it is life itself, it is voice. No doubt it is also life
which is working through an instrument by the touch, but
in singing it is direct life, the breath touching the heart of the
listener. But what must be behind this voice? There must be a
heart prepared with the help of the battery that it needs. What
is that battery? That battery is what we call love and sympathy
– the greatest power there is.

A person who is material, who is struggling for himself
from morning to evening, who is looking for his own benefit,
who is in trouble and bitter, who is in the midst of fighting
and is fighting himself – he cannot heal. The healer must
be free, free to sympathize, free to love his fellowman even
more than himself.

What teaches this love? Where can one learn it? Where can
one get it? The key to this love element is God. As we look
upon life today with all its progress, what is lacking? It is
God. God is the key to the unlimited store of love which is
in the heart of man.

Once I was very amused and surprised at an answer that a
very godly and good natured maid gave me. Working in the
house, she could not answer a knock at the door as quickly as
it should have been answered, and the lady visitor who was

waiting at the door became very impatient and spoke crossly to the maid. When I asked her what had happened, she was not cross at all. She smiled and said: 'Yes, yes, that lady was very cross with me'. I asked: 'Well, what was the matter with her, what made her cross, what was the reason?', and this maid, with innocence in her face, replied: 'The reason? There was no God'. A beautiful answer. Where God is lacking, there is no love. Wherever there is love, there is God. Wherever there is God, there is love.

If we interpret it rightly, what causes pain and suffering? It is lack of life. What is life? It is love. And what is love? It is God. What every individual wants, what the world wants, is God. All we have to attain by music, by harmony, by tone, by the science of right tuning, by a life of goodness – all we have to gain to bless our lives is God. This is the central theme of all good.

CHAPTER XXII

Spiritual Attainment by the Aid of Music

BEFORE COMMENCING this subject I should like to explain first what the word spiritual means. Is it goodness which may be called spiritual, or is it wonderworking, a power to produce miracles, or a great intellectual power? The answer is: No. The whole of life in all its aspects is one music, and to tune one's self to the harmony of this perfect music is the real spiritual attainment.

You may ask: 'What is it that keeps man back from spiritual attainment?' The answer is that it is the denseness of this material existence, and the fact that man is unconscious of his spiritual being – divided into limitations. This prevents that free flow and free movement which are the nature and character of life.

What do I mean by this denseness? There is a rock, and you want to produce sound from it. It does not give resonance, it does not answer your desire to produce sound, but the string or wire will give an answer to the tone you want. You strike it, and it answers. There are objects which give resonance to sound. You wish to produce a sound in them, and they resound; they make your music complete.

So it is with human nature. One person is heavy and dull. You tell him something, he cannot understand; you speak to him, he will not hear. He will not respond to music, to beauty, or to art. What is it? It is denseness. There is another person who is ready to appreciate and understand music and poetry, or beauty in any form. In character, in manner – in every form – beauty is appreciated by such a person. It is this which is the awakening of the soul, which is the living condition of the heart, and it is this which is the real spiritual attainment. Spiritual attainment is to make the spirit live, to become conscious. When man is not conscious of soul and spirit, and is only conscious of the material being, he is dense, he is away from spirit.

You may ask: 'What is spirit, and what is matter?' The difference between spirit and matter is as the difference between water and snow. Frozen water is snow, and melted snow is water. It is spirit in its denseness which we call matter; it is matter in its fineness which may be called spirit. Once a materialist said to me: 'I do not believe in any spirit or soul or hereafter. I believe in eternal matter'. I said to him: 'Your belief is not very different from mine. Only, that which you call eternal matter, I call spirit. It is a difference in terms. That is not a thing to dispute about, because we both believe in eternity. So long as we meet in eternity, what difference does it make if the one calls it matter and the other calls it spirit? It is one life from beginning to end'.

Beauty is born of harmony. What is harmony? Harmony is right proportion, in other words, right rhythm. And what is life? Life is the outcome of harmony. At the back of the whole creation is harmony, and the whole secret of creation is harmony. Intelligence longs to attain to the perfection of harmony. What man calls happiness and comfort, or profit and gain – all he longs for and wishes to attain – is harmony. In smaller or greater proportion he is longing for harmony; even in attaining the most mundane things he always wishes for harmony. But often he does not adopt right methods. Often his methods are wrong. The object attained by both good and bad methods is the same, but the way one tries to attain it turns the object into right or wrong. It is not the object which is wrong, it is the way one adopts to attain it. No one, whatever his station in life, wishes for disharmony, for all suffering, pain and trouble are disharmony.

To attain spirituality is to realize that the whole universe is one symphony in which every individual is one note. His happiness lies in becoming perfectly harmonious with the symphony of the universe. It is not following a certain religion that makes one spiritual, or having a certain belief, or being a fanatic in regard to one idea, or by becoming too good to live in this world. Many good people there are, who do not even understand what spirituality means. They are very good, but they do not yet know what ultimate good is. Ultimate good is harmony itself. For instance, all the different principles and beliefs of the religions of this world taught and proclaimed by priests and teachers – but which men are not always able to follow and express – come naturally from the heart of a man who attunes himself to the rhythm of the universe. His every action, every word he speaks, every feeling he has, every sentiment he expresses, is all harmonious; it is all virtue, it is all religion. It is not following a religion, it is living a religion, making one's life a religion, which is necessary.

Music is the miniature of the whole harmony of the universe, for the harmony of the universe is music itself, and man, being the miniature of the universe, must show the same harmony. In his pulsation, in the beat of his heart, and in his vibration he shows rhythm and tone, harmonious or inharmonious chords. His health or illness, his joy or discomfort – all show the music or lack of music in his life.

What does music teach us? Music helps us to train ourselves in some way or other in harmony, and it is this which is magic, or the secret behind music. When you hear music that you enjoy, it tunes you and puts you in harmony with life. Therefore man needs music; he longs for music. Many say that they do not care for music, but these have not heard music! If they really hear music it will touch their souls, and then certainly they cannot help loving it. If not, it only means that they have not heard music sufficiently, and have not made their heart calm and quiet in order to listen to it, to enjoy and appreciate it. Besides, music develops that faculty by which one learns to appreciate all that is good and beautiful. In the form of art and science, in the form of music and poetry, in every aspect of beauty one can then appreciate it. What deprives man of all the beauty around him is his heaviness of body, or heaviness of heart. He is pulled down to earth, and by that everything becomes limited. When he shakes off that heaviness and feels joyous, he feels light. All good tendencies, such as gentleness and tolerance, forgiveness, love and appreciation – all these beautiful qualities – come by being light, light in mind, soul and body.

Where does music come from? Where does the dance come from? It all comes from the natural spiritual life which is within. When that spiritual life springs forth, it lightens all the burdens that man has. It makes his life smooth, floating on the ocean of life. The faculty of appreciation makes one light. Life is just like the ocean. When there is no appreciation, no receptivity, man sinks like a piece of iron to the bottom of the sea. He cannot float like the boat which is hollow, which is receptive.

The difficulty in the spiritual path is always what comes from ourselves. Man does not like to be a pupil, he likes to be a teacher. If man only knew that the greatness and perfection of the great ones, who have come from time to time to this world, was in their pupilship, and not in teaching! The greater the teacher, the better pupil he was. He learned from everyone, the great and the lowly, the wise and the foolish, the old and the young. He learned from their lives, and studied human nature in all its aspects.

The one who learns to tread the spiritual path must become as an empty cup in order that the wine of music and harmony may be poured down into his heart. You may ask: 'How can one become an empty cup?' I shall tell you how cups show themselves filled instead of being empty. Often a person comes to me and says: 'Here I am. Can you help me spiritually?', and I answer: 'Yes'. But then he says: 'I want to know first of all what you think about life and death, or about the beginning and the end'. And then I wonder what his attitude will be if his previously conceived opinion does not agree with mine. He wants to learn, yet he does not want to be empty. That means, going to the stream of water with one's cup covered up: wanting the water, and yet the cup is closed, filled with preconceived ideas. Where have the preconceived ideas come from? No idea can be called one's own! All ideas have been learned from one source or another, but in time one comes to think that they are one's own. For these ideas one will argue and dispute, although they do not satisfy fully. At the same time they are one's battleground, and all the time they will keep the cup covered up.

Mystics therefore have adopted a different way. They have learned a different course, and that course is self-effacement or, in other words, unlearning what one has learned. They say in the East that the first thing that is learned is to understand how to become a pupil. They do not first learn what God is, or what life is. The first thing to learn is how to become a pupil. One may think that in this way one loses one's individuality. But what is individuality? Is it not that which is collected? What are one's ideas and opinions? They are just collected knowledge. This should be unlearned.

How can one unlearn? You would say that the character of the mind is such that what one learns is engraved upon it, and how then can one unlearn it? Unlearning is completing knowledge. To see a person and say: 'That person is wicked' – that is learning. To see further, and recognize something good in that person – that is unlearning. When you see the goodness in someone whom you have called wicked, you have unlearned. You have unravelled that knot. You have once said: 'I hate that person' – that is learning. And then you say: 'Oh no, I can like him, or I can pity him'. When you say that, you have seen with two eyes. First you learn by seeing with one eye; then you learn to see with two eyes. That makes sight complete.

All that we have learned in this world is partial knowledge, and when this is uprooted by another point of view, then we have knowledge in its completed form. That is called mysticism. Why is it called mysticism? Because it cannot be put into words. Words will show us one side of it, but the other side is beyond words.

The whole manifestation is duality, the duality which makes us intelligent, and behind the duality is unity. If we do not rise beyond duality and go towards unity, we do not attain the perfection which is called spirituality.

This does not mean that our learning is of no use. It is of great use. It gives us the power of discrimination and of discerning differences. This makes the intelligence sharp and the sight keen, so that we understand the value of things and their use. It is all part of human evolution, and all useful. So we must learn first, and unlearn afterwards. You do not look first at the sky when you are standing on the earth. First look at the earth, and see what it offers you to learn and to observe, but at the same time do not think that your life's purpose is fulfilled by looking only at the earth. The fulfilment of life's purpose is in looking at the sky.

What is wonderful about music is that it helps man to concentrate or meditate independently of thought. Therefore music seems to be the bridge over the gulf between the form and the formless. If there is anything intelligent, effective, and at the same time formless, it is music. Poetry suggests form, line and colour suggest form, but music suggests no form.

Music also produces that resonance which vibrates through the whole being. It lifts the thought above the denseness of matter; it almost turns matter into spirit, into its original condition, through the harmony of vibrations touching every atom of one's whole being.

Beauty of line and colour can go so far and no further. The joy of fragrance can go a little further. Music touches our innermost being, and in that way produces new life, a life that gives exaltation to the whole being, raising it to that perfection in which lies the fulfilment of man's life.

APHORISMS

APHORISMS

Love produces harmony and harmony creates beauty.
Therefore the chief motto in life is 'Love, harmony and
beauty'. Love in all things and beings the beloved God, in
harmony with all in the right understanding, and beautify
your life by observing the beauty within and without. By
love, harmony and beauty you must turn the whole of life
into a single vision of divine glory.

Life is a symphony, and the action of every person in this
life is the playing of his particular part in the music.

The best moral is to learn from all that sounds inharmonious
to us that we may not use it for another, and to use that
which sounds harmonious to us for others. Thus should
the ears be trained.

The further we advance, the more difficult and the more
important becomes our part in the symphony of life; and
the more conscious we are of this responsibility, the more
efficient we become in accomplishing our task.

Once a soul has awakened to the continual music of life,
that soul considers it as his responsibility, his duty, to play
his part in the outer life, even if it be contrary to his inner
condition at the moment.

The secret of seeking the will of God lies in cultivating
the faculty of sensing harmony, for harmony is beauty
and beauty is harmony. The lover of beauty in his further
progress becomes the seeker of harmony, and by trying
always to maintain harmony he will tune his heart to the
will of God.

There is nothing in this world which does not speak. Every
thing and every being is continually calling out its nature,

its character, its secret; the more the inner sense is open,
the more capable it becomes of hearing the voice of all
things.

If the soul were awakened to feel what the birds feel when
singing in the forest at dawn, man would know that their
prayer is even more exalting than his own, for it is more
natural.

There is nothing in the world which is not the instrument of
God.

Sound is the sign of life; in the temples of gods and
goddesses, in Hindu churches, bells ringing show life even
in the silence.

Sound is hidden under words, and words are hidden
under sound. When one perceives the words, one does not
perceive the sound underneath, and when one perceives
sound, one does not perceive the words underneath. When
the poet perceives words, the musician perceives sound
underneath. The mystic perceives even in that sound a
Word which was God.

Tone continues, time expires.

Tone lives on time, time assimilates tone.

God is not in time. Therefore He is in the silence. Sound is
part of the world of time.

Rhythm cannot exist without tone, nor tone without
rhythm. They are interdependent for their existence, and it
is the same with time and space.

Noisiness comes from restlessness, and restlessness is the
destructive rhythm.

Man's atmosphere explains the condition of his soul.

The further we go, so the more our disputes and arguments cease. They fade away until there is no colour left in them; and when all the colour has gone, the white light comes which is the light of God.

Nirvana means no colour. What is colour? Right or wrong, sin or virtue – all this is colour, and in the realm of truth they fade away, as every colour fades in the brightness of light. He who has realized this has entered *nirvana*.

A Sufi must always recognize in God the source of all things and the origin of all beings.

A Sufi must observe in the continual unfoldment of the spirit the birth of the soul.

THE MYSTICISM OF SOUND

CHAPTER I

The Silent Life

THE LIFE absolute from which has sprung all that is felt, seen and perceived, and into which all again merges in time, is a silent, motionless and eternal life which among Sufis is called *Dhat* (zat). Every motion that springs forth from this silent life is a vibration and a creator of vibrations. Within one vibration are created many vibrations.

As motion causes motion so the silent life becomes active in a certain part, and creates every moment more and more activity, losing thereby the peace of the original silent life. It is the grade of activity of these vibrations that accounts for the various planes of existence. These planes are imagined to differ from one another, but in reality they cannot be entirely detached and made separate from one another. The activity of vibrations makes them grosser, and thus the earth is born of the heavens.

The mineral, vegetable, animal and human kingdoms are the gradual changes of vibrations, and the vibrations of each plane differ from one another in their weight, breadth, length, colour, effect, sound and rhythm.

Man is not only formed of vibrations, but he lives and moves in them: they surround him as the fish is surrounded by water, and he contains them within him as the tank contains water. His different moods, inclinations, affairs, successes and failures, and all the conditions of life depend upon a certain activity of vibrations, whether these be thoughts, emotions or feelings. It is the direction of the activity of vibrations that accounts for the variety of things and beings. This vibratory activity is the basis of sensation and the source of all pleasure and pain; its cessation is the opposite of sensation. All sensations are caused by a certain grade of activity of vibration.

There are two aspects of vibrations, fine and gross, both containing varied degrees. Some are perceived by the soul, some by the mind, and some by the eyes. What the soul perceives are the vibrations of the feelings; what the mind conceives are the vibrations of the thoughts; what the eyes see are the vibrations solidified from their ethereal state and turned into atoms which appear in the physical world, constituting the elements ether, air, fire, water and earth. The finest vibrations are imperceptible even to the soul. The soul itself is formed of these vibrations; it is their activity which makes it conscious.

Creation begins with the activity of consciousness, which may be called vibration, and every vibration starting from its original source is the same, differing only in its tone and rhythm caused by a greater or lesser degree of force behind it. On the plane of sound vibration causes diversity of tone, and in the world of atoms diversity of colour. It is by massing together that the vibrations become audible, but at each step towards the surface they multiply and, as they advance, they materialize.

Sound gives to the consciousness an evidence of its existence, although it is in fact the active part of consciousness itself which turns into sound. The knower, so to speak, becomes known to himself; in other words the consciousness bears witness to its own voice. It is therefore that sound appeals to man. All things being derived from and formed of vibrations have sound hidden within them, as fire is hidden in flint. And each atom of the universe confesses by its tone: 'My sole origin is sound'. If any solid or sonorous body is struck it will answer back: 'I am sound'.

Sound has its birth, death, sex, form, planet, god, colour, childhood, youth and age. But that volume of sound which is in the abstract – beyond the sphere of the concrete – is the origin and basis of all sound.

Both sound and colour make their effect on the human soul according to the law of harmony: to a fine soul colour appeals, and to a still finer soul sound. Tone has either a warm or a cold effect, according to its element, since all elements are made of different degrees of vibrations. Therefore sound can produce an agreeable or a disagreeable effect upon man's mind and body, and has its healing effect in the absence of herbs and drugs – which also have their origin in vibrations.

Manifestations being formed of vibrations, the planets are the primal manifestations, each planet having its peculiar tone;

therefore every note represents one planet. Every individual therefore has a note peculiar to himself which is according to his birth planet. For this reason a certain tone appeals to a particular person according to the grade of his evolution.

Every element has a sound peculiar to itself. In the finer elements the circle of sound expands, and in the grosser elements it narrows. It is therefore distinct in the former and indistinct in the latter.

The earth has various aspects of beauty as well as of variety in its sound. Its pitch is on the surface, its form is crescent-like, and its colour is yellow. The sound of the earth is dim and dull, and produces a thrill, activity and movement in the body. All instruments of wire and gut, as well as the instruments of percussion – such as the drum, cymbals, etc. – represent the sound of earth.

The sound of water is deep, its form is serpent-like, its colour green, and it is best heard in the roaring of the sea. The sound of running water, of mountain rills, the drizzling and pattering of rain, the sound of water running from a pitcher into a jar, from a pipe into a tub, from a bottle into a glass – all have a smooth and lively effect, and a tendency to produce imagination, whim, dream, affection and emotion. The instrument called *jalatarang* is an arrangement of china bowls or glasses graduated in size and filled with water in proportion to the desired scale: more water lowers the tone, and less raises it. These instruments have a touching effect upon the emotions of the heart.

The sound of fire is high-pitched, its form is curled, and its colour red. It is heard in the falling of the thunderbolt and in a volcanic eruption, in the sound of a fire when blazing, in the noise of squibs, crackers, rifles, guns and cannons. All these have a tendency to produce fear.

The sound of air is wavering, its form zigzag, and its colour blue. Its voice is heard in storms, when the wind blows, and in the whisper of the morning breeze. Its effect is breaking, sweeping and piercing. The sound of air finds expression in all wind instruments made of wood, brass and bamboo. It has a tendency to kindle the fire of the heart, as Rumi writes in his Mathnavi about the flute. Krishna is always portrayed in Indian art with a flute. The air sound overpowers all other sounds, for it is living, and in every aspect its influence produces ecstasy.

The sound of ether is self-contained, and it holds all forms and colours. It is the base of all sounds, and is the undertone which is ever continuous. Its instrument is the human body, because it can be audible through it. Although it is all-pervading, yet it is unheard. It manifests to man as he purifies his body from material properties. The body can become its proper instrument when the space within is opened, when all the tubes and veins in it are free. Then the sound which exists eternally in space becomes manifest inwardly also. Ecstasy, illumination, restfulness, fearlessness, rapture, joy and revelation are the effects of this sound. To some it manifests of itself, to others when they are in a negative state caused by weakness of the body or mind; to neither of these is it a benefit, but on the other hand it causes them to become abnormal. This sound only elevates those who open themselves to it by the sacred practices known to the mystics.

The sound of earth and water commingled has a tenderness and delicacy. The sound of earth and fire produces harshness. The sound of earth and air has strength and power. The sound of water and fire has a lively and animating effect. The sound of water with ether has a soothing and comforting effect. The sound of fire and air has a terrifying and fearsome effect. The sound of fire with ether has a breaking and freeing effect. The sound of air with ether produces calm and peace.

CHAPTER II

Vibrations

THE SILENT life experiences on the surface by reason of activity. The silent life appears as death in comparison with the life of activity on the surface. Only to the wise the life eternal seems preferable on account of the ever-changing and momentary nature of mortal life. The life on the surface seems to be the real life, because it is in this life that all joy is experienced.

In the silent life there is no joy but only peace. The soul's original being is peace and its nature is joy, both of which work against each other. This is the hidden cause of all life's tragedy. The soul originally is without any experience; it experiences all when it opens its eyes to the exterior plane, and keeps them open enjoying the life on the surface until satisfied. The soul then begins to close its eyes to the exterior plane, and constantly seeks peace, the original state of its being.

The inward and essential part of each and every being is composed of fine vibrations, and the external part is formed of gross ones. The finer part we name spirit and the grosser part matter, the former being less subject to change and destruction and the latter more so. All that lives is spirit and all that dies is matter; and all that dies in spirit is matter and all that lives in matter is spirit. All that is visible and perceptible appears to be living, although subject to death and decay and becoming every moment resolved into its finer element but the sight of man is so deluded by its awareness of the seeming world, that the spirit which really lives is covered under the garb of matter and its true being is hidden.

It is the gradual increasing activity which causes vibrations to materialize, and it is the gradual decrease of the same which transmutes them again into spirit. As has been said, vibrations pass through five distinct phases while changing from the fine to the gross, and the elements of ether, air, fire, water and earth – each has a savour, colour and form peculiar to itself. Thus the elements form a wheel which brings them all in time to the surface. At each step in their activity they vary and become distinct from each other, and it is the grouping of these vibrations which causes variety in the objective world. The law, which causes them to disperse, man calls destruction.

Vibrations turn to atoms and atoms generate what we call life; thus it happens that their grouping, by the power of nature's affinity, forms a living entity. And as the breath manifests through the form so the body becomes conscious. In one individual there are many fine and small beings hidden: in his blood, in his brain cells, in his skin, and in all planes of his existence.

As in the physical being of an individual many small germs are born and nourished which are living beings, so in his mental plane also there are many beings, termed *muwakkals* – elementals. These are still finer entities born of man's own thoughts, and as the germs live in his physical body so the elementals dwell in his mental sphere. Man often imagines that thoughts are without life; he does not see that they are more alive than the physical germs and that they have a birth, childhood, youth, age and death. They work for man's advantage or disadvantage according to their nature. The Sufi creates, fashions and controls them. He drills them and rules them throughout his life; they form his army and carry out his desires. As the germs constitute man's physical being and the elementals his mental life, so do the angels constitute his spiritual existence. These are termed *farishtas*.

Vibrations as a rule have length as well as breadth, and they may last the least fraction of a moment or the greater part of the age of the universe. They make different forms, figures and colours as they shoot forth, one vibration creating another; thus myriads arise out of one. In this way there are circles under circles and circles over circles, all of which form the universe. Every vibration after its manifestation becomes merged again in its original source. The reach of vibrations is according to the fineness of the plane of their starting-point. To speak more plainly, the word uttered by the lips can only reach the ears of the hearer, but the thought proceeded from the mind reaches far, shooting from mind to mind. The vibrations of mind are much stronger than those of words. The earnest feelings of one heart can pierce the heart of another; they speak in the silence, spreading out into the sphere, so that the very atmosphere of a person's presence proclaims his thoughts and emotions. The vibrations of the soul are the most powerful and far-reaching; they run like an electric current from soul to soul.

All things and beings in the universe are connected with each other – visibly or invisibly – and through vibrations a communication is established between them on all the planes of existence. As an ordinary instance: if one person coughs in an assembly, many others begin to do the same, and the same is the case with yawning. This also applies to laughter, excitement and depression. This shows that vibrations convey the condition of one being to another. The seer therefore knows of the past, present and future, and perceives conditions on all planes of existence. Vibrations work through the chord of sympathy existing between man and his surroundings, and reveal past, present and future conditions. This explains why the howling of dogs foretells death, and the neighing of horses the approach of danger. Not only animals show this, but even the plants in times of sorrow begin to die and the flowers to fade, while during times of happiness they grow and flourish. The reason why plants and animals can perceive the vibrations and know of coming events while man is ignorant of them, is because he has blinded himself with egotism. The influence of vibrations is left on the chair on which one sits, in the bed where one has slept, in the house where one lives, in the clothes one wears, in the food one eats, and even in the street where one walks.

Every emotion arises from the intensity of the vibrations which, when active in different directions, produce different emotions, the main cause of every emotion being activity alone. Every vibration while active raises the consciousness to the outermost surface, and the mist caused by this activity collects clouds which we call emotions. The clouds of emotion obscure the clear sight of the soul. Therefore passion is called blind. The excess of activity of vibrations not only blinds, but weakens the will, and a weak will enfeebles the mind and body.

It is the state of vibrations to which man is tuned that accounts for his soul's note. The different degrees of these notes form a variety of pitch divided by the mystics into three distinct grades. First, the grade which produces power and intelligence and may be pictured as a calm sea. Secondly, the grade of moderate activity which keeps all things in motion and is a balance between power and weakness, which may be pictured as the sea in motion. Thirdly, the grade of intense activity which destroys everything and causes weakness and blindness; it may be pictured as a stormy sea.

In the activity of all things and beings the pitch is recognized by the seer, as a musician knows the key in which any particular music is written. Man's atmosphere tells of the grade of activity of his vibrations.

If vibratory activity is properly controlled man may experience all life's joy and at the same time not be enslaved by it. It is most difficult to control activity when it is once started and on the increase, for it is like trying to control a runaway horse. But yet in the control abides the whole of what is called mastership.

The saints and sages spread their peace not only in the place where they sit, but even in the neighbourhood where they dwell; the town or the country where they live is at peace, in accordance with the power of the vibrations they send out from their soul. This is the reason why association with good or bad and with those of the upper or lower classes has a great influence upon the life and character of man.

The vibrations of thought and feeling create, procure and prepare of themselves all the necessary means for their manifestation on the surface. For example a person may desire to eat fish and, instead of ordering it, might think strongly of it. His thought-vibrations thus speaking to the mental ears of the cook transmit this desire, and perhaps his strong feeling would even attract a fishmonger to the house. In this way the thoughts of sages work out their destiny according to the strength, power and purity of their minds. A certain degree of thought-power is needed to bring about a certain result, as so much dynamite is required to blast a single rock, and an infinitely greater quantity is necessary to make a tunnel through a mountain.

The length of time that the thought is held has also much to do with its accomplishment, for the thought-vibrations have to be active for a certain time to bring about a certain result. A certain length of time is required for the baking of a cake:

if it is hurried the cake will be uncooked, with too great a heat it will burn. If the operator of the mental vibrations lacks patience then the power of thought will be wasted, even if it were half-way to its destiny, or still nearer to a successful issue. If too great a power of thought is given to the accomplishment of a certain thing it destroys while preparing it.

In order to reflect thought and feeling on another, man should observe the same rule as in voice and word. The louder a person speaks in an assembly the more attention he attracts, and all those present perforce give him a hearing. In the same way, if a Sufi sends forth the vibrations of his thought and feeling, they naturally strike with a great strength and power on any mind on which they happen to fall. As sweetness of voice has a winning power, so it is with tenderness of thought and feeling. Thought-vibrations to which the spoken word is added are double in strength, and with a physical effect this strength is trebled.

Reason is like fire: it gives light to the thought, but thought overheated loses its power, as heat weakens the physical body. Reason gives birth to doubt which destroys the thought-power before it is able to fulfil its destiny. The strength of thought-power consists in confidence or faith. Reason confuses, and doubts scatter the waves of thought-vibrations which disperse and go off in different directions from lack of the strength that binds.

One should never think or speak against one's desire, for it weakens the thought-vibrations and often brings about contrary results. A variety of thoughts springing up at the same time naturally enfeebles the power of mind, for none of them has a chance to mature, just as twins are often imperfect and triplets seldom live. The disharmony between one's desire and one's ideal always causes a great confusion in life, for they constantly work against each other.

When a person speaks, thinks or feels either harshly or kindly of another, it reaches the spirit of that one, either consciously or unconsciously, by the power of vibration. If we happen to be offended with someone and do not show it in speech or action, yet it still cannot be hidden, for the vibrations of our feeling will reach directly to the person in question, and he will begin to feel our displeasure, however far away he may be. The same is the case with our love and pleasure: however we may try to conceal it in speech or action, it cannot be hidden. This explains the old adage that even walls have ears, which really means that even the wall is not impervious to vibrations of thought.

Sufis give special attention to the good and bad wishes of people. They strive continually to attract the good wishes of others, whether worthy or unworthy, by every means in their power.

Intensity of activity produces strong vibrations named in Sufi terms *jelal*; gentleness of activity causes mild vibrations called *jemal*. The former activity works as strength and power, the latter as beauty and grace. The conflict of both these forces is termed *kemal*, and causes nothing but destruction.

The standard of right and wrong, the conception of good and evil, and the idea of sin and virtue are understood differently by the people of different races, nations and religions; therefore it is difficult to discern the law governing these opposites. It becomes clear, however, by understanding the law of vibrations. All things and beings on the surface of existence seem separate from one another, but in every plane, beneath the surface, they approach nearer to each other, and in the innermost plane they all become one. Every disturbance, therefore, caused to the peace of the smallest part of existence on the surface, inwardly affects the whole. Thus any thought, speech or action that disturbs peace is wrong, evil and a sin. If it brings about peace it is right, good and a virtue. Life being like a dome, its nature is also dome-like. Disturbance of the slightest part of life disturbs the whole and returns as a curse upon the person who caused it. Any peace produced on the surface comforts the whole, and thence returns as peace to the producer. This is the philosophy of the reward of good deeds and the punishment of bad deeds given by the higher powers.

CHAPTER III

Harmony

HARMONY IS the source of manifestation, the cause of its existence, and the medium between God and man.

The peace for which every soul strives, and which is the true nature of God and the utmost goal of man, is but the outcome of harmony. This shows that all life's attainments without a sense of harmony are but vain. It is the attainment of harmony which is called heaven, and it is the lack of it which is termed hell. The master of harmony alone understands life, and he who lacks it is foolish in spite of all other knowledge that he may have acquired.

The Sufi gives great importance to the attainment of harmony, believing that light is for angels and darkness for the devil, but that harmony is necessary for the human being in order to keep a balance in life.

There are three aspects of harmony: eternal, universal and individual.

Eternal harmony is the harmony of consciousness. As it is in itself eternal, all things and beings live and move in it; yet it remains remote, undisturbed and peaceful. This is the God of the believer and the God of the knower. All vibrations, from the finest to the grossest, as well as each atom of manifestation, are held together by this harmony. Both creation and destruction take place in order to uphold it. Its power ultimately attracts each being towards the everlasting peace.

Man is drawn in two opposite directions by the power of harmony: towards the Infinite and towards manifestation. He is less conscious of the former than of the latter, and by facing towards one direction he loses sight of the other. The Infinite being, the essential spirit of all, finally attracts all to itself. The Sufi gives the greatest importance to harmony with the Infinite, which he realizes through resignation to the will of God, the Beloved.

The existence of land and water, the land for the water and the water for the land, the attraction between the heavens and the earth – all demonstrate a universal harmony. The attraction of the sun and moon to each other, the cosmic order of the stars and the planets, all connected and related with each other, moving and working under a certain law; the regular rotation of the seasons; the night following the day, and the day in its turn giving place to the night; the dependence of one being on another; the distinctiveness, attraction and assimilation of the five elements – all prove the universal harmony.

The male and female, beast and bird, vegetable and rock – all classes of things and beings – are linked together and attracted to each other with a chord of harmony. If one being or thing, however apparently useless, were missing in this universe of endless variety, it would be as it were a note missing in a song. As Sa'adi says: 'Every being is born for a certain purpose, and the light of that purpose is kindled within his soul'. All famines, plagues and disasters such as storms, floods, volcanic eruptions, wars and revolutions, however bad they appear to man, are in reality for the adjustment of this universal harmony.

There is a story told in India how once all the inhabitants of a village which had suffered from drought gathered together before the temple of their God, praying that for this year an abundance of rain might fall. A voice from the unseen replied: 'Whatever We do is for the betterment of Our purpose. Ye have no right to interfere with Our work, Oh ye men!' But they again cried for mercy, and continued to do so more persistently. Then came the answer saying: 'Your prayers, fastings and sacrifices have induced Us to grant for this one year as much rain as ye desire'. They all returned home rejoicing. In the autumn they worked vigorously on their farms, and after having prepared the ground and sown the seed they prayed for rain. When they considered that sufficient had fallen they again had recourse to prayer, and the rain ceased. In this way an ideal crop of corn was produced and all the inhabitants of that country made merry over it.

This year more crop was grown than ever before. After the crops were gathered in however, all those who ate the corn died and many were the victims. In perplexity they again sought the God bowing low before the temple, crying: 'Why hast Thou shown such wrath to us, after having shown so

great a mercy?' The God replied: 'It was not Our wrath, but
your folly for interfering with Our work. We sometimes send
a drought, and at other times a flood, so that a portion of
your crops may be destroyed. But We have Our reasons for
so doing, for in this way all that is poisonous and undesirable
in them is also destroyed, leaving only what is beneficial for
the preservation of your life'.

The villagers prostrated themselves in humble prayer,
saying: 'We shall never again try to control the affairs of the
universe. Thou art the Creator, and Thou art the Controller.
We are Thine innocent children, and Thou alone knowest
what is best for us'. The Creator knows how to control His
world, what to bring forth, and what to destroy.

There are two aspects of individual harmony: the
harmony between body and soul, and the harmony
between individuals.

The soul rejoices in the comforts experienced by the
external self, yet man becomes so engrossed in them that the
soul's true comfort is neglected. This keeps man dissatisfied
through all the momentary comforts he may enjoy, but not
understanding this he attributes the cause of his dissatisfaction
to some unsatisfied desire in his life. The outlet of all
earthly passions gives a momentary satisfaction, yet creates a
tendency for more. In this struggle the satisfaction of the soul
is overlooked by man who is constantly busied in the pursuit
of his earthly enjoyment and comfort, depriving the soul of
its true bliss. The true delight of the soul lies in love, harmony
and beauty, the outcome of which is wisdom, calm and peace;
the more constant they are the greater is the satisfaction of the
soul.

If man in his daily life would examine every action which
has reflected a disagreeable picture of himself upon his soul
and caused darkness and dissatisfaction, and if on the other
hand he would consciously watch each thought, word or
deed which had produced an inward love, harmony and
beauty, and each feeling which had brought him wisdom,
calm and peace, then the way of harmony between soul and
body would be easily understood, and both aspects of life
would be satisfied, the inner as well as the outer. The soul's
satisfaction is much more important than that of the body for

it is more lasting. In this way the thought, speech and action can be adjusted, so that harmony may be established first in the self by the attunement of body and soul.

The next aspect of individual harmony is practised in one's contact with another. Every being has an individual ego produced from his own illusion. This limits his view which is led in the direction of his own interest; and he judges of good and bad, high or low, right or wrong in relation to himself and others through his limited view, which is generally partial and imaginary rather than true. This darkness is caused by the overshadowing of the soul by the external self. Thus a person becomes blind to his own infirmities as well as to the merits of another: the right action of another becomes wrong in his eyes and the fault of the self seems right. This is the case with mankind in general, until the veil of darkness is lifted from his eyes.

The *nafs*, the ego of an individual, causes all disharmony with the self as well as with others, thus showing its unruliness in all aspects of life. The lion, the sovereign among all animals, most powerful and majestic, is always unwelcome to the inhabitants of the forest, and he is even unfriendly to his own kind. Two lions will never greet one another in a friendly way, for their *nafs* is so strong. Although the lion is the ruler of all other animals, he is a slave to his own passions which make his life restless. The *nafs* of herbivorous animals such as sheep and goats is subdued; for this reason they are harmless to one another, and are even harmonious enough to live in herds. The harmony and sympathy existing among them makes them mutually partake of their joys and sorrows, but they easily fall a victim to the wild animals of the forest. The masters of the past, like Moses and Muhammad, have always loved to tend their flocks in the jungles, and Jesus Christ spoke of himself as the Good Shepherd, while St. John the Baptist spoke of the Lamb of God, harmless and innocent, ready for sacrifice.

The *nafs* of the bird is still milder; therefore upon one tree many and various kinds can live as one family, singing the praise of God in unison, and flying about in flocks of thousands. Among birds are to be found those who recognize their mate and who live together harmoniously, building the nest for their young, each in turn sitting on the eggs and bearing their part in the upbringing of their little ones. Many times they mourn and lament over the death of their mate.

The *nafs* of the insects is still less; they walk over each other without doing any harm, and live together in millions as one family without distinction of friend or foe. This proves how the power of *nafs* grows at each step in nature's evolution, and culminates in man, creating disharmony all through his life unless it is subdued, producing thereby a calm and peace within the self, and a sense of harmony with others.

Every human being has an attribute peculiar to his *nafs*. One is tiger-like, another resembles a dog, while a third may be like a cat, and a fourth like a fox. In this way man shows in his speech, thoughts and feelings the beasts and birds, and the condition of his *nafs* is akin to their nature; at times his very appearance resembles them. Therefore his tendency to harmony depends upon the evolution of his *nafs*. As man begins to see clearly through human life, the world begins to appear as a forest to him, filled with wild animals, fighting, killing and preying upon one another.

There are four different classes of men who harmonize with each other in accordance with their different states of evolution: angelic, human, animal and devilish.

The angelic seeks for heaven, and the human being struggles along in the world. The man with animal propensities revels in his earthly pleasures, while the devilish man is engaged in creating mischief, thereby making a hell for himself and for others. Man after his human evolution becomes angelic, and through his development in animality arrives at the stage of devil.

In music the law of harmony is that the nearest note does not make a consonant interval. This explains the prohibition of marriage between close relatives because of the nearness in merit and blood. As a rule harmony lies in contrast. Men fight with men and women quarrel with women, but the male and the female are as a rule harmonious with each other and a complete oneness makes a perfect harmony.

In every being the five elements are constantly working, and in every individual one especially predominates. The wise have therefore distinguished five different natures in man according to the element predominant in him. Sometimes two elements or even more predominate in a human being in a greater or lesser degree.

The harmony of life can be learned in the same way as the harmony of music. The ear should be trained to distinguish both tone and word, the meaning concealed within, and to know from the verbal meaning and the tone of the voice whether it is a true word or a false note; to distinguish between sarcasm and sincerity, between words spoken in jest, and those spoken in earnest; to understand the difference between true admiration and flattery; to distinguish modesty from humility, a smile from a sneer, and arrogance from pride, either directly or indirectly expressed. By so doing the ear becomes gradually trained in the same way as in music, and a person knows exactly whether his own tone and word, as well as those of another, are false or true.

Man should learn in what tone to express a certain thought or feeling as in voice cultivation. There are times when he should speak loudly, and there are times when a soft tone of voice is needed; for every word a certain note, and for every speech a certain pitch is necessary. At the same time there should be a proper use of a natural sharp or flat note, as well as a consideration of key.

There are nine different aspects of feeling, each of which has a certain mode of expression:

> mirth, expressed in a lively tone
> grief, expressed in a pathetic tone
> fear – in a broken voice
> mercy – in a tender voice
> wonder – in an exclamatory tone
> courage – in an emphatic tone
> frivolity – in a light tone
> attachment – in a deep tone
> indifference – in the voice of silence.

An untrained person confuses these. He whispers the words which should be known, and speaks out loudly those which should be hidden. A certain subject must be spoken in a high pitch, while another requires a lower pitch. One should consider the place, the space, the number of persons present, the kind of people and their evolution, and speak in accordance with the understanding of others, as it is said: 'Speak to people in their own language'. With a child one must have childish talk, with the young only suitable words should be spoken, with the old one should speak in accordance with their understanding. In the same way there should be a graduated expression of our thought, so that everybody may not be driven with the same whip. It is consideration for others which distinguishes man from the animals.

It must be understood that rhythm is the balance of speech and action. One must speak at the right time, otherwise silence is better than speech: a word of sympathy with the grief of another, and a smile at least when another laughs. One should watch the opportunity for moving a subject in society, and never abruptly change the subject of conversation, but skilfully blend two subjects with a harmonious link. Also one should wait patiently while another speaks, and keep a rein on one's speech when the thought rushes out uncontrollably, in order to keep it in rhythm and under control during its outlet. One should emphasize the important words with a consideration of strong and weak accent. It is necessary to choose the right words and mode of expression, to regulate the speed and to know how to keep the rhythm. Some people begin to speak slowly and gradually increase the speed to such an extent that they are unable to speak coherently.

The above named rules apply to all actions in life.

The Sufi, like a student of music, trains both his voice and ear in the harmony of life. The training of the voice consists in being conscientious about each word spoken, about its tone, rhythm, meaning and the appropriateness for the occasion. For instance the words of consolation should be spoken in a slow rhythm, with a soft voice and sympathetic tone. When speaking words of command a lively rhythm is necessary, and a powerful distinct voice.

The Sufi avoids all unrhythmic actions; he keeps the rhythm of his speech under the control of patience, not speaking a word before the right time, not giving an answer until the question is finished. He considers a contradictory word a discord unless spoken in a debate, and even at such times he tries to resolve it into a consonant chord. A contradictory tendency in man finally develops into a passion, until he contradicts even his own idea if it be propounded by another.

In order to keep harmony the Sufi even modulates his speech from one key to another; in other words, he falls in with another person's idea by looking at the subject from the speaker's point of view instead of his own. He makes a base for every conversation with an appropriate introduction, thus preparing the ears of the listener for a perfect response. He watches his every moment and expression, as well as those of others, trying to form a consonant chord of harmony between himself and another.

The attainment of harmony in life takes a longer time to acquire and a more careful study than does the training of the ear and the cultivation of the voice, although it is acquired in the same manner as the knowledge of music. To the ear of the Sufi every word spoken is like a note which is true when harmonious and false when inharmonious. He makes the scale of his speech either major, minor or chromatic as occasion demands, and his words – either sharp, flat or natural – are in accord with the law of harmony. For instance, the straight, polite and tactful manner of speech is like his major, minor or chromatic scale, representing dominance, respect and equality. Similarly he takes arbitrary or contrary motions to suit the time and situation by following step by step, by agreeing and differing, and even by opposing, and yet keeping up the law of harmony in conversation. Take any two persons as two notes; the harmony existing between them forms intervals either consonant or dissonant, perfect or imperfect, major or minor, diminished or augmented, as the two persons may be.

The interval of class, creed, caste, race, nation or religion, as well as the interval of age or state of evolution, or of varied and opposite interests shows the law here distinctly. A wise man would be more likely to be in harmony with his foolish servant than with a semi-wise man who considers himself infallible. Again it is equally possible that a wise man be far from happy in the society of the foolish, and vice versa.

The proud man will always quarrel with the proud while he will support the humble. It is also possible for the proud to agree on a common question of pride, such as pride of race or birth.

Sometimes the interval between the disconnected notes is filled by a middle note forming a consonant chord. For instance the discord between husband and wife may be removed by the link of a child, or the discord between brothers and sisters may be taken away by the intervention of the mother or father. In this way, however inharmonious two persons may be, the forming of a consonant chord by an intervening link creates harmony. A foolish person is an unpliable note whereas an intelligent person is pliable. The former sticks to his ideas, likes, dislikes and convictions, whether right or wrong, while the latter makes them sharp or flat by raising or lowering the tone and pitch, harmonizing with the other as the occasion demands. The key-note is always in harmony with each note, for it has all notes of the scale within it. In the same way the Sufi harmonizes with everybody, whether good or bad, wise or foolish, by becoming like the key-note.

All races, nations, classes and people are like a strain of music based upon one chord, when the key-note, the common interest, holds so many personalities in a single bond of harmony. By a study of life the Sufi learns and practises the nature of its harmony. He establishes harmony with the self, with others, with the universe and with the infinite. He identifies himself with another, he sees himself, so to speak, in every other being. He cares for neither blame nor praise, considering both as coming from himself. If a person were to drop a heavy weight, and in so doing hurt his own foot, he would not blame his hand for having dropped it, realizing himself in both the hand and the foot. In like manner the Sufi is tolerant when harmed by another, thinking that the harm has come from himself alone. He uses counterpoint by blending the undesirable talk of the friend and making it into a fugue.

He overlooks the fault of others, considering that they know no better. He hides the faults of others, and suppresses any facts that would cause disharmony. His constant fight is with the *nafs*, the root of disharmony and the only enemy of man. By crushing this enemy man gains mastery over himself; this wins for him mastery over the whole universe, because the wall standing between the self and the Almighty has been broken down.

Gentleness, mildness, respect, humility, modesty, self-denial, conscientiousness, tolerance and forgiveness are considered by the Sufi as the attributes which produce harmony within one's own soul as well as within that of another. Arrogance, wrath, vice, attachment, greed and jealousy are the six principal sources of disharmony. *Nafs*, the only creator of disharmony, becomes more powerful the more it is gratified, the more it is pleased. For the time being it shows its satisfaction at having gratified its demands, but soon after it demands still more until life becomes a burden. The wise detect this enemy as the instigator of all mischief, but everybody else blames another for his misfortunes in life.

CHAPTER IV

Name

THE VARIETY of things and beings and the peculiarities which make them differ cause the necessity of name. Name produces the picture of a form, figure, colour, size, quality, quantity, feeling and sense of things and beings – not only perceptible and comprehensible, but even of those beyond perception and comprehension. Therefore its importance is greater than all things. There is a great secret hidden in name, be it the name of a person or a thing, and it is formed in relation to the past, present and future conditions of its object; the right horoscope tells you about the conditions of a person.

All mystery is hidden in name. The knowledge of everything rests on first knowing its name, and knowledge is not complete which is devoid of name. Mastery depends upon knowledge; man cannot master a thing of which he has no knowledge. All blessings and benefits derived from earth or heaven are gained by mastery which depends upon knowledge, knowledge depending upon name. Man without the knowledge of the name of a thing is ignorant, and the ignorant is powerless, for man has no hold over any thing of which he has no knowledge.

The reason of man's greatness is the scope of the knowledge with which he is gifted, all the mystery of which lies in his recognition of the differences between things and beings. This gives man superiority not only over all creatures of the earth, but it even makes him excel the angels, the hosts of heaven.

The Qur'an explains it in the following words: 'When the Lord said unto the angels, "We are going to place a substitute on earth", they said: "Wilt Thou place there one who will do evil therein and shed blood, while we celebrate Thy praise and sanctify Thee?" God answered: "Verily We know that which ye know not", and He taught Adam the names of all things, and then proposed them to the angels, and said: "Declare unto Me the names of these things if ye say truth". They answered: "Praise be unto Thee; we have no knowledge but what Thou teaches us, for Thou art all-knowing and wise". God said: "O

Adam, tell them their names". And when Adam came he told their names'.

Every name reveals to the seer the past, present and future of that which it covers. Name is not only significant of form but of character as well. The meaning of name plays an important part in man's life, and the sound, the vowels in the name, the rhythm, number and nature of the letters which compose it, the mystical numbers, symbol and planet, as well as the root from which it is derived and the effect which it produces, all disclose their secret to the seer.

The meaning of a name has a great influence upon its possessor as well as upon others. From the sound of the letters and the word they compose the mystic can understand much about the character and the fate of a person. An intelligent person generally gets the idea from the sound of letters that compose a name, whether it is beautiful or ugly, soft or hard, consonant or dissonant, but does not know what makes it so; the one who understands knows why it is so.

Letters singly or together are either pronounced smoothly or with difficulty and have their effect accordingly upon oneself and upon another. Names that are smooth and soft-sounding make a soft effect upon the speaker and listener, whereas hard-sounding names have a contrary effect. Man naturally calls soft things by smooth names and hard things by hard-sounding names, as for instance flower and rock, wool and flint, etc.

Language, and especially name, shows the class of people and character of families, communities and races. Vowels play a great part in the name and its influence. E and I denote *jemal*, the feminine quality of grace, wisdom, beauty and receptivity. O and U denote *jelal*, the masculine quality of power and expression. A denotes *kemal*, which is significant of the perfection in which both these qualities are centred. The above-named vowels in the composition of the name have an effect according to their place in the name, whether in the beginning, centre or end.

Fate in Sanskrit is called *karma*, meaning the rhythm of past actions. The influence of rhythm suggested by a name has an effect upon the entity whose name it is, as well as upon those who call him by that name. Evenness of rhythm gives balance, while unevenness causes lack of balance. The beauty of rhythm beautifies the character of man.

By rhythm is meant the way in which the name begins and how it ends, whether evenly or unevenly, on the accent or before the accent. The accent falling on the beginning, middle or end varies the effect which plays a part in a person's character and fate. The rhythm of the name suggests the main thing in life: balance or its lack. Lack of balance is a deficiency in character, and causes adversity in life.

The number of letters plays a great part in the name of a person. An even number shows beauty and wisdom, and an odd number shows love and power. Number plays a great part in life, and especially in name. Each letter in the constitution of a name has a numerical value; in oriental science it is called *jafr*. By this system not only are names given to buildings, objects and people, conveying their period of commencement and completion, but the combination of these numbers conveys to the seer its mystical effect.

Names have a psychic effect upon their owners and even upon surroundings. The names of elementals and *jinn*, the sacred names of God, and the holy names of the prophets and saints, written according to the law of their numerical value, act as a magical charm for the accomplishment of different objects in life, and by the combination of such names, written or repeated in their numerical form, wonders are performed.

Every letter, either singly or when grouped in a word, produces a picture which tells its secret to the seer. For instance X makes a cross, and 0 zero, both of which have a meaning. The alphabet used in modern times is a corruption of the original ones. The old Arabian and Persian writings which are found on arches, walls, hems of garments, on brass vessels and carpets, are of most perfect and beautiful design. A great symbolic significance may be seen in the Chinese, Japanese, Sanskrit and other ancient scripts. Every line, dot and curve has a meaning. The ancient used to write every name not with different letters, but as a picture signifying what they wished to express. The picture was divided into different parts and each part was used to represent a certain sound, and in this way the alphabets were made. By this break the true picture was lost, but a certain likeness may still be traced. Even in the present day, although we have a most corrupted form of writing, still from the appearance of a certain name a person's life, fate or character may be read in whatever language it may be written. For instance, a name beginning with I shows a steadfast and righteous ego, uniqueness and love of God and the pursuit of truth. E shows a shy and backward nature and an interest in three directions.

As one letter makes a picture, in the same way a whole word makes a picture. The idea of *Allah* has come from man, and one can read in the form of the hand the word *Allah*.

The Christian name has a greater influence than the surname. Sometimes a nickname has a still greater effect. The effect of the name is according to its use; the more it is used the greater the effect. Shortened names such as May for Mary, Bill or Willie for William lessen the effect of the name. The names given by the holy ones have a double effect: that of the name itself and that of the will of the one who gave it. Maula Bakhsh, the greatest musician of his day in India, was given his name by a *faqir* who was charmed on hearing his music. It means 'God bless'. After taking this name he had success wherever he went and was blessed with merit and reward, both of which are the rare gifts of God. There are many instances to be found where a change of name has brought an entire change in a man's life. We read in the Bible that the blessing of Jacob was the name of Israel given to him by the angel.

In the Qur'an Muhammad is constantly addressed by a special name having its effect not only on the life of the Prophet, but on his followers who adopted and worked psychologically with any of these names. Sufis have for ages experienced the mystical value of these names. Among Sufis the *Murshid* gives to his pupils the name *Talib*, or *Mureed*, which is to give him in time the identity of the name.

CHAPTER V

Form

THE LIGHT from which all life comes exists in three aspects, namely the aspect which manifests as intelligence, the light of the abstract, and the light of the sun. The activity of this one light functions in three different aspects. The first is caused by a slow and solemn activity in the eternal Consciousness which may be called consciousness or intelligence. It is intelligence when there is nothing before it to be conscious of; when there is something intelligible before it, the same intelligence becomes consciousness. A normal activity in the light of intelligence causes the light of the abstract at the time when the abstract sound turns into light. This light becomes a torch for the seer who is journeying towards the eternal goal. The same light in its intense activity appears as the sun.

No person would readily believe that intelligence, abstract light and the sun are one and the same – yet language does not contradict itself, and all three have always been called by the name of light. These three aspects of the one light form the idea that lies behind the doctrine of the Trinity, and that of *Trimurti* which existed thousands of years before Christianity among the Hindus, and which denotes the three aspects of the One: the One being three.

Substance commences to develop from radiance to atom, but before this it exists as a vibration. What man sees he accepts as something existent, and what he cannot see does not exist for him. All that man perceives, sees, and feels is matter, and that which is the source and cause of all is spirit.

The philosophy of form may be understood by the study of the process by which the unseen life manifests into the seen. As the fine waves of vibrations produce sound, so the gross waves produce light. This is the manner in which the unseen, incomprehensible and imperceptible life becomes gradually known: first becoming audible, and then visible. This is the origin and only source of all life.

The sun, therefore, is the first form seen by the eyes, and it is the origin and source of all forms in the objective world; as such it has been worshipped by the ancients as God, and we can trace the origin of all religions in that mother-religion. We may trace this philosophy in the words of Shams-e-Tabriz: 'When the sun showed his face, then appeared the faces and forms of all worlds. His beauty showed their beauty; in his brightness they shone out; so by his rays we saw and knew and named them'.

All the myriad colours in the universe are but the different grades and shades of light, the creator of all elements, which has decorated the heavens so beautifully with sun, moon, planets and stars; which has made the land and water with all the beauties of the lower spheres, in some parts dull and in some parts bright, which man has named light and shade. The sun, moon, planets and stars, the brilliance of electricity, the lesser light of gas, lamp, candle, coal and wood, all show the sun reappearing in different forms. The sun is reflected in all things, be they dull pebbles or sparkling diamonds, and their radiance is according to their capability of reflection. This shows that light is the one and only source, and the cause of the whole creation. 'God is the light of the heavens and of the earth', the Qur'an says, and we read in Genesis: 'And God said: "Let there be light", and there was light'.

All forms, on whatever plane they exist, are moulded under the law of affinity. Every atom attracts toward itself the atom of its own element; every positive atom attracts the negative atom of its own element, and the negative attracts the positive. Yet each attraction is different and distinct. These atoms group together and make a form. The atoms of the abstract plane group together and make forms of light and colour. These and all different forms of the finer forces of life are seen by the seer. The forms of the mental plane are composed of the atoms of that plane; these are seen by the mind's eye and called imagination. On the physical plane this process may be seen in a more concrete form.

The mystic sees on the abstract plane one or other element predominating at a certain time, either ether, air, fire, water or earth. Every element in the finer forces of life is rendered intelligible by the direction of its activity and colour, and the various forms of light show its different rates of activity. For instance the feeling of humour develops into greater humour, and sadness into a deeper sorrow, and so it is with the imagination: every pleasant thought develops pleasure and expands into a still pleasanter thought, and every disagreeable imagination grows and becomes more intense. Again, on the physical plane we not only see men dwelling together in cities and villages, but even beasts and birds living in flocks and herds; coal is found in the coal-mine, and gold in the gold-mine, the forest contains thousands of trees, whereas the desert holds not a single one. All this proves the power of affinity which collects and groups the atoms of like kind and makes of them numerous forms, thereby creating an illusion before the eye of man who thus forgets the one source in the manifestation of variety.

The direction taken by every element to make a form depends upon the nature of its activity. For instance an activity following a horizontal direction shows the earth element, a downward direction the water element, an upward direction the fire element; the activity that moves in a zigzag direction shows the air element, and the form taken by the ether is indistinct and misty. Therefore the nature of all things is made plain to the seer by their form and shape, and from their colour their element is known, yellow being the colour of earth, green of water, red of fire, blue of air, and grey of ether. The mingling of these elements produces mixed colours which vary into innumerable shades and tones, and the variety of colour in nature bears evidence of the unlimited life behind it.

Every activity of vibrations produces a certain sound according to its dome of resonance, and according to the capacity of the mould in which the form is shaped. This explains the idea behind the ancient Hindu word *Nada Brahma*. which means: Sound, the Creator-God.

By the law of construction and destruction, as well as by addition and reduction, the different forms in this objective world group together and change. A close study of the constant grouping and dispersing of the clouds will reveal many different forms within a few minutes, and this is a key to the same process which can be seen all through nature. The construction and destruction, addition and reduction in forms all take place under the influence of time and space. Each form is shaped and changed subject to this law, for the substance differs according to the length, depth, height, figure and shape of the mould wherein the form is modelled, and the features are formed according to the impression pressed upon it. It takes time to make a young and tender leaf green, and again to change it from green to red and yellow, and it is space that makes of water either a ditch, well, pond, stream, river or ocean.

The dissimilarity in the features of various races in different periods can be accounted for by the law of time and space together with climatic and racial causes. The Afghans resemble the natives of the Panjab, and the Singalese the people of Madras; Arabs are similar in feature to the Persians, and the Chinese resemble the Japanese; Tibetans resemble the natives of Bhutan, and the Burmese closely resemble the Siamese. All this proves that the proximity of the lands which they inhabit is largely the cause of likeness in feature. As wide as is the distance of space, so wide is the difference in feature among people. The similarity in form of germs, worms and insects is accounted for by the same reason. Twin-born children as a rule resemble each other more closely than other children.

Form depends mostly upon reflection; it is the reflection of the sun in the moon that makes the moon appear round like the sun. All the lower creation evolves by the same law. Animals which begin to resemble man are among those which are in his surroundings and see him daily. A man who has the care of animals begins to resemble them, and we see that the butler of a colonel has the bearing of a soldier, and a maid working in a nunnery in time becomes like a nun.

As all things are subject to change, no one thing is the same as it was a moment before, although the change may not be noticeable; only a definite change is perceptible. In a flower there is a change from bud to blossom, and in a fruit from the unripe to the ripe state. Even stones change, and some among them have been known to become perceptibly altered even in the course of twenty-four hours.

Time has a great influence upon all things and beings, as may be seen by the change from infancy to youth, and from middle age to old age. In Sanskrit, therefore, time is called *kala*, which means destruction, as no change is possible without destruction; in other words, destruction may be described as change. All things natural and artificial that we see today differ vastly in their form from what they were several thousand years ago, and not only can this be noticed in such things as fruit, flowers, birds and animals, but also in the human race; for from time to time the structure of man has undergone various changes.

The form of man is divided into two parts, each part having its special attributes. The head is the spiritual body, and the lower part the material body. Therefore, in comparison with the body, the head has far greater importance. Thereby one individual is able to recognize another, as the head is the main distinctive part of man. The face is expressive of man's nature and his condition of life, also of his past, present and future. When asked if the face would be burned in the fire of hell, the Prophet answered: 'No, the face will not be burned, for Allah hath said: "We have modelled man in Our own image"'.

The likeness between things and beings, as well as between beast and birds and man, can tell us a great deal about the secret of their nature. The sciences of phrenology and physiognomy were discovered not only by examining the lives of men of various features, but chiefly by studying the similarity that exists between them and animals. For instance, a man having the features of a tiger will have a dominant nature, coupled with courage and cruelty. A man with a face resembling a horse is by nature subservient; a man with a face like a dog will have a pugnacious tendency, while a mouse-like face shows timidity.

There are four sources from which the human face and form are derived, and these account for the changes which take place in them. These are: the inherent attributes of his soul; the influence of his heritage; the impressions of his surroundings; and lastly the impression of himself and of his thoughts and deeds, of the clothes he wears, the food he eats, the air he breathes, and the way he lives.

In the first of these sources man is helpless for he has no choice. It was not the desire of the tiger to be a tiger, neither did a monkey choose to be a monkey, and it was not the choice of the infant to be born a male or a female. This proves that the first source of man's form depends upon the inherent attributes brought by his soul. Words never can express adequately the wisdom of the Creator who not only fashioned and formed the world, but has given to each being the form suited to his needs. The animals of the cold zone are provided with thick fur as a protection against the cold; to the beasts of the tropics a suitable form is given; the birds of the sea have wings fit for the sea, and those of the earth are provided with wings suitable for the earth. Birds and animals have forms which accord with their habits in life. The form of man proclaims his grade of evolution, his nature, his past and present, as well as his race, nation and surroundings, character and fate.

In the second instance man inherits beauty or its opposite from his ancestors, but in the third and fourth his form depends upon how he builds it. The build of his form depends upon the balance and regularity of his life, and upon the impressions he receives from the world; for in accordance with the attitude he takes towards life his every thought and action adds, or takes away, or removes to another place the atoms of his body, thus forming the lines and muscles of form and feature. For instance the face of a man speaks his joy, sorrow, pleasure, displeasure, sincerity, insincerity, and all that is developed in him. The muscles of his head tell the phrenologist his condition in life. There is a form in the thoughts and feelings which produces a beautiful or ugly effect.

It is the nature of evolution for all beings, from the lowest to the highest stage of manifestation, to evolve by being connected with a more perfect form. Animals approaching man in their evolution resemble primitive man, and animals in contact with man acquire in their form traces of the likeness of man. This may be understood by a close study of the features of man in the past, and of the improvement which has been made in them.

The nature of creation is that it is progressing always towards beauty. 'God is beautiful, and He loves beauty', says the Qur'an. The nature of the body is to beautify itself; the nature of the mind is to have beautiful thoughts; the longing of the heart is for beautiful feelings. Therefore an infant should grow more beautiful every day, and ignorance seek to become intelligence. When the progress is in a contrary direction, it shows that the individual has lost the track of natural progress. There are two forms: the natural and the artificial, the latter being a copy of the former.

CHAPTER VI

Rhythm

MOTION IS the significance of life, and the law of motion is rhythm. Rhythm is life disguised in motion, and in every guise it seems to attract the attention of man: from a child, who is pleased with the moving of a rattle and is soothed by the swing of its cradle, to a grown person whose every game, sport and enjoyment has rhythm disguised in it in some way or another, whether it is a game of tennis, cricket or golf, as well as boxing and wrestling. Again in the intellectual recreations of man, both poetry and music – vocal or instrumental – have rhythm as their very spirit and life. There is a saying in Sanskrit that tone is the mother of nature, but that rhythm is its father.

An infant once given the habit of a regular time for its food demands it at that time, although it has no idea of time. This is accounted for by the fact that the very nature of life is rhythm. The infant begins its life on earth by moving its arms and legs, thus showing the rhythm of its nature, and illustrating the philosophy which teaches that rhythm is the sign of life. The inclination to dance shown by every man illustrates also that innate nature of beauty which chooses rhythm for its expression.

Rhythm produces an ecstasy which is inexplicable, and incomparable with any other source of intoxication. This is why the dance has been the most fascinating pastime of all people, both civilized and savage, and has delighted alike saint and sinner.

The races which show a tendency for strongly accentuated rhythm must be vigorous by nature. Jazz has come from the negroes, and the syncopation is the secret of its charm and is the natural expression of their racial rhythm. Its rhythm arouses a kind of life among performers and audience alike, and it is the love of this life that has given such popularity to the jazz-band.

The dances among many wild tribes in different parts of the world show a most pronounced rhythm, which proves that rhythm is not a culture, but natural. Among Europeans the

Spanish, Poles, Hungarians and Russians show the greatest tendency toward rhythm. The secret of the success of the Russian ballet and the Spanish dance lies in their exquisite rhythm.

Among the Asiatic races the music of the Mongolians is chiefly based on rhythm, it being more pronounced than melody in their music. In Turkish and Persian music rhythm is also pronounced, and among the Arabs the variety of rhythms is very vast. In India however the culture of rhythm has reached perfection. An expert musician in India improvises a melody, keeping the same time throughout the whole improvisation. In order to become a master musician in India one must master thoroughly not only *Raga*, the scale, but also *tala*, the rhythm. Indians as a race are naturally inclined to rhythm; their dance *Tandeva Nrutya*, the dance of the South, is an expression of rhythm through movement.

In the Hindu science of music there are five different rhythms which are generally derived from the study of nature:

1. *Chatura*, the rhythm of four beats which was invented by *devas* – divine men.
2. *Tisra*, the rhythm of three beats, invented by *rishis* – saints.
3. *Khanda*, the rhythm of five beats, invented by the *rakshasas*.
4. *Misra*, the rhythm of seven beats, invented by the people.
5. *Sankrian*, the rhythm of nine beats, invented by the commercial class.

Mahadeva, the great Lord of the Yogis, was the dancer of *Tandeva Nrutya* and his consort Parvati danced the *Lassia Nrutya*.

The traditions of the Hindus have as a most sacred record the mystical legend of their Lord Shri Krishna dancing with the *gopis*. The story relates how Krishna, the charming youthful Lord of the Hindus, was moving among the dwelling of the cowherds, and every maiden, attracted by his beauty and charm, asked him to dance with her on the night of the full moon. On the night of the full moon there assembled sixteen hundred *gopis*, and the miracle of Krishna was performed when he appeared as a separate Krishna to each *gopi*, and all of them danced with their beloved Lord at one and the same time.

There is a tradition in Islam, where music, dancing and all amusements and light occupations are strictly prohibited, that on one occasion – it being a holiday – the Prophet called his wife Ayesha to look at the dance and listen to the music of some street musicians. In the meantime his great *Khalif* happened to come by and was shocked at seeing the Prophet, who had prohibited such things, himself permitting music in front of his house. When he stopped the music of the street players, pointing out to them that this was the house of the Prophet, Prophet Muhammad requested that they might continue, saying that it was a holiday, and: 'There is no heart that does not move with the motion of rhythm'.

In the traditions of the Sufis *Raqs*, the sacred dance of spiritual ecstasy which even now is prevalent among the Sufis of the East, is traced to the time when contemplation of the Creator impressed the wonderful reality of His vision so deeply on the heart of Jelal-ud-Din Rumi that he became entirely absorbed in the whole and single immanence of nature, and took a rhythmic turn which caused the skirt of his garment to form a circle, and the movements of his hands and neck made a circle. It is the memory of this moment of vision which is celebrated in the dance of dervishes.

Even in the lower creation among beasts and birds their joy is always expressed in dance. A bird like the peacock, when conscious of his beauty and the beauty of the forest around him, expresses his joy in dance. Dance arouses passion and emotion in all living creatures.

In the East, and especially in India where the life of the people for centuries has been based on psychological principles, in the royal processions or at *darbars*, the beating of the drums is taken as the means of making an impression of kingly grandeur upon the minds of people, and the same beating of drums takes place at wedding ceremonies and at the services in the temples.

Sufis, in order to awaken in man that emotional nature which is generally asleep, have a rhythmic practice which sets the whole mechanism of body and mind in rhythm.

There exists in all people, either consciously or unconsciously, a tendency toward rhythm. Among European nations the expression of pleasure is shown by the clapping of the hands. A farewell sign is made by the waving of the hand, which makes rhythm.

All labour and toil, however hard and difficult, is made easy by the power of rhythm in some way or other. This idea opens to the thinker a still deeper scope for the study of life.

Rhythm in every guise, be it called game, play, amusement, poetry, music or dance, is the very nature of man's whole constitution. When the entire mechanism of his body is working in a rhythm, the beat of the pulse, of the heart, of the head, the circulation of the blood, hunger and thirst – all show rhythm, and it is the breaking of rhythm that is called disease.

When the child is crying and the mother does not know what ails it, she holds it in her arms and pats it on the back. This sets the circulation of the blood, the pulsations and the whole mechanism of the body in rhythm; in other words sets the body in order, and soothes the child. The nursery rhyme 'Pat-a-cake', which is known all the world over in some form or other, cures a child of fretfulness by setting its whole being in rhythm.

Therefore physicians depend more upon the examination of the pulse than on anything else in discovering the true nature of disease, together with the examination of the beat of the heart and the movement of the lungs in the chest and back.

Rhythm plays a most important part not only in the body, but in the mind also. The change from joy to sorrow, the rise and fall of thoughts, and the whole working of the mind show rhythm, and all confusion and despair seem to be accounted for by the lack of rhythm in mind.

In ancient times healers in the East, and especially those in India, when healing a patient of any complaint of a psychological character known either as an obsession or an effect of magic, excited the emotional nature of the patient by the emphatic rhythm of their drum and song, at the same time making the patient swing his head up and down in time to the music. This aroused his emotions and prompted him to tell the secret of his complaint, which hitherto had been hidden under the cover of fear, convention and forms of society. The patient confessed everything to the healer under the spell produced by the rhythm, and the healer was enabled to discover the source of the malady.

The words 'thoughtful' and 'thoughtless' signify a rhythmic or unrhythmic state of mind, and balance, which is the only upholding power in life, is kept by rhythm. Respiration which keeps mind and body connected, and which links the mind and soul, consists in keeping rhythm every moment when awake or asleep; inhaling and exhaling may be likened to the moving and swinging of the pendulum of a clock. As all strength and energy is maintained by breath, and as breath is the sign of life and its nature is to flow alternatively on the right and left side, all this proves rhythm to be of the greatest significance.

As rhythm is innate in man and maintains his health, so upon rhythm depend all a man's affairs in life; his success, his failure, his right acts and his wrong acts, all are accounted for in some way or other by a change of rhythm.

The instinct of flying in the bird is a rhythmic movement of the wings, and it is the same tendency of rhythmic contraction which makes the fish swim and the snake glide.

A keen observation shows that the whole universe is a single mechanism working by the law of rhythm; the rise and fall of the waves, the ebb and flow of the tide, the waxing and waning of the moon, the sunrise and the sunset, the change of the seasons, the moving of the earth and of the planets – the whole cosmic system and the constitution of the entire universe are working under the law of rhythm. Cycles of rhythm, with major and minor cycles interpenetrating, uphold the whole creation in their swing. This demonstrates the origin of manifestation: motion has sprung from the still life, and every motion must necessarily result in a dual aspect. As soon as you move a stick, the single movement will make two points: the one where it starts and the other where it ends, the one strong and the other weak. To these a music conductor will count '*one, two*'; *one*, two: a strong accent and a weak accent, one motion with two effects, each distinct and different from the other. It is this mystery that lies hidden under the dual aspects in all phases and forms of life. And the reason, cause and significance of all life is found in rhythm.*

There is a psychological conception of rhythms used in poetry or music which may be explained thus: every rhythm has a certain effect, not only upon the physical and mental bodies of the poet or on him for whom the poetry is written, on the musician or on him to whom the song is sung, but even upon their life's affairs. The belief is that it can bring good or bad luck to the poet and musician, or to the one who listens. The idea is that rhythm is hidden under the root of every activity, constructive or destructive, so that on the rhythm of every activity the fate of the affair depends. Expressions used in everyday speech such as: 'he is too late', or 'it was done too soon', or 'that was done in time', all show the influence of rhythm upon the affair. Events such as the sinking of the *Titanic*, and the amazing changes that took place during the late war†, if keenly studied, can be accounted for by rhythm working in both mental and physical spheres.

There is a superstition among Indians that when somebody yawns, someone else who is present must either snap his fingers or clap his hands. The hidden meaning of this is that a yawn is significant of the slowing down of the rhythm, and that by clicking the fingers or clapping the hands one is supposed to bring the rhythm back to its original state.

A Muslim child when reading the Qur'an moves his head backwards and forwards; this is popularly supposed to be a respectful bow to the sacred words that he reads, but psychologically speaking it helps him to memorize the Qur'an by regulating the circulation and making the brain a receptive vehicle, as when filling a bottle one sometimes must shake it in order to make more room. This also may be seen when a person nods the head in accepting an idea, or shakes it when he cannot take it in.

* For a further explanation of the law of rhythm see Volume XI
† The first World War.

The mechanism of every kind of machinery that works by itself is arranged and kept going by the law of rhythm, and this is another proof of the fact that the whole mechanism of the universe is based on the law of rhythm.

CHAPTER VII

Music

WHEN WE pay attention to nature's music we find that every
thing on the earth contributes to its harmony. The trees
joyously wave their branches in rhythm with the wind; the
sound of the sea, the murmuring of the breeze, the whistling
of the wind through the rocks, hills and mountains, the flash
of the lightning, and the crash of the thunder, the harmony of
the sun and moon, the movements of the stars and planets,
the blooming of the flower, the fading of the leaf, the regular
alternation of morning, evening, noon and night – all reveal to
the seer the music of nature.

The insects have their concerts and ballets, and the choirs
of birds chant in unison their hymns of praise. Dogs and
cats have their orgies, foxes and wolves have their *soirées
musicales* in the forest, while tigers and lions hold their operas
in the wilderness. Music is the only means of understanding
among birds and beasts. This may be seen by the gradation
of pitch and volume of tone, the manner of tune, the number
of repetitions, and the duration of their various sounds. These
convey to their fellow-creatures the time for joining the flock,
the warning of coming danger, the declaration of war, the
feeling of love, and the sense of sympathy, displeasure,
passion, anger, fear and jealousy – making a language of itself.

In man breath is a constant tone, and the beat of the heart,
pulse and head keeps the rhythm continuously. An infant
responds to music before it has learned how to speak; it
moves its hands and feet in time, and expresses its pleasure
and pain in different tones.

In the beginning of human creation no language such as we
now have existed, but only music. Man first expressed his
thoughts and feelings by low and high, short and prolonged
sounds. The depth of his tone showed his strength and
power, and the height of his pitch expressed love and
wisdom. Man conveyed his sincerity, insincerity, inclination,
disinclination, pleasure or displeasure by the variety of his
musical expressions.

The tongue touching various points in the mouth, and the opening and the closing of the lips in different ways produced the variety of sounds. The grouping of the sounds made words conveying different meanings in their various modes of expression. This gradually transformed music into a language, but language could never free itself from music.

A word spoken in a certain tone shows subservience, and the same word spoken in a different tone expresses command; a word spoken in a certain pitch shows kindness, and the same word spoken in a different pitch expresses coldness. Words spoken in a certain rhythm show willingness, and the same words express unwillingness when spoken at a different degree of speech. Up to the present day the ancient languages Sanskrit, Arabic and Hebrew cannot be mastered by simply learning the words, pronunciation and grammar, because a particular rhythm and tonal expression is needed. The word in itself is frequently insufficient to express the meaning clearly. The student of language by keen study can discover this. Even modern languages are but a simplification of music. No words of any language can be spoken in one and the same way without the distinction of tone, pitch, rhythm, accent, pause and rest. A language, however simple, cannot exist without music in it; music gives it a concrete expression. For this reason a foreign language is rarely spoken perfectly; the words are learned, but the music is not mastered.

Language may be called the simplification of music; music is hidden within it as the soul is hidden in the body. At each step towards simplification the language has lost some of its music. A study of ancient tradition reveals that the first divine messages were given in song, as were the Psalms of David, the Song of Solomon, the *Gathas* of Zoroaster and the *Gita* of Krishna.

When language became more complex, it closed as it were one wing, the sense of tone – keeping the other wing, the sense of rhythm, outspread. This made poetry a subject distinct and separate from music. In ancient times religions, philosophies, sciences and arts were expressed in poetry. Parts of the Vedas, Puranas, Ramayana, Mahabharata, Zendavesta, Kabala and Bible are to be found in verse, as well as different arts and sciences in the ancient languages. Among the scriptures the only work in prose is the Qur'an, and even this is not devoid of poetry. In the East, even in recent times, not only manuscripts of science, art and literature were written in poetry, but the learned even discoursed in verse.

In the next stage man freed the language from the bond of rhythm and made prose out of poetry. Although man has tried to free language from the trammels of tone and rhythm, yet in spite of this the spirit of music still exists. Man prefers to hear poetry recited and prose well read, which is in itself a proof of the soul seeking music even in the spoken word.

The crooning song of the mother soothes the infant and makes it sleep, and lively music gives it an inclination to dance. It is music which doubles the courage and strength of a soldier when marching towards the field of battle. In the East, when the caravans travel from place to place on a pilgrimage, they sing as they go. In India the coolies sing when at work, and the rhythm of the music makes the hardest labour become easy for them.

An ancient legend tells how the angels sang at the command of God to induce the unwilling soul to enter the body of Adam. The soul, intoxicated by the song of the angels, entered the body which it regarded as a prison.

All spiritualists who have really sounded the depths of spirituality have realized that there is no better means of attracting the spirits from their plane of freedom to the outer plane than by music. They make use of different instruments which appeal to a certain spirit, and sing songs that have a special effect upon the particular spirit with whom they wish to communicate. There is no magic like music for making an effect upon the human soul.

The taste for music is inborn in man, and it first shows in the infant. Music is known to a child from its cradle, but as it grows in this world of delusion its mind becomes absorbed in so many and various objects that it loses the aptitude for music which its soul possessed. When grown-up, man enjoys and appreciates music in accordance with his grade of evolution and with the surroundings in which he has been born and brought up. The man of the wilderness sings his wild lays, and the man of the city his popular songs. The more refined man becomes, the finer the music he enjoys. The character in every man creates a tendency for music akin to it; in other words the gay man enjoys light music, while the serious minded person prefers classical; the intellectual man takes delight in technique, while the simpleton is satisfied with his drum.

There are five different aspects of the art of music: the popular, that which induces motion of the body; technical, that which satisfies the intellect; artistic, that which has beauty and grace; appealing, that which pierces the heart; uplifting, that in which the soul hears the music of the spheres.

The effect of music depends not only on the proficiency, but also upon the evolution of the performer. Its effect upon the listener is in accordance with his knowledge and evolution; for this reason the value of music differs with each individual. For a self-satisfied person there is no chance of progress, because he clings contentedly to his taste according to his state of evolution, refusing to advance a step higher than his present level. He who gradually progresses along the path of music, in the end attains to the highest perfection. No other art can inspire and sweeten the personality like music. The lover of music attains sooner or later to the most sublime field of thought.

India has preserved the mysticism of tone and pitch discovered by the ancients, and its music itself signifies this. The Indian music is based upon the principle of the *Raga*, which shows it to be akin to nature. It has avoided limitations of technique by adopting a purely inspirational method.

The *Ragas* are derived from five different sources: the mathematical law of variety, the inspiration of the mystics, the imagination of the musicians, the natural lays peculiar to the people residing in different parts of the land, and the idealization of the poets. These made a world of *Ragas*, calling one *Rag* – the male, another *Ragini* – the female, and others *Putras* – sons, and *Bharyas* – daughters-in-law.

Raga is called the male theme because of its creative and positive nature; *Ragini* is called the female theme on account of its responsive and fine quality. *Putras* are such themes as are derived from the mingling of *Ragas* and *Raginis*; in them can be found a likeness to the *Raga* and the *Ragini* from which they are derived. *Bharya* is the corresponding theme to *Putra*.

There are six *Ragas* and thirty-six *Raginis*, six belonging to each *Raga*; there are forty-eight *Putras* and forty-eight *Bharyas* which constitute this family.

Each *Raga* has an administration of its own, including a chief – *Mukhya*, the key-note; a king – *Wadi*, a principal note; a minister – *Samwadi*, the subordinate note; a servant – *Anuwadi*, an assonant note; an enemy – *Vivadi*, a dissonant note. This gives to the student of the *Raga* a clear conception of its use. Each *Raga* has its image distinct from the other. This shows the highest reach of imagination.

Just as the picture of each aspect of life is clear in the imagination of the intelligent, so the poets have depicted the images of the *Ragas*. The ancient gods and goddesses were simply images of the different aspects of life, and in order to teach the worship of the immanence of God in nature these various images were placed in the temples, in order that God in His every aspect of manifestation might be worshipped. The same idea has been worked out in the images of *Ragas*, which create with delicate imagination the type, form, action, expression and effect of the idea.

Every hour of the day and night, every day, week, month and season has its influence upon man's physical and mental condition. In the same way each *Raga* has power upon the atmosphere as well as upon the health and mind of man, the same effect as that shown by the different times in life, subject to the cosmic law. By the knowledge of both time and *Raga* the wise have connected them to suit each other.

There are instances in ancient tradition when birds and animals were charmed by the flute of Krishna, rocks were melted by the song of Orpheus, and the *Dipak Raga* sung by Tansen lighted all the torches, while he himself was burned by reason of the inner fire his song produced. Even today snakes are charmed by the *pungi* of the snake-charmers in India. All this shows us how the ancients must have dived into the most mysterious ocean of music.

The secret of composition lies in sustaining the tone as solidly and as long as possible through all its different degrees. A break destroys its grace, power and magnetism, just as the breath holds life and has all grace, power and magnetism. There are some notes that need a longer life than others, according to their character and purpose.

In a true composition a miniature of nature's music is seen. The effects of thunder, rain and storm, and the picture of hills and rivers make music a real art. Although art is an improvisation on nature, yet it is only genuine when it keeps close to nature.

The music which expresses the nature and character of individuals, nations or races is still higher. The highest and most ideal form of composition is that which expresses life, character, emotions and feelings, for this is the inner world which is only seen by the eye of the mind. A genius uses music as a language to express fully, without the help of words, whatever he may wish to be known; for music, a perfect and universal language, can express feeling more comprehensively than any tongue.

Music loses its freedom by being subject to the laws of technique, but mystics in their sacred music, regardless of the world's praise, free both their composition and improvisations from the limitations of technicality.

The art of music in the East is called *kala*, and has three aspects: vocal, instrumental, and expressing movement.

Vocal music is considered to be the highest, for it is natural; the effect produced by an instrument which is merely a machine cannot be compared with that of the human voice. However perfect strings may be, they cannot make the same impression on the listener as the voice which comes direct from the soul as breath, and has been brought to the surface through the medium of the mind and the vocal organs of the body. When the soul desires to express itself in voice, it first causes an activity in the mind, and the mind, by means of thought, projects finer vibrations in the mental plane. These in due course develop and run as breath through the regions of the abdomen, lungs, mouth, throat and nasal organs, causing air to vibrate all through, until they manifest on the surface as voice. The voice therefore naturally expresses the attitude of mind: whether true or false, sincere or insincere. The voice has all the magnetism which an instrument lacks, for voice is nature's ideal instrument upon which all other instruments of the world are modelled.

The effect produced by singing depends upon the depth of feeling of the singer. The voice of a sympathetic singer is quite different from that of one who is heartless. However artificially cultivated a voice may be, it will never produce feeling, grace and beauty unless the heart be cultivated also. Singing has a twofold source of interest: the grace of music, and the beauty of poetry. In proportion as the singer feels the words he sings, an effect is produced upon the listeners; his heart, so to speak, accompanies the song.

Although the sound produced by an instrument cannot be produced by the voice, yet the instrument is absolutely dependent upon man. This explains clearly how the soul makes use of the mind, and how the mind rules the body. Yet it seems as though the body works, not the mind, and the soul is left out. When man hears the sound of the instrument and sees the hand of the player at work, he does not see the mind working behind, nor the phenomenon of the soul. At each step from the inner being to the surface there is an apparent improvement, which appears to be more positive. Yet every step toward the surface entails limitation and dependence.

There is nothing which is unable to serve as a medium for sound, although tone manifests more clearly through a sonorous body than through a solid one, the former being open to vibrations, while the latter is closed. All things which give a clear sound show life, while solid bodies choked up with substance seem dead. Resonance is the reserving of tone; in other words it is the rebound of tone which produces an echo. On this principle all instruments are made, the difference lying in the quality and quantity of the tone, which depend upon the construction of the instrument. The instruments of percussion, such as the *tabla* or the drum, are suitable for practical music, and stringed instruments like the *sitar*, violin or harp are meant for artistic music. The *vina* is especially constructed to concentrate the vibrations; as it gives a faint sound, audible to the player only, it is used in meditation.

The effect of instrumental music also depends upon the evolution of man who expresses with the tips of his fingers upon the instrument his grade of evolution; in other words, his soul speaks through the instrument. Man's state of mind can be read by his touch upon any instrument, for however great an expert he may be, he cannot produce by mere skill, without a developed feeling within himself, the grace and beauty which appeal to the heart.

Wind instruments, like the flute and the *algosa*, especially express the heart quality, for they are played with the breath which is the very life; therefore they kindle the heart's fire.

Instruments stringed with gut have a living effect, for they come from a living creature which once had a heart. Those stringed with wire have a thrilling effect, and the instruments of percussion, such as the drum, have a stimulating and animating effect upon man.

After vocal and instrumental music comes the motional music of the dance. Motion is the nature of vibration. Every motion contains within itself a thought and feeling. This art is innate in man. An infant's first pleasure in life is to amuse itself with the movement of hands and feet; a child on hearing music begins to move. Even beasts and birds express their joy in motion. The peacock, proud in the vision of its beauty, displays its vanity in dance; likewise the cobra unfolds its hood and rocks its body on hearing the music of the *pungi*. All this proves that motion is the sign of life, and when accomplished with music it sets both the performer and onlooker in motion.

The mystics have always looked upon this subject as a sacred art. In the Hebrew Scriptures we find David dancing before the Lord, and the gods and goddesses of the Greeks, Egyptians, Buddhists and Brahmans are represented in different poses, all having a certain meaning and philosophy relating to the great cosmic dance which is evolution.

Even up to the present time among Sufis in the East dancing, called *sam'a*, takes place at their sacred meetings, for dancing is the outcome of joy. The dervishes at the *sam'a* give an outlet to their ecstasy in *Raqs*, which is regarded with great respect and reverence by those present, and is in itself a sacred ceremony.

The art of dancing has greatly degenerated owing to its misuse. People for the most part dance either for the sake of amusement or exercise, often abusing the art in their frivolity.

Tune and rhythm tend to produce an inclination for dance. To sum up, dancing may be said to be a graceful expression of thought and feeling without uttering a word. It may be used also to impress the soul by movement, by producing an ideal picture before it. When beauty of movement is taken as the presentment of the divine ideal, then the dance becomes sacred.

The music of life shows its melody and harmony in our daily experiences. Every spoken word is either a true or a false note, according to the scale of our ideal. The tone of one personality is hard like a horn, while the tone of another is soft like the high notes of a flute.

The gradual progress of all creation from a lower to a higher evolution, its change from one aspect to another, is shown as in music where a melody is transposed from one key into another.

The friendship and enmity among men, their likes and dislikes, are as chords and discords. The harmony of human nature, and the human tendency to attraction and repulsion, are like the effect of the consonant and dissonant intervals in music.

In tenderness of heart the tone turns into a half-tone, and with the breaking of the heart the tone breaks into microtones. The more tender the heart becomes, the fuller the tone becomes; the harder the heart grows, the more dead it sounds.

Each note, each scale, and each strain expires at the appointed time, and at the end of the soul's experience here the *finale* comes. But the impression remains, as a concert in a dream, before the radiant vision of the consciousness.

With the music of the absolute the bass, the undertone, is going on continuously, but on the surface and under the various keys of all the instruments of nature's music the undertone is hidden and subdued. Every being with life comes to the surface and again returns whence it came, as each note has its return to the ocean of sound. The undertone of this existence is the loudest and the softest, the highest and the lowest. It overwhelms all instruments of soft or loud, high or low tone, until all gradually merge in it. This undertone always is, and always will be.

The mystery of sound is mysticism; the harmony of life is religion. The knowledge of vibration is metaphysics, and the analysis of atoms science; their harmonious grouping is art. The rhythm of form is poetry, and the rhythm of sound is music. This shows that music is the art of arts, and the science of all sciences, and it contains the fountain of all knowledge within itself.

Music is called a divine or celestial art, not only because it is in itself a universal religion, but because of its fineness in comparison with all other arts and sciences. Every sacred scripture, holy picture or spoken word produces the impression of its identity upon the mirror of the soul, but music stands before the soul without producing any impression of this objective world in either name or form, thus preparing the soul to realize the infinite.

Recognizing this the Sufi names music *giza-i-ruh*, the food of the soul, and uses it as a source of spiritual perfection; for music fans the fire of the heart, and the flame arising from it illumines the soul. The Sufi derives much more benefit from music in his meditations than from anything else. His devotional and meditative attitude makes him responsive to music, which helps him in his spiritual unfoldment. The consciousness, by the help of music, first frees itself from the body and then from the mind. This once accomplished, only one step more is needed to attain spiritual perfection.

Sufis in all ages have taken a keen interest in music in whatever land they may have dwelt. Rumi especially adopted this art by reason of his great devotion. He listened to the verses of the mystics on love and truth sung by the *qawwals*, the musicians, to the accompaniment of the flute.

The Sufi visualizes the object of his devotion in his mind, which is reflected upon the mirror of his soul. The heart, the factor of feeling, is possessed by everyone, although with everyone it is not a living heart. This heart is made alive by the Sufi who gives an outlet to his intense feelings in tears and in sighs. By so doing the clouds of *jelal*, the power which gathers with his psychic development, fall in tears as drops of rain, and the sky of his heart is clear, allowing the soul to shine.

This condition is regarded by the Sufi as the sacred ecstasy. The masses in general, owing to their narrow orthodox view, have cast out Sufis, and opposed them for their freedom of thought, misinterpreting the Prophet's teaching which prohibited the abuse of music, not music in the real sense of the word. For this reason a language of music was made by the Sufis, so that only the initiated could understand the meaning of the songs. Many in the East hear and enjoy these songs not understanding what they really mean.

Since the time of Rumi music has become a part of the devotions in the Mevlevi Order of the Sufis. A branch of this order came to India in ancient times, and was known as the Chishtia school of Sufis. It was brought to great glory by Khwaja Moin-ud-Din Chishti, one of the greatest mystics ever known to the world. It would not be an exaggeration to say that he actually lived on music. Even at the present time, although his body has been in the tomb at Ajmer for many centuries, yet at his shrine there is always music given by the best singers and musicians in the land. This shows the glory of a poverty stricken sage compared with the poverty of a glorious king: the one during his life had all things, which ceased at his death, while with the sage the glory is ever increasing. At the present time music is prevalent in the school of the Chishtis, who hold meditative musical assemblies called *sam'a* or *qawwali*. During these they meditate on the ideal of their devotion, which is in accordance with their grade of evolution, and they increase the fire of their devotion while listening to the music.

Wajad, the sacred ecstasy which the Sufis experience as a rule at *sam'a*, may be said to be union with the Desired One. There are three aspects of this union which are experienced by Sufis of different stages of evolution.

The first is union with the revered ideal from the plane of earth, present before the devotee; either the objective plane or the plane of thought. The heart of the devotee, filled with love, admiration and gratitude, then becomes capable of visualizing the form of his ideal of devotion whilst listening to the music.

The second step in ecstasy and the higher part of union is union with the beauty of character of the ideal, irrespective of form. The song in praise of the ideal character helps the love of the devotee to gush forth and overflow.

The third stage in ecstasy is union with the divine Beloved, the highest ideal, who is beyond the limitation of name and form, virtue or merit; with whom the soul has constantly sought union and whom it has finally found. This joy is unexplainable. When the words of those souls who have already attained union with the divine Beloved are sung before the one who is treading the path of divine love, he sees all the signs on the path described in those verses, and it is a great comfort to him. The praise of the One so idealized, so unlike the ideal of the world in general, fills him with joy beyond words.

Ecstasy manifests in various aspects. Sometimes a Sufi may be in tears, sometimes a sigh may manifest; sometimes it expresses itself in *Raqs*, motion. All this is regarded with respect and reverence by those present at the *sam'a* assembly, as ecstasy is considered divine bliss. The sighing of the devotee clears a path for him into the world unseen, and his tears wash away the sins of ages. All revelation follows the ecstasy, all knowledge that a book can never contain and that a language can never express, nor a teacher teach, comes to him of itself.

CHAPTER VIII

Abstract Sound

ABSTRACT SOUND is called *sawt-e-sarmad* by the Sufis; all space is filled with it. The vibrations of this sound are too fine to be either audible or visible to the material ears or eyes, since it is even difficult for the eyes to see the form and colour of the ethereal vibrations on the external plane.

It was the *sawt-e-sarmad*, the sound of the abstract plane, which Muhammad heard in the cave of Ghar-e-Hira when he became lost in his divine ideal. The Qur'an refers to this sound in the words: 'Be! and all became'.

Moses heard this sound on Mount Sinai when in communion with God, and the same word was audible to Christ when absorbed in his heavenly Father in the wilderness. Shiva heard the same *anahad nada* during his *samadhi* in the cave of the Himalayas. The flute of Krishna is symbolic of the same sound. This sound is the source of all revelation to the Masters to whom it is revealed from within. It is because of this that they know and teach one and the same truth.

The Sufi knows of the past, present and future, and about all things in life, by being able to know the direction of sound. Every aspect of one's being in which sound manifests has a peculiar effect upon life, for the activity of vibrations has a special effect in every direction. The knower of the mystery of sound knows the mystery of the whole universe. Whoever has followed the strains of this sound has forgotten all earthly distinctions and differences, and has reached that goal of truth in which all the blessed ones of God unite.

Space is within the body as well as around it; in other words, the body is in the space and the space is in the body. This being the case, the sound of the abstract is always going on within, around and about man. Man does not hear it as a rule, because his consciousness is entirely centred in his material existence. Man becomes so absorbed in his experiences in the external world through the medium of the physical body that space, with all its wonders of light and sound, appears to him blank.

This can be easily understood by studying the nature of colour. There are many colours that are quite distinct by themselves; yet, when mixed with others of still brighter hue, they become altogether eclipsed. Even bright colours, when embroidered with gold, silver, diamonds or pearls, serve merely as a background to the dazzling embroidery. So it is with the abstract sound compared with the sounds of the external world. The limited volume of earthly sounds is so concrete that it dims the effect of the sound of the abstract to the sense of hearing, although in comparison to it the sounds of the earth are like that of a whistle to a drum. When the abstract sound is audible, all other sounds become indistinct to the mystic.

The sound of the abstract is called *anahad* in the Veda, meaning unlimited sound. The Sufis name it *sarmad*, which suggests the idea of intoxication. The word intoxication is here used to signify upliftment, the freedom of the soul from its earthly bondage. Those who are able to hear the *sawt-e-sarmad* and meditate on it are relieved from all worries, anxieties, sorrows, fears and diseases, and the soul is freed from captivity in the senses and in the physical body. The soul of the listener becomes the all-pervading consciousness, and his spirit becomes the battery which keeps the whole universe in motion.

Some train themselves to hear the *sawt-e-sarmad* in the solitude, on the sea shore, on the river bank and in the hills and dales; others attain it while sitting in the caves of the mountains, or when wandering constantly through forests and deserts, keeping themselves in the wilderness apart from the haunts of men. Yogis and ascetics blow *sing* – a horn, or *shanka* – a shell, which awakens in them this inner tone. Dervishes play *nai* or *alghoza* – a double flute – for the same purpose. The bells and gongs in the churches and temples are meant to suggest to the thinker the same sacred sound, and thus lead him towards the inner life.

This sound develops through ten different aspects because of its manifestation through ten different tubes of the body. It sounds like thunder, the roaring of the sea, the jingling of bells, running water, the buzzing of bees, the twittering of sparrows, the *vina*, the whistle, the sound of *shanka* – until it finally becomes *Hu*, the most sacred of all sounds.

This sound *Hu* is the beginning and end of all sounds, be they from man, bird, beast, or thing. A minute study will prove this fact, which can be realized by listening to the sound of the steam engine or of a mill, while the echo of bells or gongs gives a typical illustration of the sound *Hu*.

The Supreme Being has been called by various names in different languages, but the mystics have known him as *Hu*, the natural name, not man-made, the only name of the nameless which all nature constantly proclaims.

The sound *Hu* is most sacred; the mystics of all ages called it *Ismi-Azam*, the name of the most High, for it is the origin and end of every sound as well as the background of each word. The word *Hu* is the spirit of all sounds and of all words, and is hidden under them all, as the spirit in the body. It does not belong to any language, but no language can help belonging to it.

This alone is the true name of God, a name that no people and no religion can claim as their own. This word is not only uttered by human beings, but is repeated by animals and birds. All things and beings exclaim this name of the Lord, for every activity of life expresses distinctly or indistinctly this very sound. This is the word mentioned in the Bible as existing before the light came into being: 'In the beginning was the word, and the word was with God, and the word was God'.

The mystery of *Hu* is revealed to the Sufi who journeys through the path of initiation.[7] The more a Sufi listens to *sawt-e-sarmad*, the sound of the abstract, the more his consciousness becomes free from all the limitations of life. The soul floats above the physical and mental plane without any special effort on man's part, which shows its calm and peaceful state; a dreamy look comes into his eyes and his countenance becomes radiant; he experiences the unearthly joy and rapture of *wajad* or ecstasy. When ecstasy overwhelms him he is neither conscious of the physical existence nor of the mental. This is the heavenly wine to which all Sufi poets refer, which is totally unlike the momentary intoxications of this mortal plane.

A heavenly bliss then springs in the heart of a Sufi, his mind is purified from sin, his body from all impurities, and a pathway is opened for him towards the world unseen. He begins to receive inspirations, intuitions, impressions and revelations without the least effort on his part. He is no longer dependent upon a book or a teacher, for divine wisdom – the light of his soul, the Holy Spirit – begins to shine upon him.

'I, by the light of soul, realize that the beauty of the heavens and the grandeur of the earth are the echo of Thy magic flute'. (Sherif)

COSMIC LANGUAGE

CHAPTER I

Voices

1

THE WHOLE of manifestation in all its aspects is a record upon which the voice is reproduced, and that voice is a person's thought. There is no place in the world, neither desert, forest, mountain nor house, town or city, where there is not a voice continually going on – a voice which was once engraved upon it and which since then has continued. No doubt every such voice has its limit: one voice may continue for thousands of years, another voice for several months, another for some days, another for some hours or moments. For everything that is created, intentionally or unintentionally, has a life, it has a birth and so it has a death. Plainly speaking, it has a beginning and an end.

One can experience this by feeling the atmosphere of different places. Sitting upon the rocks of the mountains one often feels the vibrations of the one who has been sitting there before. Sitting in a forest, in a wilderness, one can feel what has been the history of that place. It may be that there was a city, that there was a house, that people lived there, and now it has turned into a wilderness. One begins to feel the history of the whole place; it communicates with one.

Every town has its own particular voice. It is, so to speak, telling aloud who lived in the town and how they lived, what was their life. It tells of their grade of evolution, it tells of their doings, it tells of the results produced by their actions. People perceive the vibrations of haunted houses, because the atmosphere is stirred, and therefore it is often felt distinctly. But there is no house, there is no place which has not got its own voice: the voice that has been engraved upon it, so that it has become a record reproducing what has been given to it, consciously or unconsciously.

When Abraham returned from Egypt after his initiation into the mysteries of life, he arrived at Mecca. A stone was set there in memory of the initiation which he had just received from the ancient esoteric school of Egypt, and the voice that was put into the stone by the singing soul of Abraham continued and became audible to those who could hear. The prophets and seers have since that time made pilgrimages to this stone of Ka'ba. This continued and is still going on.

A place like Mecca, a desert with nothing of interest: the ground not fertile, the people not very evolved, no business or industry flourishing, no science nor art developed – has had an attraction for millions of people who have gone there for only one purpose, and that was pilgrimage. What was it, and what is it? It is the voice which has been put into the place, into a stone. A stone has been made to speak, and it speaks to those whose ears are open.

Every place where a person sits and thinks for a moment on any subject takes in the thought of man; it takes the record of what has been spoken, so that no man can hide his thought or feeling. It is recorded even in the seat he has been sitting on while thinking and many persons, by sitting in that place, begin to feel it. Sometimes, the moment he sits on a certain seat, a person may feel a thought quite foreign to him, a feeling which does not belong to him, because on that seat there was that thought vibrating. As a seat can hold the vibrations of the thought for a much longer time than the life of the person who has thought or has spoken, so an influence remains in every place where one sits, where one lives, where one thinks or feels, where one rejoices, or where one sorrows. This voice continues for a time incomparably longer than the life of the person who spoke or thought there.

Question: When many people have lived somewhere for a long time, would there not be a confusion of voices, or would one voice predominate?
Answer: There is a dominating voice which is more distinct than the other voices. But at the same time, as one feels what a composer wishes to convey through the whole music he writes, through all the instruments, so even the different voices which are going on together make one result, and that result comes as a symphony to the person who can hear them together. A collective thought comes, when one can perceive it, especially in a town, in a new city. It is a kind of voice of the past and a voice of the present, the

ll as one music. It has its peculiar and particular

Would the thought of people coming afterwards
p.... _ the initial thought?
Answer: No, it would add to it. For instance, if there is a flute,
then a clarionet, a trumpet or a trombone, added to it, make
up the volume of sound, but there is always one instrument
which plays the first part. The main voice stands as a breath,
and all the other voices, attracted to it, build around it a form.
The breath remains as life. The form may be composed and
decomposed, but the breath remains as life.

Question: Does the duration of the impression that Abraham
made upon the Ka'ba stone depend upon its intensity, or upon
the sacredness of the thought?
Answer: When the thought comes from an evolved person,
this has a greater power than the thought itself, than what
the thought contains, because the person is the life of that
thought; the thought is the cover over that life. Perhaps
Abraham would not have been able to engrave any other
stone with that same power he had when he came with
his fresh impression after his initiation. At that time the
impression was perhaps more intense than at any other time
of his life, before or after.

Abraham said: 'This stone I set here in memory of
initiation, as a sign of God to be understood as One God.
This stone will remain for ever as a temple'. He was not a
king, nor a rich man; he could not build a temple, he could
only put up this one stone. But this stone has remained for a
much longer time than many temples built with riches.[8]

This is only one example, but there are numberless
examples to be found. There is the atmosphere of Benares,
and there are the vibrations of Ajmer where Khwaja Moin-
ud-Din Chishti lived, meditated and died. There is the tomb
of the saint where a continual voice is going on, a vibration
so strong that a person who is meditative would sit there
and would like to sit there for ever. It is in the midst of the
city, and yet it has a feeling of wilderness, because in that
place the saint sat and meditated on *sawt-e-sarmad*, the cosmic

symphony. And hearing that cosmic music continually, cosmic music has been produced there.

There was a wonderful experience during the lifetime of the Khwaja of Ajmer. To visit this saint a great master, Khwaja Abdul Qadir Jilani, who was also an advanced soul, came from Baghdad. A remarkable meeting took place between them in Ajmer. Now the latter was very strict in his religious observances, and the religious people would not have music. So naturally in order to respect his belief the Khwaja of Ajmer had to sacrifice his everyday musical meditation. But when the time came the symphony began by itself. The great master felt that, without anyone playing, music was going on, and he said to the saint: 'Even if religion prohibits it, it is for others, not for you'.

Question: What is the character of remote places that have always been uninhabited, or very little inhabited? Is the attraction that such places possess due to the absence of distracting voices?
Answer: In remote places sometimes the voices have become buried, and there is a kind of overtone which is most gentle and soothing, for the voices have gone, and the vibration remains as an atmosphere. If the place has always been a desert it is still more elevating, because it has its own natural atmosphere which is most uplifting. And if some travellers have passed through it and if this brings their voice to us, even that is much better than what one perceives and feels in cities, in towns, because in nature man is quite a different person. The more he approaches nature, the more that is artificial falls away from him; he becomes more and more free from the superficial life and at one with nature. Therefore his predisposition which is nature and truth and which is goodness, all comes up and makes life a kind of dream for him, a romance, a lyric; so even his thought there, as a human thought, begins to sing through nature.

Question: Does a tomb keep the voice of the person who is buried there?
Answer: No, not the tomb, but the place where the person lived. In ancient times people made a mark where a person

had lived; they made the tomb where the vibrations of that person had been recorded. Ancient tombs were mostly made in places where the person sat, thought and meditated. In this case the tomb is an excuse; it is only a mark which shows that here the person sat.

In India, where cremations take place, they often make a seat to mark the place where the one who died meditated and produced his vibrations. He may not be buried there, but a mark has been made just to keep that seat, that place.

2

The secret of the idea of a blessing to be found in holy places lies in the principle that the holy place is no longer a place: it has become a living being. The prophets having proclaimed for ages the name of God and the law of the divine Being in the Holy Land make it still living, and it has attraction for the whole world.

It is said that for ages roses have sprung up on Sa'adi's grave, and that his grave has never been without them. It is credible, for in *The Rosegarden* that he has written in the thought of beauty the beauty of his thought, once voiced, is still continuing, although the mortal body of Sa'adi has perished. If this maintained roses in the place of his burial for centuries it is not astonishing.

People often wonder why the Hindus with their great philosophical mind, with their deep insight into mysticism, should believe in such a thing as a sacred river. But besides being symbolical there is another meaning in it. The great Mahatmas live on the heights of the Himalayas where the Ganges and Jumna streams rise, which then take different directions till they unite again and become one. This is really a phenomenon deep in its symbolism as well as in its actual nature. It is symbolical that the rivers begin as one and then turn into duality; that after the two streams have been separated for miles they are attracted to each other. Then they meet in a place at Allahabad, called Sangam, which is a place of pilgrimage. This gives us in its interpretation the idea of the whole manifestation, which is one in the beginning, then manifests as dual, and unites in the end.

Besides this the thoughts of the great Mahatmas flow with the water and come into the world combined with this living stream of the Ganges. This brought the vibrations of the great ones and spoke as a voice of power, of wakening, of blessing, of purity and of unity to those who heard it. Nevertheless, those unconscious of the blessing have also been blessed by bathing in the sacred river, for it was not only water: there was a thought besides, a most vital thought, a thought of power with life in it. Those who have perceived that, have perceived its secret, for in many poems in the Sanskrit language one reads how, in the waves of the Ganges and the Jumna, the seers heard the voice of the evolved souls and felt the atmosphere of those advanced beings as a breath current coming through the water.

There is a tank in Mecca, called Zemzem, from which the prophets of all ages have drunk. They did not only drink water; they received from it what had been put into it, and then they charged it with what they had to give to it. Even now pilgrims go there and receive that water as a blessing.

I once had an amusing experience during my travels in India when I happened to arrive at the place of the tomb of a most powerful person. I learned that often when a person visited this tomb he got fever. This amused me, and I asked: 'What is the reason of it?' I was told: 'This great personality was hot tempered. Although most spiritual, he could not tolerate anyone; he would keep everyone at a bamboo's distance. So now anyone going near this tomb gets fever'. I thought: 'I must bow from a distance and leave!'

I also happened to see a place where a great healer, Miran Datar, used to sit. Throughout all his life he healed thousands of patients; many he healed instantly. In the same place his grave was made, and till this day people are attracted to his tomb; those who touch this place are healed instantly.

There is a story in the East of five brothers who were travelling and arrived at a place where they found that each one had lost his merit; for each was gifted in something. They were confused, disappointed and they were wondering about the reason for such an experience, until the wise one among them found in the end, through the power of concentration, that it was the effect of the place. The place had lost its life, it was a dead place, and everyone who came there felt as if he had no life in him. The inner life had gone. We see this in land which, after having been used for many thousands of years, has lost the strength, the vitality of the earth. If outwardly the land can lose it, then inwardly the vitality, the breath of the land can also be lost.

Often one feels most inspired in one place, in another most depressed; in one place confused, in another place dull, one finds nothing of interest, nothing to attract one. One might think it is the effect of the weather, but there are places outwardly most beautiful in nature, with a wonderful climate and yet one does not feel inspired.

If an artist is born in a dead country, his talent cannot be developed there. There is no nourishment; his artistic impulse will become paralysed. Even a plant cannot live on itself; it must have air, sun, water. Yet a prophet can inspire a dead land just by passing through it.

Jelal-ud-Din Rumi said centuries ago that before everyone fire, water, earth and air are objects; before God they are living beings that work at His command. The meaning of what Rumi said is that all objects, all places, are as gramophone records. What is put into them they speak; either one's soul hears it or one's mind, according to one's development.

It seems that people are now beginning to believe in what they call psychometry. What is it? It is learning the language that objects speak. Apart from the colour or form an object has, there is something in it that speaks to one; either this belongs to that object, or it belongs to the one who has used it, but it is in that object. Sometimes one may bring an object into the house, and the moment one has brought it other objects begin to break. As long as that object is there, there is always a kind of loss. It can bring disharmony in the house; an object can bring illness, it can bring bad luck.

Those who knew the psychological effect that comes from objects therefore always avoided getting old objects, however beautiful and precious. They always bought a new object for their use. Of course one cannot do this with jewels. They have to be old, but most often one finds that jewels have more effect upon a person, on his character, on his life, on his affairs, on his environment, than anything else. One may obtain a pearl which could bring good luck of every kind from the moment the jewel was bought, or it may produce a contrary effect. Very often a person does not think of it, yet the effect is just the same; it is continual. Besides this, what one wears has an effect upon one's health, on one's condition of mind, on one's feeling. If it is a jewel it may have the voice of thousands of years. As old as a jewel is, so much traditions does it have behind it, and it explains it. Intuitive persons who are sensitive and feeling can easily perceive the vibrations of old stones; it seems as if they speak to them.

Also with all one gives to another in the form of food, sweet, drink, fruit, or flower one gives one's thought, one's feeling; it has an effect. Among the Sufis in the East there is a custom of giving to someone either a piece of cloth, a flower, a fruit, or some grains of corn. There is a meaning behind it: it is not what is given *in* that object, but what is given *with* it.

How little we know when we say: 'I believe in what I see'. If one can see how influence works, how thought and feeling speak, how objects partake of them and give them to one another, how thought and feeling, life and influence are conveyed by the medium of an object – it is most wonderful.

Question: Can any object be charged with good vibrations when in itself it is a bad omen?
Answer: There are certain bitter things which can be made sweet, but at the same time the bitterness is there. There are eatables in which people put different things in order to take away a certain smell, but the smell is still there.

Question: Can the bad influences attached to places and beings be got rid of and turned to good?
Answer: Certainly, since at the depth of all things and beings there is goodness.

Question: Is it in the power of a human being to change the influence of an object?
Answer: The answer to this is given in the first four lines of the Gayan:

'When a glimpse of Our image is caught in man,
when heaven and earth are sought in man, then
what is there in the world that is not in man?
If one only explores him there is a lot in man'.

CHAPTER II

Impressions

THERE ARE many ancient places where one finds stones engraved, woods carved with some artistic designs. Sometimes there are letters engraved on the rock of a mountain, on a stone; letters which today no one can read. Yet one endowed with the gift of intuition can read them from the vibrations, from the atmosphere, from the feeling that comes from them. Outwardly, they are engravings, inwardly they are a continual record, a talking record which is always expressing what is written upon it. No traveller with intuitive faculties open will deny the fact that in the lands of ancient traditions he will have seen numberless places which, so to speak, sing aloud the legend of their past.

One sees the same in the atmosphere of the trees in the forests, in the gardens, which also express the past – the impressions that have been given to them by those who sat under them. Often people have superstitions about a tree being haunted, and this one finds much more in the East. Actually a vibration has been created, consciously or unconsciously, by someone who has lived there, who has taken shelter under the tree and pondered upon a certain thought, upon a certain feeling which the tree has taken up, and which the tree is expressing. Perhaps the person has forgotten about it, but the tree is still repeating the thought that has been given to it; for the tree can express the voice that was put into it more clearly than a rock.

In tropical countries where in ancient times people used to travel on foot through the forests and woods, and take shelter under a certain tree, all that they thought and felt has been taken up by the tree. Those with intuitive faculties open have heard it more clearly than if they had heard it from a living person.

One finds the same thing among animals, the pet animals which live and partake thought and feeling through their contact with man. There especially exists a superstition about horses. Those who know horses are very particular in buying one which has good vibrations, apart from considering its health and breed. Often a horse of a very good breed and perfectly sound may prove to be unlucky. The reason is that the disappointment of someone who has been riding upon this horse has been left there, recorded upon the heart of the horse. Perhaps the condition of the person has changed, but that which the horse has kept is still continuing.

I myself was once very impressed in Nepal by seeing a horse and an elephant which were kept only for the Maharaja of Nepal to ride on. It seemed as if those two animals were conscious of their rider. One could see from their dignity that they knew that they belonged to the Maharaja. In every movement of the horse, in the look that the elephant gave, one would feel the presence of a Maharaja. And not only that, but all that belonged to the Maharaja, as pain or pleasure, as life and experience, all seemed to have been recorded upon the horse and the elephant. The most surprising thing was that the elephant was not larger than other elephants; it was even smaller, and most often it is the size that gives dignity to the elephant. Nor was the horse any larger than other horses, but the size did not count. It was the spirit in those animals, a life that one could see, expressing the feeling they possessed in their heart.

This wakens us again to another field of thought, and that is what association can create in us – the association of a sad person or of a happy one, of a foolish or of a wise person, the association of a noble minded person or of one who is low. The associate partakes of the one he associates with and vibrates what he partakes of. You can almost hear it spoken in the atmosphere of that person, in his expression, in his thought, speech and action. A person, however happy, will have a line of melody of wretchedness if he has associated with someone who is miserable. It continues, it sings its song separate from the whole symphony. It has its peculiar tone, one can always distinguish it. A wise person who has associated with a foolish one has kept a line; it is quite a different melody, it is in a different key, it has a different pitch from his original song. In a person who has associated with someone who is noble minded, someone of high quality, in spite of all his shortcomings one will see a line marked, distinctly audible to the hearts that listen.

It is not a thing of little importance to consider association. It is of great importance from a psychological point of view; it makes all the difference. For a wise person is not always positive against a foolish person, nor is a good person always positive against a wicked one. The one who is positive cannot always be positive; he has his times when he must be negative for a change. Therefore association certainly brings to one that which is received by the contact, and there is a great wisdom in the saying that a person is known by his associates.

In the East much thought has been given to this, especially from a spiritual point of view. For those who seek after spiritual truth association with friends in the same path is more precious than anything in the world. Everything else comes after. Association is held as the first and most important thing.

Question: How can we overcome the disagreeable vibrations of people of our immediate surroundings with whom we daily have to live?
Answer: By being positive. It is true that one cannot always be positive. At such times one may retire from one's associates. But as you evolve so your contact becomes more powerful than the influence of the other person. Therefore the other person receives more benefit from you, while the harm you receive is less. If by receiving a little harm you are able to do more good to the other person, it is just as well. It is only a matter of self-discipline, and love can conquer all things. In every person, however wicked, there is a good string somewhere; you must know where to find it. If one always thought about it, one could always touch the best point of the other person and overlook the other points. Nevertheless, it is a struggle!

Question: How can we protect ourselves from association with a wicked person?
Answer: In order to answer this we must go into the law of harmony. A person harmonizes with his like, and he harmonizes with his opposite. A wise person may harmonize

with a thoughtful person, and he may harmonize with a foolish person. The half wise is a greater trouble for him than the foolish one, because the half wisdom makes a barrier. The foolish person is open, so a harmony can be established at once. The wisdom of another wise person makes him closer, and there is a kind of response between the two; so there is harmony.

It is not surprising that one often finds two persons becoming most harmonious or great friends in whose evolution there is so vast a difference that one cannot understand how it can be possible. But, as said before, association must have an effect. However thoughtful and wise a person may be, there can come a cloud upon his thought and wisdom through association. Perhaps that cloud may be dispersed after a time, but it can cover the light of the sun. The cloud is much smaller compared to the sun, but often it can cover the whole sun from our sight. The influence of a wicked person may cover the light of a good and wise person, and this may remain until the clouds have dispersed.[9]

CHAPTER III

The Magnetism of Beings and Objects

IN PREPARING a thing one not only puts one's magnetism into it, but the voice of one's soul is produced in the thing one prepares. For instance, it is not difficult for an intuitive person to feel in the food that comes before him the thoughts of the cook. It is not only the grade of evolution of the cook that is produced in it, but also what the cook was thinking at that particular time. If the cook is irritated while cooking, if he or she is grumbling or sighing, if he or she is miserable, wretched – all that is prepared in the food that comes before you.

It is the knowledge of this fact which made the Hindus accept a high-caste *Brahmin* as a cook: that person was taken as a cook whose evolution was great, whose life was pure, whose thoughts were elevated. It is not a custom of the past, it is a custom even of today. The Brahmin who is sometimes the *Guru*, the teacher of other castes, may also be the cook.

Besides this, in ancient times when human psychology was keenly observed in all one did, every person, whatever his rank or position in life, was equipped for cooking and preparing dishes for himself and for his friends. A great mark of appreciation and affection was shown by people who invited some relations or friends to their house by placing before them dishes that they themselves had prepared. It was not the dish, it was the thought that was put into it.

Life at the present day seems to have taken away many considerations of psychological character. There was a time when, whether in the East or in the West, knitting or weaving clothes was known to every little girl, and to give to one's brother, or sister, or beloved, or relation some little thing made by one's own hand was a custom. Now a thing is easily bought at a shop; no one knows who has made it, whether it was made grudgingly or with grumbling, or how! Especially at this time when the working man is in revolt, what the workman has put into the objects he has made for you is open to question. In sewing for the person one loves a thought has gone naturally with every stitch that one has made. If it is done with love and affection every stitch produces a new thought, and completes that living thought of love, thus giving inwardly that great help that every soul is in need of.

But then also the wagons, carriages and ships which are used at the risk of man's life, by whom are they made? Who knows what was the condition of the mind of the builders of the *Titanic*? Was there a peacemaker teaching them to keep a certain rhythm of mind while making her? Everything that is made has a magical influence in it. If it is made with a thought quite contrary to what is needed, it only means dangers awaiting the ship, the train, the wagon, the car. Often, without apparent cause, you will find a boat in danger, something breaking without substantial reason. This is because in its make-up the thought of destruction has been given. It is working through it; it is something more living than the object itself. So it is when a house is built. The thoughts given to it by the one who was building it, or by those who worked on it, all count. In short, we understand by this that there is a thought attached to all things prepared either by an individual or by a multitude, and that thought must give results accordingly.

In all things there is God, but the object is the instrument, and the person is life itself. Into the object the person puts life. When a certain thing is being made, it is at that time that a life is put into it, which goes on and on as a breath in a body. This also gives us a hint that, when we take flowers to a patient and we have a healing thought with them, the flowers convey the thought of healing. As the patient looks at the flowers he will receive from them the healing which was put there. Any eatable or sweet, anything that we take to a friend with a thought of love – its use must create a harmonious, happy result for him. Therefore every little thing given and taken in love, with a harmonious and good thought, has a greater value than the object itself; for it is not the object, it is what is behind it. Does this not teach us that it is not always doing or preparing things in our everyday life that counts, but that it is giving these things a life with a harmonious, constructive thought, so that our work may become a thousand times greater in effect and real value?

This also teaches us that while doing a small thing we should be accomplishing something very great if we did it with this attitude, with this idea at the back of it: that we are not only making a thing, but we are making it living. Does this not open before us a vast field of work that we could do easily without much cost or effort? In its result that work could be of a much greater importance than anyone could think or imagine. Is it not at the same time a great blessing to be able to do a thing of great importance without any outward pretence?

Even while writing a letter a person sometimes puts in it what words cannot explain – and yet the letter conveys it. There may be one word written with a living thought behind it; that word will have a greater effect than a thousand pages. Do we not almost hear a letter speaking? It is not always what is written in it; the letter brings the one who wrote it to us, what mood he was in, his evolution, his pleasure, his displeasure, his joy and his sorrow. The letter conveys more than what was written in it.

Consider the great souls who have come on earth at different times. Conditions opposed them, and they found difficulties at every move in accomplishing what they wanted to. Yet they have produced the voice, a living voice. That living voice continued long after they had left, and in time it spread throughout the whole universe, accomplishing what they had once wished. The effect of their one moment of thought took perhaps centuries to build something, but it was something worthwhile, something beyond man's comprehension.

If we could only understand what spirit is, we would esteem the human being much more than we do now. We trust man so little, we believe in man so little, we respect man so little, we esteem the possibilities he has so little. If we only knew what was at the back of every strong and weak soul, we should know that there is every possibility, and we should never underestimate anyone, nor fail to respect man in spite of all he may lack. We should recognize that it is the Creator who creates through all the different forms. But it is one Creator, and all that is built and prepared and made and composed, is all made by that one Being working through this world of variety.

Question: Does the life and influence put into things decrease with the passing of time?
Answer: Its life is according to the intensity of the feeling. A note resounds according to the intensity with which you strike it. You may strike a note on the piano and it will continue to resound for so long. If you strike it with less intensity it resounds for a shorter time. But it is at the same time according to the strength with which you strike it and according to the instrument on which you strike. There may be one instrument the string of which will continue to vibrate for a very long time, and there may be another instrument whose string will vibrate for not very long, and then will quieten down. So it is also according to the medium which you take in striking vibrations that the effect is made.

Question: Is the thought attached to things a vibratory power?
Answer: It is a life power, but in order to define it I would call it a vibratory power. From a mystical conception vibrations may be considered to have three aspects: audible, visible and perceptible. Now the vibrations put into an object are neither audible nor visible; they are only perceptible. Perceptible to what? To the intuitive faculty of man. But it is not meant by this that the one who lacks intuitive faculty does not perceive it. He perceives it too, but unconsciously.

CHAPTER IV

The Influence of Works of Art

IN WORKS of art that have been made – independently
of the skill that has been put into them and the ideas they
convey to us – there is a feeling which is in them and behind
them. When I was visiting Berlin I saw statuary set around
the Kaiser's palace. Everywhere around it was some work of
art suggestive of horror, of terror, of destruction. As soon as
I saw it I thought: 'No wonder things happened as they did,
for this statuary was produced beforehand'.

A work of art may be beautiful to look at, it may have great
skill in it, but with it the mind of the artist is working, and
the effect that the picture will have is not what it suggests
outwardly, but what it speaks aloud as the voice of its heart.
In every picture, in every statue, in every artistic construction
one can see this; there is a voice hidden in it continually telling
for what purpose the work of art was created. Sometimes an
artist is unaware of what he is creating; he is following his
imagination. He may be working against his own work of
art; he may be bringing about an effect which he had not
desired for himself nor for the person to whom the work of
art is to be given.

Once I went to see a temple. I could not call that temple
beautiful, but it was wonderful, unique in its kind. No sooner
did my eyes fall on the colour-scheme and the pictures
which stood there as its prominent features, than I was
surprised, thinking: 'How could such a temple have existed
so long!' Not long afterwards I heard that the temple had
been destroyed. The idea is that the constructor of the temple
was so absorbed in his scheme that he forgot the harmony of
the spirit which had to make its plan, and so it resulted in
failure.

A friend once took me to see the pictures made by her
husband. I no sooner saw them, than it brought to me the
whole history of that person: how his soul had repeated
throughout his life the agonies he had undergone. The whole
thing was expressed in those pictures. And what was the

condition of the possessor of those pictures? Nothing but sorrow and depression.

It is the same with poetry. Among the Hindus there is a psychology of poetry which is taught before one is allowed to write poetry. For it is not only the rhythm and the swing of mind and thought that should be expressed, but to write poetry means to construct something: to make something or to mar something. Poetry has sometimes the effect of bringing prosperity or decline to great ones in whose praise it has been written. There is a science attached to it; a poet may speak highly of a personality in his poetry, yet the construction of his words or the idea behind it may be harmful. It does not only harm the person for whom it was made, but sometimes – if that personality is strong – the effect falls back upon the poet, thus destroying him for ever.

So it is with music. It seems a very good idea for a musician to imagine in a kind of magical music that a flood came and a city was destroyed, and everybody who lived in that city was drowned. For the moment it might seem an amusement to him, a queer imagination – but it has its influence!

The most interesting thing is that through art, poetry or music, or through the movements one makes in dance, a thought or feeling is created, the effect of which is the outcome of the whole action. The art is, so to speak, a cover. How wonderful it is to notice that art in its every aspect is something living, something speaking. It is either good or evil, but it is not without meaning.

One sees in frescoes in old houses in Italy, and in the art produced in statuary in ancient times that these works of art almost speak to us of the history of the past. They tell us of the person who made them, of his stage of evolution, his motive, his soul, and of the spirit of that time.

This teaches us that unconsciously our thought and feeling are produced upon all things we use: a place, a rock, a tree, a seat, upon the things we prepare – but in art an artist completes the music of his soul, of his mind. It is not produced automatically, it is very often a conscious effort, an effort which results in a certain effect. This shows that it is not enough to learn art, or to practise art. In order to complete art one must understand the psychology of it, through which one accomplishes the purpose of one's life.

Question: Would not an artist be afraid of making a work that might produce something undesirable?
Answer: It is better that he should be afraid, for then he will be careful.

Question: But if he does not know the effect it may have?
Answer: If he will try to know the effect, then he will know it.

One day a person brought me a record and took the trouble of explaining it to me. In the absence of his master the pupil of a magician called the forces of water and then found he could not stop the flood. Afterwards the teacher came and stopped it. On that idea the music was made. I said: 'It is an interesting idea, but please, don't play it!' It is very easy to enjoy a picturesque idea, but one never stops to think that it is not the idea that is important, but that it is the outcome of it: will it be destructive or constructive.

Another example one sees in steamers, especially in the Channel; as soon as one goes into one's cabin the first thing one sees is a picture of a person about to sink and putting on a lifebelt. It is the first thing one is impressed with as the first omen. Certainly it is instructive, but it is not a psychological instruction. Even if the person in the picture is not drowned, the impression is not a good one. If such an instruction is needed, it would be better to distribute picture cards after the ship has started, after people have become accustomed to it.

Question: Is it not unwise to fill a schoolroom or a chapel with scenes of death, even of saints and masters?
Answer: It is more than unwise. I could use some other word for it – especially when it is in connection with saints and masters who never died.

Question: Does the idea of beauty and ugliness account for the constructive or destructive nature of art?
Answer: Certainly. Harmony is beauty, and lack of harmony is ugliness. Harmony is constructive and disharmony is destructive.

Question: Is it not a mistake of modern art to take its subjects from the earth instead of making a reproduction of the higher worlds?
Answer: Artists would do it today also if they could reach the higher worlds; the condition is to be able to reach them. The same old wine which was before is here now. The one who drinks it will obtain the same intoxication which people in the past used to experience. If a man becomes more earthly, it is not the fault of heaven. The past did not hold any bliss which is not to be found in the present. The bliss which is the most valuable is eternal; it is always there. It is for us to prepare ourselves to obtain it.

Question: Do not drama and tragedy do harm?
Answer: There are many things that harm us, but there are many things which at the same thing are interesting. Besides this, there are minds that are more attracted to tragedy than to anything else. It is natural, for when there is a sore that sore feels alive for the moment, a sensation which is perhaps agreeable. It may be called pain, but it is an agreeable pain when the sore is scratched. Tragedy has that effect. No doubt too much tragedy is not desirable for anybody, but an artistic nature, a person who loves poetry, finds something in tragedy. It would be depriving oneself of a great joy not to read Shakespeare. But when people write poetry in connection with some personality, a king or a sovereign, or anyone, then there is a direct effect, whereas the poetry of Shakespeare is general. However, a play has an effect, and a serious effect too!

The above is according to the psychological point of view; it is not meant to say that it is the point of view of the Sufi. For Sufis are very fond of poetry, and their passion for poetry goes sometimes very far in expressing the sentiment of longing, yearning, heartbreak, disappointment. However, that is not psychological; according to psychology it is not right!

Question: How does one learn the inner meaning of a certain piece of music?

Answer: Once you have read 'The Soul Whence and Whither' you begin to feel that in every plane the cover of that particular plane is required in order to experience the life in that plane. And so, music being a world, poetry being a world and art being a world, a person who lives in the world of art, in the world of poetry, in the world of music knows music, poetry or art, he appreciates it. In order to have an insight into music one must live in it and observe that world most keenly. It is not sufficient that a person should be musical, and that he should occupy his heart and soul with music, but he should also develop intuition that he may see music keenly.

CHAPTER V

The Life of Thought

GOD IS omniscient, omnipotent, all-pervading, and the Only Being. This suggests to us that the absolute is living being – the Only Being – that there is no such thing as death, that there is no such thing as an end, that every thing, every being, every particle has a continuity, because life is continuous.

End or death is only a change. Therefore every thought that has once crossed the mind, every feeling that has once passed through the heart, every word that is once spoken and perhaps never thought about any longer, every action once done and forgotten, is given a life and it continues to live. It is just like a traveller who is journeying and who on his way has some seeds in his hands which he throws on the ground. When the plants grow in that place, he never sees them. He just threw the seeds and they are there. The earth has taken them, the water has reared them, and the sun and the air have helped them to grow.

This life is an accommodation, and in it everything – thought, word, action or feeling – once given birth, is taken care of, is raised, and brought to fruitfulness. One would hardly think that it could be so. One thinks: it is spoken and gone, or done and finished with, or it was felt and now it is no longer there. But it is only a change, and it is the change of which we are conscious. We know of something, and then it is no longer before us. We think it is gone – but it is still there. It remains, and it pursues its course, for it is life. In everything there is life, and life lives. As all is life, there is no death.

No doubt birth and death, beginning and end are the names of the different aspects of this mechanical working of the whole universe. It is a kind of automatic working that gives us an idea of something beginning and something ending. When we ring a bell the action takes only a moment, but the resonance lasts. It lasts to our knowledge as long as it is audible; then it passes on further and is no longer audible to us – but it exists. It exists somewhere, it goes on.

If a little pebble thrown into the sea puts the water in action, one hardly stops to think to what extent this vibration acts upon the sea. What one can see is the little waves and circles that the pebble produces before one. One sees these, but the vibration which has been produced in the sea reaches much further than man can ever imagine. What we call space is a much finer world. If we call it sea, it is a sea with the finest fluid. If we call it land, it is a land which is incomparably more fertile than the land we know. This land takes everything in it and brings it up, it rears it, it allows it to grow – our eyes do not see it, our ears do not hear it.

Does this idea not make us responsible for every movement we make, for every thought we think, for every feeling that passes through our mind or heart? There is not one moment of our life wasted, if we only know how to utilize our activity here, how to direct our thought, how to express it in words, how to further it with our movement, how to feel it, so that it may make its own atmosphere. What responsibility! The responsibility that every man has is greater than a king's responsibility. It seems as if every man has a kingdom of his own for which he is responsible – a kingdom which is in no way smaller than any kingdom known to us, but incomparably larger than the kingdoms of the earth. This teaches us to be thoughtful and conscientious and to feel our responsibility at every move we make. When a man does not feel this, he is unaware of himself, he is unaware of the secret of life. He goes on as a drunken man walking in a city. He does not know what he is doing, either for himself, or against himself.

Now one might ask: 'How can a thought live? In what way does it live? Has it a body to live in, has it a mind, has it a breath?' Yes. The first thing we should know is that a breath which comes directly from the source seeks a body, an accommodation in which to function. A thought is as a body. The breath which runs from the source – as a ray of the spirit which may be likened to the sun – makes the thought an entity; it lives as an entity.

It is these entities that are called in Sufi terms *muwakkals*, which means elementals. They live, they have a certain purpose to accomplish. They are given birth by man, and behind them there is a purpose to direct their life. Imagine how terrible it is if in a moment's absorption a person expresses his wrath, his passion, his hatred! A word expressed at such a moment must live and carry out its purpose. It is like creating an army of enemies around oneself. Perhaps one thought has a longer life than another; it depends on what body has been given to it. If the body is stronger, then it lives longer. On the energy of the mind the strength of the body of that thought depends.

Elementals are created by man. When the winds blow and the storms rage, creating all destruction, one looks on it as a mechanical action of nature. But it is not only mechanical action, it is directed by man's feelings, by the intense feelings of human beings. These feelings turn into huge lives. They push as a battery behind winds and storms, floods and volcanoes.

And so other thoughts which call for blessing, such as rainfall, must bring the mercy of God upon the earth. In the East they call the rain the divine mercy. The sunshine, when the sky is clear, and all other blessings of nature – the pure air that is exhilarating, the spring, good crops, fruits, flowers and vegetables, all different blessings from the earth or heaven which are given to us – are also directed by forces behind them.

As the mechanical working of nature raises the vapours to the sky which all form together in clouds and cause rain, so the thoughts and feelings, words and actions also have their mechanical work to do. That work directs the action of the universe. This shows to us that it is not only a mechanical work of nature, but human intelligence, mechanically working, which directs the whole working of nature.

This gives us an idea that man's responsibility is greater than that of any other being in the world. It is told in the Qur'an that God said: 'We laid our trust on the mountains, and they could not bear the load; we laid our trust on the trees, and they were unable to take it; we then laid our trust on man, and it is man who has borne it'. This trust is our responsibility; not only our responsibility to those around us, to those whom we meet in everyday life, or to the work that we are engaged in, or to the interest that we have in life – but our responsibility towards this whole creation: what we contribute to this creation, whether it is something agreeable to bring about better and harmonious conditions in the sphere, in the world, on the earth. If we do so then we know our responsibility. If we are unaware of it, we have not yet learned the purpose of our being here.

There is childhood, when a child knows nothing. He destroys things of value and beauty owing to his curiosity, his fancy. But when he grows up the child begins to feel his responsibility. The sign of maturity is the feeling of responsibility. So when a soul matures it begins to feel its responsibility, and it is from that moment that a person begins his life. It is from that moment that the soul is born again, and so long as the soul is not born again it will not enter the kingdom of God. The kingdom of God is here. As long as man is not conscious of his responsibility he does not know the kingdom of God. It is his becoming conscious of his responsibility which wakens him to the kingdom of God, in which is the birth of the soul.

Furthermore, in support of this idea there is a word that in the Sanskrit language is used for the God-conscious people. That word is *Brahman*, meaning creator. No sooner has a soul realized this idea than he begins to know that every moment of his life is creative, either automatically or intentionally. And if he is responsible for his creation, he is responsible for every moment of his life. Then there is nothing in life that is wasted. Whatever be the condition of man, however helpless or miserable, yet his life is not wasted, for there is the creative power working through every move that he makes, every thought that he thinks, every feeling that he has. He is always doing something.

There is another word in Sanskrit for *Brahman* which is *Duija*, meaning the soul who is born again. For the moment one has realized all this, the soul is born again: one's realization of life is different then, one's plan of life becomes different, one's action becomes different.

Now going a little further, there are sometimes souls who seem to be doing nothing, and one thinks: 'Yes; they are most spiritual people, I suppose – but what do they do?' – for what

we know about doing is hustling and bustling, being busy all
the time. However unimportant, yet that is something done!
That is the thought. But when a person is evolved, even if
outwardly he may not seem to be doing something, he is
doing and can do much greater works inwardly than can be
noticed outwardly.

There is a story of a *madzub*. A *madzub* is someone who
is not considered to be an active person in the world. Many
think of him as someone who is not quite balanced. In the East
there are some who know about such beings, and they have
regard for them. There used to be a *madzub* in Kashmir some
centuries ago, who was allowed by the Maharaja to roam
about in the palace and the gardens wherever he wanted to
go, and he was given a piece of ground where he could dwell.
He used to walk in every corner of the Maharaja's gardens that
he was allowed to enter. There was a miniature toy cannon
in the garden, and sometimes this *madzub* got a fancy to play
with it. He used to take this gun and turn it, either toward
the south or toward the north or elsewhere. Then he would
turn it again and make all sorts of gestures. After making
those gestures he would be delighted. It seemed as if he were
fighting and as if after that fighting he was now victorious
and delighted. It was at such times that the Maharaja Ranjit
Singh used to give the order to his army: 'Now prepare for
fight!', and there was success. The war had been going on for
many, many years, and it was going on slowly; nothing had
happened, but every time the *madzub* played with the cannon
results were achieved.

I myself have seen in Hyderabad a *madzub* whose habit it
was to insult everybody, to call people such names that they
would go away from him. Still one man dared go there in
spite of all the insults. The *madzub* said to him: 'What do you
want?' He said: 'My case is coming on in the court six days
from now, and I have no money, no means. What shall I do?'
'Tell me what is the condition', said the *madzub*, 'but tell me
the truth'. So the man told him all. The *madzub* listened to
it; then he wrote on the ground: 'There seems to be nothing
in this case; so it must be dismissed'. Then he said: 'Go, it is
done'. The man went to the court. On the opposite side were
many barristers and pleaders; on his part there were none,

because he was a poor man. The judge heard the case from both sides, and then spoke the same words that the *madzub* had written on the ground.

What does this mean? It only explains to us the words that Christ spoke: 'Enter the kingdom of God'; meaning that every soul has in himself a kingdom of God. To become conscious of this mystery of life is to open one's eyes to the kingdom of God, and then whatever one does has a meaning, an influence. It is never lost. If it is not materialized, it does not matter: it is spiritualized. Nothing is gone, nothing here is lost. If it has not been produced on this plane, it is produced on another plane – but then it is reflected on this plane, because there is always an action and reaction between both planes. It only means that what one does – if it is not materialized on this plane – is reflected from the other plane on this plane, and then materialized. That is all. If a person thinks: 'I have thought and thought on a certain subject, and yet it has not been realized', it only means that the time and the conditions have not allowed it to materialize. But if it is once sent out, it must ultimately be materialized.

CHAPTER VI

The Form of Thought

THE MIND has five aspects, but the aspect that is best known is that for which we use the word 'mind'. Mind means: the creator of thought and imagination. The mind is a soil upon which, in the form of thoughts and imaginations, plants grow. They live there but, as they are continually springing up, only the newly created plants are before one's consciousness, and those plants and trees which were created before are hidden from one's eyes. Therefore, when thoughts and imaginations are forgotten, they are no longer before one; one does not think about them any more, but whenever one wishes to find a thought which has once been shaped, it can immediately be found, for it still exists in the mind.

That part of the mind which our consciousness does not see immediately is called subconsciousness. It is called so because the consciousness remains on the surface, making clear to us that part of our thoughts and imaginations which we have just shaped and at which we are busy looking.

Nevertheless once a person has had an imagination, a thought, it still exists. In what form does it exist? In the form which the mind gave it. As the soul takes a form in the physical world, a form borrowed from this world, so the thought takes a form which is borrowed from the world of mind. A clear mind, therefore, can give a distinct body, a distinct form to the thought; a mind which is confused produces indistinct thoughts. One can see the truth of this in dreams: the dreams of the clear-minded are clear and distinct, the dreams of those whose mind is unclear are confusing. Besides, it is most interesting to see that the dreams of artists, poets, musicians – who live in beauty, who think of beauty – are beautiful, whereas the dreams of those whose mind contains doubt, fear or confusion are of the same character.

This gives proof that the mind gives a body to the thought. The mind supplies form to each thought, and with that form the thought is able to exist. The form of the thought is not only known to the person who thinks, but also to the one who reflects the thought, the one in whose heart it is reflected. That is why there is a silent communication between people: the thought-forms of one person reflecting in the mind of another. These thought-forms are more powerful and clearer than words. They are often more impressive than a spoken word, because language is limited, while thought has a greater scope of expression.

Someone asked me what elementals look like. I answered: 'Elementals are exactly like your thoughts. If you have the thoughts of human beings then the elementals have human form. If you have the thoughts of birds then the elementals have the form of birds. If your thoughts are of the animals then the elementals have the form of animals, for elementals are made of your thoughts'.

There is another most interesting aspect in studying the nature of the mind: that every mind attracts and reflects thoughts of its own kind – just as there is a part of the earth which is more suitable for flowers to grow in, and another part of the earth more suitable for fruits, and yet another part where weeds grow. Thus a reflection that falls from one mind upon another only falls upon the mind which attracts it. This is the reason why like is attractive to like. If a robber or a thief goes to Paris, he will certainly meet with another thief. He will easily find out where the thief lives; he will recognize him at once, because his mind has become a receptacle for thoughts of the same kind. As soon as their glances meet a communication is established: their thoughts are alike.

One sees in everyday life how like attracts like. The reason is that the mind has developed a certain character, and the thought-pictures of that particular character appeal to it. It is so very interesting for a person who sees this phenomenon in everyday life that there is not one moment when he does not see the truth of it.

High minds will always reflect and attract higher thoughts; from wherever it comes it will come to them. It will be attracted to the mind the ground of which is prepared for it. An ordinary mind is attracted to ordinary thoughts. For instance, a person who has a habit of criticizing people is very eager to open his ears to criticism, because that is the subject which interests him, his pleasure is there. He cannot resist the temptation of hearing ill of another, because this is most dear to his heart, for he speaks ill of others himself. When that thought does not belong to a person it is a foreign note to his ears; he does not want to hear it. His heart has no pleasure in it; it wants to throw off anything that is inharmonious. Therefore the mind-world is man's kingdom, his property. Whatever he sows, that he reaps. Whatever he keeps that property for, that is produced in it.

Now going into deeper metaphysics, what is it that forms the thought-picture? It is a very subtle question. A materialistic scientist will say that there are thought-atoms which group and make the form: joining together they compose the thought-form. If he wants to make it more objective he will say that in the brain there are little thought-pictures, just like moving pictures, and that, moving successively, they complete the form. For this person does not see further than his body, and so he wants to find out the secret of the whole life in his body and in the physical world. In reality the brain is only an instrument to make thoughts clearer. Thought is greater, vaster, deeper and higher than brain.

There is no doubt that the picture of thoughts is made by the impressions of the mind. If the mind has had no impressions thoughts will not be clear. For instance, a blind person who has never in his life seen an elephant, will not be able to form an idea of an elephant, because his mind has no form ready to compose it at the command of his will. For the mind must know it first in order to compose it. Therefore the mind is a storehouse of all forms which a person has ever seen.

One might ask: 'Cannot a form be reflected upon a blind person's mind?' Yes, but it will remain incomplete. If a thought is projected on a blind person he takes only half of it, for he will not have that part which he should give from his own mind, and so he only takes the reflection which is projected upon him. Therefore he has a vague idea of the thing, but he cannot make it clear to himself, because his mind has not yet formed that idea.

The form of a thought which the mind holds is reflected upon the brain, and made clearer to the inner sense. By inner sense is meant the inner part of the five senses. For it is outwardly that these five organs give us an idea of five senses, but in reality there is only one sense. Through the five different outer organs we experience different things, and this gives us the idea that there are five senses.

There are visionary people who have conceptions of the different colours of thoughts and imaginations and feelings. This is symbolical rather than astral. The colour of a thought corresponds with the condition of the mind. It shows the element to which the thought belongs: whether the thought belongs to the fire element, to the water element, or to the earth element. This means that it is the feeling which is behind the thought that produces its colour around it as an atmosphere which surrounds it. When such visionary people see the thought-form in the form of colour, it is what surrounds the thought, it is the atmosphere of the thought, and this is according to the element belonging to that thought.

A thought connected with earthly gain is of the earth element; a thought of love and affection represents the water element, it is spreading out sympathy; a thought of revenge and destruction, hurt and harm represents fire; a thought of enthusiasm, courage, hope and aspiration represents air; a thought of retirement, solitude, quiet and peace represents ether. These are the predominant characteristics of thought in connection with the five elements.

The form of a thought is also its effect: its effect upon the form and expression of a person. For a thought has a particular language which manifests as a kind of letter – if one could read it. This language can be read in the face and form of a person. Everyone reads this to a certain extent, but it is difficult to define the letters, the alphabet of this language. There is one mystery which opens a door into the thought-language, and that is the vibrations: what direction the vibrations take. A thought works upon and around a person's form, and becomes manifest to the eyes upon his visible being. There is a certain law which governs its work, and that law is the law of direction: whether the forces are going to the right or to the left, upward or downward. It is this direction of the vibrations of thought which produces a picture, so that a seer can see this picture as clearly as a letter.

No doubt for a seer it is not necessary to read the thought from the visible form of a person, because he cannot be a seer if he is not open to reflection. Every thought is reflected in him, which makes things even clearer. Besides that, he need not see the picture of the thought on its visible form in order to know it; the atmosphere tells him. The thought itself calls out: 'I am this thought!', whatever it may be, for thought has a language, a voice, thought has breath and has life.

Question: What is imagination?
Answer: Imagination is uncontrolled thought.

Question: Is it good to have strong imagination?
Answer: It is good to be strong oneself. If one has strength, then imagination is strong, and thought is strong, and one is strong oneself. Furthermore, a strong imagination means a strength going out from oneself, reaching out without control. Therefore strong imagination is not always promising. It is strength of thought which is desirable. For what is thought? Thought is a self-directed and controlled imagination.

Question: If thought has a body, is it bound to a place, or does it spread through the whole universe?
Answer: This is a subtle question. One could ask: 'If a person is in prison, is his mind in prison too, or can it reach beyond, can it go out of prison?' Certainly it can. It is the body of the man that is in prison. His mind can reach everywhere. Perhaps a thought produced in the mind-world is made captive by its object or motive, by its source, or by its application in a sphere, within a horizon where it is working out its destiny. Nevertheless it is a thought, it is capable of reaching every part of the universe in a moment's time.

Question: How should undesirable thoughts be destroyed? Must this always be done by the person who created them?
Answer: Yes, it is the creator of the thought who must destroy it, and it is not in every person's power to do it. Yet the mind

which has reached mastery, which can create as it wishes, this same mind can destroy.

Question: Would you explain further what role the brain plays in thinking?

Answer: The brain may be likened to a photographic plate. The thought falls upon the brain just as a reflection falls upon the photographic plate – both one's own thought and the thought of another. Then there is another process, and that is that the thought is developed like the photographic plate. What is it developed with? Is there some solution in which the photographic plate is to be put? Yes, and that is the intelligence. Through one's own intelligence it is developed and made clearer.

Question: Has one element superiority over another? For instance, is a thought coloured by fire superior to a thought coloured by another element?

Answer: There is no superiority of one element over another. The superiority of a thought is according to the outlook of the mind. For instance, one person standing on the ground sees the horizon just before him; this is one outlook. Another person stands on the top of a tower and from there he looks at the wide horizon; his outlook is different. It is according to the outlook that the thought is superior or inferior. Besides, no one can take a thought, any thought-picture before himself and say: 'This is an inferior thought', or: 'This is a superior thought'. Thought is not an earthly coin which can be inferior or superior. What makes it inferior or superior is the motive behind it.

CHAPTER VII

Memory

MEMORY IS a mental faculty, a distinct aspect of the mind. It is a recording mechanism which records all that falls upon it through any of the five senses. What one sees, hears, smells, touches and tastes is recorded upon the memory. A form, a picture, an image, once seen, sometimes remains in the memory for the whole of one's life if it is well recorded. In the life of the world one hears so many words during the day – yet some words which the memory has recorded remain for one's whole life, as living as ever.

So it is with music. Once a person has heard wonderful music, and it is recorded upon his memory, it remains for ever and ever. Memory is such a living machine that one can produce that music at any time; it is all there. A good perfume once experienced, once perceived, is remembered; the feeling of taste remains, also the feeling of touch. Memory holds it all.

It does not remain in the memory as in a notebook. For as the notebook is dead, so what remains in the notebook is dead, but memory is living, and so whatever is recorded upon the memory is also living and gives a living sensation. A record of a pleasant memory is sometimes so precious that one wishes to sacrifice this objective world for such a record.

I was very touched once by seeing a widow whose relatives wished me to tell her to go into society, to mix with people, to live a more worldly life. I went to advise her on that subject, but when she told me gently: 'All experiences of this world's life, however pleasant, do not afford me pleasure. My only joy is the memory of my beloved; other things give me unhappiness, other things make me miserable. If I find joy, it is in the thought of my beloved', I could not say one word to change her mind. I thought it would be a sin on my part to take her away from her joy. If her memory had been a misery for her, I should have preached to her otherwise, but it was happiness for her, it was her only happiness. I thought that here was a living *Sati*. I had only a great esteem for her, and could not speak one word.

In the memory the secret of heaven and hell is to be found. As Omar Khayyam said in his *Rubayat*: 'Heaven is the vision of fulfilled desire, and hell the shadow of a soul on fire'. What is it? Where is it? It is only in the memory. Therefore memory is not a small thing. It is not something which is hidden in the brain. It is something living, and it is something so vast that a limited mind cannot conceive it. It is something which is a world in itself.

People might ask: 'What is it then, if a person has lost his memory? Is it caused by disorder in the brain?' In the first place no one really loses his memory. A person may lose it, but his memory does not lose him, because the memory is his own being. What happens is that the disorder of the brain makes him incapable of distinguishing what the memory contains. Therefore a person who has lost his memory in his life-time, owing to a disorder in the brain, has memory just the same. That memory will become clearer to him after death. Also, if he lifted himself off his objective being he would find his memory intact. Only, the memory cannot function in a brain which is out of order.[10]

To have a good memory is not only a good thing, it is a bliss. It is a sign of spirituality because it shows that the light of the intelligence is clear and is illuminating every particle of the brain. A good memory is a sign of great souls. Besides, memory is the treasury where one's knowledge is stored. If a person cannot draw the knowledge that he has collected from his memory, then dependence upon books is of little worth.

One day, six months after I had been received by my *Murshid* as his pupil, he began to speak on metaphysics. Being metaphysically inclined myself I jumped at the thought of it. During those six months I was never impatient, I had never shown any eagerness to know something more than what I was allowed to know. I was quite contented at the feet of the master. That was everything to me. Nevertheless it was a great stimulus to my mind to hear from him something about metaphysics. But as soon as I took out my notebook from my pocket my *Murshid* ended the subject. He said nothing, but from that day I learned a lesson: 'By this he means that my notebook must not be the storehouse of my knowledge. There is a living notebook, and that is my memory, a notebook which I shall carry with me all through life and through the hereafter'.

No doubt we always write down on paper things belonging to the earth: the figures of ten, twenty and hundred – but things pertaining to the spiritual order of things, to the divine law, are of much greater importance. The notebook cannot contain them, it is not made for them. It is in the memory that they must be treasured, for memory is not only a recording machine. It is a fertile ground at the same time. What is put there is continually creative, it is doing something there. So one does not only possess something that one has deposited, there is its interest also.

Sometimes memory is weakened by too great a strain put upon it. When one tries to remember, this puts a strain upon a process which is natural. It is the nature of memory to remember, but when you put a strain upon it: 'You must remember!', then it will forget. The very fact that you have strained it will make it forget. One must not try to impress one's mind more deeply than it naturally becomes impressed. One's attention is quite enough. Will-power must not be used to remember things; it is a wrong method that people are applying at present when they say that in order to remember things one must will it. By willing one weakens the memory. Besides this, a balance between activity and repose is necessary.

Memory is never lost. What happens is that, when the mind is upset, the memory becomes blurred. It is the stillness of the mind which makes one capable of distinguishing all that one's memory contains. When the mind is upset, when a person is not tranquil, then naturally – in spite of all the record the memory has – one is not able to read it. It is not true that memory gives away what is stored in it. It is only man who loses the rhythm of his life by over-excitement, nervousness, weakness of nerves, anxiety, worry, fear, confusion; and it is that which causes a kind of turmoil in the mind: one cannot distinctly find the things which were once recorded in the memory.

One need not work with one's memory in order to make it clear. What is required is to make oneself tranquil, rhythmical and peaceful in order to make the memory distinct.

Question: Should one then not use the brain when trying to remember something?
Answer: It is not necessary to use the brain when trying to remember something, because by using the brain one only strains it. The memory is at the command of the person. If he wants to know about something, instantly, without his straining the brain, it must come. It is an automatic mechanism; it must bring before him automatically all that he wishes to know.

Question: What should a person do who cannot easily learn by heart?
Answer: He should make his mind tranquil. This is the first thing. It is the mental way of making memory better. A physical way of making the memory better is to eat less and sleep normally. One should not work too much, not worry very much, and keep all anxiety and fear away.

Question: Through what vehicle does the memory function after death?
Answer: The mind is distinctly different from the body; it is something apart, standing independent of the body. The mind depends on the body for perceiving the outer experiences which it takes in through the senses, but the mind is independent of the body for holding its treasures which it has collected through the outer world, and retaining them. As we are accustomed to experience everything through the vehicle of the body – even our feelings – this makes us dependent for some time upon the body. But this does not mean that we cannot experience all that belongs to the mind without the help of the body.

Question: Is there not a danger in losing oneself in the memory of that which lies behind us?
Answer: There is an answer to this in the Gayan where it is said: 'If you live in the vision of the past, dream on, do not

open your eyes to the present. If you live in the eternal, do not worry about the morrow. But if you live for the time to come, do all you can to prepare for the future'.

Question: How should one erase from the record a living memory of something of the past?
Answer: That is what we learn in the Sufi path. It is the work which we accomplish by concentration and meditation. It is not an easy thing to do; it is the most difficult, but also the most valuable thing there is. That is why we keep our teachings free from speculations, beliefs, doctrines and dogmas, for we believe in actual work with ourselves. What if you were told a thing one day and you believed it one day, and next day you doubted and did not believe it any more? If you were told that there is a house in the sixth heaven and a palace in the seventh, what would that do for you? It would only answer your curiosity; it would take you nowhere. It is therefore by the way of meditation that we attain to this: that we can erase from the memory what we wish to. In this way we are able to make our heaven ourselves.

The whole secret of esotericism lies in controlling the mind, and in working with it as an artist would work on a canvas producing whatever he likes. When we are able to produce on the canvas of our heart all that we wish, and to erase all we wish, then we arrive at that mastery for which our soul craves. We fulfil the purpose for which we are here. Then we become the masters of our destiny. It is difficult, but that is the object that we pursue in life.

CHAPTER VIII

Will

WILL IS not *a* power, but it is *all* the power there is. How did God create the world? By will. Therefore what we call will-power in us is in reality God-power, a power which increases by our recognizing its potentiality, and proves to be the greatest phenomenon in life. If there is any secret behind the mystery of the world of phenomena that can be learned it is will-power, and it is by will-power that all we do, physically or mentally, is accomplished. Our hands, with all their perfect mechanism, cannot hold a glass of water if there is no will-power to support them. If will-power fails him, a person seemingly healthy will not be able to stand.

It is not the body which makes us stand upright, it is our will-power. It is not the strength of body that makes us move about, it is will-power which is holding the body, which is making it go. Therefore, in reality, birds do not fly with their wings, they fly with will-power. Fishes do not swim with their body, they swim with their will-power. And when man has the will to swim he swims like a fish.

Man has been able to accomplish tremendous things by will-power. Success and failure are its phenomena. It is only the phenomenon of will which will bring one to success, and when will fails, however qualified and intelligent the person, he fails. Therefore it is not a human power, it is a divine power in man. Its work with the mind is still greater, for no man can hold a thought in his mind for a moment if there is not the strength of his will to hold it. If a person cannot concentrate, cannot keep his thought still for a moment, it means that will-power fails him, for it is will which holds a thought.

Now coming to the question as to what will-power is made of: in poetical words will-power is love, in metaphysical terms love is will-power. If one says: 'God is love', this means in reality that God is will; for the love of God manifests after the creation, but the will of God caused the creation. So the most original aspect of love is will. When a person says: 'I love to do it', it means: 'I will to do it', which is a stronger expression and means: 'I fully love to do it'.

In the Qur'an it is said: 'We said "Be", and it became'. This is a key to the world of phenomena. To the progressive world, to advanced thought, this is the key which shows how manifestation came into existence. It came into existence in answer to that Will which expressed itself in saying: 'Be' – and it became. This phenomenon does not only belong to the origin of things, it belongs to the whole being of things, to the whole process of manifestation.

We are apt to look at this whole creation as a mechanism, and we do not stop to think how a mechanism can exist without an engineer. What is mechanism? It is only an expression of the will of the engineer who for his convenience made the mechanism. But as we do not see the engineer before us and only see the mechanism, we involve ourselves in the laws of the working of this mechanism and forget the engineer by whose command this whole mechanism is going on. As Rumi, the great inspirer and philosopher, has said in his *Mathnavi*: 'Earth, water, fire, air seem to us as things, as objects – but before God they are living beings; they stand as His obedient servants and obey the divine Will'

A part of that Will we inherit as our own divine heritage, and it is our consciousness of it which makes it greater. If we are not conscious of it, it becomes smaller. It is the optimistic attitude towards life which develops the will; the pessimistic attitude reduces it, robs it of its great power. Therefore, if there is anything that hinders our progress in life it is our own selves. It is proved a thousand times over that there is no one in the world who can be a worse enemy to us than ourselves, for at every failure we see ourselves standing in our own light.

The earth holds the seed, and the result is that a plant springs out and bears fruit. So with the heart; the heart holds the seed of thought, and there also a plant springs out and brings the fruit of fulfilment. But it is not only the thought, it is the power of holding the thought which is of very great importance. Therefore the factor of the heart, a factor which holds the thought, is of very great importance for the fulfilment of life's purpose. Often a person says: 'I try my best, but I cannot concentrate my mind; I cannot make my mind still'. It is true, but it is not true that he tries his best. 'Best' does not end there. 'Best' really brings the purpose to its fulfilment.

The mind is just like a restive horse. Bring a wild horse and yoke it to a carriage; it is such a strange experience for it that it will kick and jump and run and try to destroy the carriage. So it is a weight for the mind to carry when you make it take one thought and hold it for a while. It is then that the mind becomes restless, because it is not accustomed to discipline. There is a thought that the mind will hold by itself: a thought of disappointment, or pain, or grief, of sorrow or failure. The mind will hold it so fast that you cannot take it away from its grip; the mind holds it by itself. But when you ask the mind to hold a particular thought, then the mind will not hold it; it says: 'I am not your servant, sir!'

When once the mind is disciplined by concentration, by the power of will then the mind becomes your servant. Once the mind has become your servant, then what more can you wish? Then your world is your own, you are the king of your kingdom. No doubt, one might say: 'Why should we not let the mind be free also, as we are free?' But we and the mind are not two beings. It is like saying: 'Let the horse be free and the rider be free'. Then the horse wants to go to the south and the rider wants to go to the north. How can they go together?

There are souls who would even say: 'Let us be free, and the will be free'. But what are we then? Then we are nothing! Discipline has a place in man's life. Self-discipline, however difficult and tyrannical to ourselves it may seem in the beginning, yet is that which in the end makes the soul the master of self. It is not in vain that the great sages and adepts led an ascetic life; there was a purpose in it. It is not something to follow, but it is something to understand: what use they made of it, what they accomplished through it. It was self-discipline, it was the development of will-power.

All the lack that we find in life is the lack of will, and all the blessing that comes to us comes by the power of will.

Question: What is the best way to develop will-power?

Answer: Sufis develop will-power systematically by first putting the body into a certain discipline. It must sit in the posture that is prescribed to it; it must stand in a place where it is asked to stand. The body must not become restless, tired, fatigued by what is asked of it. The body must answer the demands of the person to whom it belongs. The moment he begins to discipline the body he begins to see how disobedient the body has always been. Then he finds out that this body which he has called 'mine', 'myself', and for whose comfort he has done everything possible, having closed his eyes to everything else in order to give his body comfort, rest, nourishment – here this infidel seems to be most faithless, most disobedient. So the body is trained by physical exercises, by sitting, standing, or walking, by doing things to which it is not accustomed and which are yet for the betterment of this physical body.

Then comes the discipline of the mind. That is done by concentration. When you wish the mind to think on one thought that you have before you while the mind is thinking about something else, then the mind becomes very restless. It does not want to stand on one spot, because it has always been moving about without discipline. As soon as you discipline it, it becomes like a wild horse. Very often people tell me that during the day they do not have such difficulty as at the moment that they want to concentrate: at that time the mind jumps, at other times it moves. This is because the mind is an entity. It becomes restive. It feels as a wild horse would feel: 'Why should I be troubled by you?' At the same time this mind is meant to be an obedient servant. This body is meant to become your tool with which to experience life. If mind and body are not in order, if they do not act as you wish them to, then you cannot hope for real comfort, for real happiness in this world.

Question: Will you please explain the difference between concentration and silence?
Answer: Concentration is holding a certain thought before you. Silence is relaxing mind and body. It is repose. It is a healing.

Question: What is the difference between concentration and meditation?

Answer: Concentration is the beginning of meditation, meditation is the end of concentration; it is an advanced form of concentration. The subtle working of the mind is called meditation. It is more profound than concentration, but once concentration is accomplished fully it becomes easy for a person to meditate.

Question: Will-power does not seem to depend on ourselves. Is it not given to some as a grace, as a blessing?

Answer: It does not depend on ourselves, but it is ourselves. It is grace and blessing no doubt, but at the same time it is to be found in ourselves, it is our very being.

Question: Are will and consciousness fundamentally the same?

Answer: Yes. It is the two expressions of one thing, and this makes them distinct. This duality comes out of unity. It is God's own Being that in expression is will, in repose consciousness. In other words: in action it is will, in stillness it is consciousness – just as fundamentally sound and light are one and the same thing. In one condition the same vibrations are audible, in another condition the friction of vibrations produces light. That is why the nature and character of sound and light are one and the same. And so are the nature and character of consciousness and will, because fundamentally both belong to God's own Being.

Question: Can the will be so strong that it controls the human body so as to make it perfectly healthy? What then is death?

Answer: Death is not something different from will-power. Death is will just the same: even death is caused by will-power. One thinks that one does not invite one's death. Yes, one does not invite it, but the personal will becomes feeble, and the greater Will impresses the feeble will, turning it into itself, for the smaller will belongs to the greater Will.

Sufis call the smaller will *Qadr*, the greater Will *Qaza*. They attribute the greater Will to God, and the smaller will to man. It is the smaller will which becomes feeble, and the greater

Will reflects its command upon it. It is this command which the smaller will, unconsciously, accepts. On the surface a person may still want to live, but in the depth of his will he has resigned himself to die. If he had not resigned himself he would not die. He has resigned himself to death before his life is taken away from him.

Question: Is it then by putting the human will in harmony with the divine Will that the world redeemers are made?
Answer: Resignation of the human will to the divine Will is the real crucifixion. After that crucifixion follows resurrection, but in order to attain to it one should first try and seek the pleasure of God. This is not so difficult when one begins to seek it, but when one does not begin to seek it, then one does not know what is the pleasure of God. Then there is another way which the Sufis have always taught: to seek the pleasure of one's fellowmen, and that is the very thing that man refuses to do. He is quite willing to seek the pleasure of God, but if one asks him to seek the pleasure of his fellowmen he refuses. In any case, either in seeking the pleasure of his fellowmen or of God, in both he is seeking the pleasure of one and the same being. It all begins very often with resignation. After having once resigned and when he is tuned to the divine Will, then a man need not resign any more, for then his wish becomes divine impulse.

Question: Is the power of will the same as the power of the soul?
Answer: Yes. It is the power of soul and spirit, and the power of man and God – all.

CHAPTER IX

Reason

WHEN WE analyse the word reason it opens before us a vast field of thought. In the first place every doer of good and every evil-doer has a reason to support his doing. When two persons quarrel, each says he is in the right, because each has a reason. To a third person perhaps the reason of the one may appear to be more reasonable than that of the other, or perhaps he will say that both have no reason and that he has reason on his side. All disputes, arguments and discussions seem to be based upon reason, and yet reason, before one has analysed it, is nothing but an illusion and keeps one continually in perplexity. The cause of all inharmony, all disagreement is the perplexity which is caused by not understanding one another's reason.

One might ask: 'What is reason? Where does it belong?' Reason belongs to both earth and heaven: its depth heavenly, its surface earthly; and that which, in the form of reason, fills the gap between earth and heaven is the middle part of it which unites them. Therefore reason can be most confusing, and reason can be most enlightening. In the language of the Hindus reason is called *Bodhi*, or *Buddh*, from which comes the title of Gautama Buddha. But what reason is this? It is the depth of reason, the most perfect reasoning which belongs to heaven.

There is another reasoning which belongs to the earth. If a person says to someone who has taken another person's raincoat: 'Why did you take it?', he may answer: 'Because it was raining'. He has a reason. Another reason is needed to think: 'Why should I take another person's raincoat? Although it is raining – it is not my raincoat'. That is another reason altogether. Do you think that thieves and robbers, or the great assassins have no reason? Sometimes they have great reasons – but reasons that are on the surface. Can a thief not say in order to justify his action: 'What is it to that rich person if he lost so much money? Here am I, a poor man, I could make better use of it. I have not robbed him of every penny. I have just taken as much as I wanted. It is useful, I can do some good with it'.

Besides, reason is the servant of the mind. The mind feels like praising a person – reason at once brings a thousand things in praise of him, in his favour. The mind has a desire to hate a person – at once reason brings perhaps twenty arguments in favour of hating him. So we see that a loving friend can find a thousand things that are good and beautiful in his friend, and an adversary will find a thousand faults in the best person in the world – and he has reasons.

In French conversation they say: 'Vous avez raison', but one can say that everyone has reason. It is not sometimes that one has a reason, everyone always has a reason. Only it depends which reason it is: is it the earthly reason, or is it the heavenly reason? It is natural that heavenly reason does not agree with earthly reason.

Now coming to the essence of things: where do we get reason, where do we learn it? The earthly reason we learn from our earthly experiences. When we say: 'This is right, and that is wrong', it is only because we have learned on the earth that this is right and that is wrong. An innocent child who is just born on earth, and who has not yet learned to distinguish between what we call right and wrong – to him it is nothing, he has not yet acquired that earthly reason.

Then there is a reason which is beyond earthly reason. The person who has taken someone's raincoat has a reason: 'because it was raining'. But there is a reason beyond that: the raincoat did not belong to him. He should rather have got wet through in the rain than have taken this raincoat. That is another reason: that is reason behind reason.

Then there is the essence of reason which is heavenly reason. It is that reason which not everyone understands. It is that reason which is discovered by the seers and sages, by the mystics and prophets within themselves. It is upon this reason that religions are founded. On the ground of this reason the ideas of mysticism and philosophy spring up as plants and bear fruits and flowers. When a pupil is expected to listen to the reason of his teacher, instead of disputing over it, it is in order to regard that heavenly reason behind it, and to know that there comes a time in one's life when one's eyes are open to the essential reason. It is that reason which is called *Bodhisatva*: *Bodhi* or *Buddh* meaning reason, and *satva* meaning essence.

How is one to arrive at that reason? By arriving at that rhythm which is called *satva*. There are three rhythms: *tammas*, *rajas* and *satva*. A person whose rhythm of life is *tammas* knows earthly reason; he whose life is *rajas* knows, beyond earthly reason, a reason which is hidden behind a reason; and the one who begins to see or live in the rhythm of *satva* begins to see the cause of every reason – which is in the profound depths of the whole being, and that is God's reason.

No doubt in the present time education is a great hindrance to children. The children are taught to reason freely with their parents. By reasoning freely, when they come to a certain age, they do not stop to think; before they think they argue, they dispute and ask: 'Why not? Why?' In this way they never attain to the heavenly reason. For in order to arrive at that heavenly reason a responsive attitude is necessary, not an exacting attitude. What today a child learns is an assertive, exerting attitude. He exerts his knowledge upon others. Through the lack of that responsive attitude he loses his opportunity of ever touching that essence of reason which is the spirit of *Bodhisatva*.

Once a *Murshid* went to the city and on his return he said: 'Oh, I am filled with joy, I am filled with joy. There was such exaltation in the presence of the Beloved'. Then his *mureed* thought: 'There was a beloved and an exaltation. How wonderful! I too must go and see if I cannot find one'. He went through the city and came back saying: 'Horrible! How terrible the world is! All seem to be at one another's throats. That was the picture I saw. I felt nothing but depression, as if my whole being was torn to pieces'. 'Yes', the *Murshid* said, 'you are right'. 'But explain to me', the *mureed* said, 'why you were so exalted after going out, and why I should be so torn to pieces. I cannot bear it. It is horrible!' The *Murshid* said: 'You did not walk in the rhythm that I walked in through the city'. This walking means not only the slow rhythm of the walk, but that rhythm with which the mind is moving, that rhythm with which the observation is gained. It is that which

makes the difference between one person and another. It is
that which brings about the difference between the reasoning
of one person and another.

The person who says: 'I will not listen to your reason', no
doubt has his reason, as everybody has a reason. But he could
have a better reason still if he were able to listen, if he were
able to understand the reason of another. The rhythm of a
person's mind is just like making circles. One person's mind
makes one circle in a minute; another person's mind makes
a circle in five minutes; his reason is different. And another
person's mind makes a circle in fifteen minutes; his reason is
different again. The longer it takes, the wider is the horizon
of his vision, and so more keen is his outlook on life.

Reasoning is a ladder. By this ladder one can rise, and by
this ladder one may fall. For if one does not go upward by
reasoning, then it will help one to go downward too, because,
if for every step one takes upward there is a reason, there is
also a reason for every step downward.

No doubt this distinction is made to enable us to understand
the three different aspects of reason. In reality there is one
reason. One may divide the human body into three parts, but
it is one body, it is one person. Reason is a great factor and has
every possibility in it of every curse and of every blessing.

Question: What may we call the middle part of the reason? Is
it the sense of discrimination?
Answer: Yes; reason is attached to an impulse, and reason is
attached to thought. The reason which is attached to thought
is the middle part of reason; the reason which is attached to
impulse is the lower part of reason. But the reason which is
inspiring, which is revealing to the soul, is heavenly reason.
This reason unfolds divine light; it comes by wakening to the
reason that one finds in the heart of God.

There is a story told about Moses who was passing
with Khidr through a country. Khidr was the *Murshid* of
Moses when Moses was being prepared for prophetship.
Moses's first lesson of discipline was to keep quiet under all
circumstances. While they were walking through the beauty
of nature both teacher and pupil were quiet. The teacher was

exalted in seeing the beauty of nature, and the pupil also felt it. So they arrived on the bank of a river, where Moses saw a little child drowning, and the mother crying aloud for she could not help. Here Moses could not keep his lips closed. He had to break that discipline and say: 'Master, save him! The child is drowning!' Khidr said: 'Quiet!', and Moses was quiet. But the heart of Moses was restless, he did not know what to think: 'Can the Master be so thoughtless, so inconsiderate, so cruel, or is the Master powerless?' He could not understand which was which. He did not dare to think such a thought, and yet it made him feel very uncomfortable.

As they went further they saw a boat sinking. Moses said: 'Master, that boat is sinking, it is going down!' The Master again ordered him to be quiet; so then Moses was quiet, but he was still more uncomfortable. When they arrived home he said: 'Master, I thought that you would have saved that little innocent child from drowning, and that you would have saved the boat which was going down in the water – but you did nothing. I cannot understand, but I should like to have an explanation'. The Master said: 'What you saw, I also saw. We both saw. So there was no use in your telling me, because I saw. You did not need to tell me what was happening, for I knew. If I had thought that it was better to interfere, I could have done it. Why did you take the trouble to tell me, and spoil your vow of silence?'

He continued: 'The child who was drowning was meant to bring about a conflict between two nations, and thousands and thousands of lives were going to be destroyed in that conflict. When he was drowned this averted the other danger which was to come'. Moses looked at him with great surprise. Then Khidr said: 'The boat that was sinking was the boat of pirates. It was sailing in order to wreck a large ship full of pilgrims, and then to take what was left in the ship and bring it home. Do you think that you and I can be judge of it? The Judge is behind. He knows what He is doing, He knows his work. When you were told to be quiet, your work was to keep your lips closed and to see everything, as I was doing, silently, in reverence'.

There is a Persian verse which says: 'It is the gardener who knows which plant to rear and which to cut down'.

You might ask me: 'Shall we all take the same attitude? If a person is troubled or in difficulty, shall we not go and help?' Yes, you may help – but at the same time, if a spiritual person does not seem to do what you expect him to do, you do not need to trouble about it, for you must know that there is some reason. You do not need to judge him, for the more you evolve the more your reason becomes different. So no one has the power to judge another, but one may do one's best oneself.

Question: Is that why the great ones have been misjudged, because the little ones tried to judge them?
Answer: This has always been the great difficulty in the lives of evolved souls. What happened with Jesus Christ? In the one place there was earthly reason, in the other place there was heavenly reason.

I shall tell you a story of my insolence that will interest you. Once I looked at my *Murshid* and there came to my restless mind a thought: 'Why should a great soul such as my *Murshid* wear gold-embroidered slippers!' I checked myself at once; it was only a thought. It could never have escaped my lips; it was under control. But there, it was known. I could not cover my insolence with my lips; my heart was open before my *Murshid* as an open book. He instantly saw into it and read my thought. And do you know what answer he gave me? He said: 'The treasures of the world are at my feet'.

CHAPTER X

The Ego

WHEN WE think of that sense, that feeling, or that inclination which makes us affirm the word 'I', we realize that it is difficult to point out what this 'I' is, what is its character. For it is something which is beyond human comprehension. That is why a person who wishes to explain, even to himself, what it is, points to what is nearest to him declaring: 'This is the one whom I have called "I"'. Therefore every soul which has, so to speak, identified itself with anything, has identified itself with the body, its own body, because that is the thing which one feels and realizes to be immediately next to one, and which is intelligible as one's being.

So what a person knows of himself as the first thing is his body. He calls himself his body, he identifies himself with his body. For instance if one asks a child: 'Where is the boy?', he will point to his body. That is what he can see or can imagine of himself.

This forms a conception in the soul. The soul conceives this deeply, so that after this conception all other objects, persons or beings, colour or line, are called by different names, and the soul does not conceive of them as itself, for it already has a conception of itself: this body, which it has first known or imagined to be itself. All else that it sees, it sees through its vehicle which is the body, and calls it something next to it, something separate and different.

In this way duality in nature is produced. From this comes 'I and you'. But as 'I' is the first conception of the soul, it is fully concerned with this 'I'; with all else it is only partly concerned. All other things that exist, besides this body which it has recognized as its own being, are considered according to their relation with this body. This relation is established by calling them 'mine', which is between 'I' and 'you': 'You are "my" brother, or "my" sister, or "my" friend'. This makes a relationship, and according to this relationship the other object or person stands nearer to or farther from the soul.

All other experiences that the soul has in the physical world and in the mental spheres become a sort of world around it. The soul lives in the midst of it, yet the soul never for one moment feels with anything that it is 'I'. This 'I' it has reserved, and made captive in one thing only: the body. Of everything else the soul thinks that it is something else, something different: 'It is near to me, it is dear to me, it is close to me, because it is related. It is mine, but it is not me'. 'I' stands as a separate entity, holding, attracting, collecting all that one has got and which makes one's own world.

As one becomes more thoughtful in life, so this conception of 'I' becomes richer. It becomes richer in this way, that one sees: 'It is not "my" body only, but it is also the thought that I think which is "my" thought; the imagination is "my" imagination; my feelings are also a part of my being. Therefore I am not only my body, but I am my mind also.' In this next step that the soul takes in the path of realization it begins to feel: 'I am not only a physical body, but also a mind'. This realization in its fullness makes one declare: 'I am a spirit', which means: body, mind and feeling, all together with which I identify myself – it is these which are the ego.

When the soul goes further in the path of knowledge it begins to find: 'Yes, there is something which feels itself, which feels the inclination to call itself "I"'. There is a feeling of 'I'–ness, but at the same time all that the soul identifies itself with is not itself. The day when this idea springs up in the heart of man he has begun his journey in the path of truth. Then analysing begins, and he begins to find out: 'When this is "my" table and this is "my" chair, all that I can call mine belongs to me, but is not really myself.' Then he also begins to see: 'I identify myself with this body, but this is "my" body, just as I say "my" table, or "my" chair. So the being which is saying "I" in reality is separate. It is something which has taken even this body for its use; this body is only an instrument.' And he thinks: 'If it is not this body which I can call "I", then what else is there that I can call so? Is it my imagination with which I should identify myself?' But even that one calls 'my' imagination, 'my' thought, or 'my' feeling. So even thought, imagination, or feeling is not the real 'I'. What affirms 'I' remains the same even after having discovered the false identity.

We read in the tenth Sufi thought that perfection is achieved by the annihilation of the false ego.* The false ego is what does not belong to the real ego, and what that ego has wrongly conceived to be its own being. When that is separated by analysing life better, then the false ego is annihilated. A person need not die for it. In order to annihilate this body, in order to annihilate the mind a person has to analyse himself and see: 'Where does "I" stand? Does it stand as a remote, exclusive being? If it is a remote and an exclusive being then it must be found out'. The whole spiritual process is to find this out.

Once this is realized, the work of the spiritual path is accomplished. As in order to make the eyes see themselves one has to make a mirror to see the reflection of these eyes, so in order to make this real being manifest, this body and mind have been made as a mirror: that in this mirror this real being may see itself and realize its being independent. What we have to achieve by the path of initiation, by the way of meditation, by spiritual knowledge is to realize this by making ourselves a perfect mirror.

In order to explain this idea the *faqirs* and dervishes have told a story. A lion roaming through the desert found a little lioncub playing with the sheep. It so happened that the little lion had been reared with the sheep, and so had never had a chance or an occasion to realize what he was. The lion was greatly surprised to see a young lioncub running away with the same fear of the lion as the sheep. He jumped in among the flock of sheep and roared: 'Halt, halt!', but the sheep ran on, and the little lion ran also. The lion pursued only the cub, not the sheep, and said: 'Wait, I wish to speak to you'. The cub answered: 'I tremble, I fear, I cannot stand before you'. 'Why are you running about with the sheep? You are a little lion yourself!' 'No, I am a sheep. I tremble, I am afraid of you. Let me go. Let me go with the sheep!' 'Come along', said the lion, 'come with me. I will take you and I will show you what you are before I let you go'. Trembling and yet helpless,

---

* There is one path, the annihilation of the false ego in the real, which raises the mortal to immortality, in which resides all perfection.

the lioncub followed the lion to a pool of water. There the lion said: 'Look at me, and look at yourself. Are we not closer, are we not near? You are not like the sheep, you are like me'.

Through the whole spiritual process what we learn is to disillusion this false ego. The annihilation of this false ego is its disillusionment. When once it is disillusioned then the true ego realizes its own merit. It is in this realization that the soul enters the kingdom of God. It is in this realization that the soul is born again, a birth which opens the doors of heaven.

Question: Must the true self have mind and body in order to be conscious of itself?
Answer: The true self need not have mind and body for its existence. It does not depend upon mind and body for its existence, for its life, just as the eyes do not depend upon the mirror to exist. They only depend upon the mirror to see their reflection. Without it the eyes will see all things, but they will never see themselves.

Another example is the intelligence. The intelligence cannot know itself unless it has something intelligible to hold; then the intelligence realizes itself. A person with poetic gift who is born a poet, never realizes himself to be a poet till he has put his idea on paper, and his verse has struck a chord in his own heart. When he is able to appreciate his poetry, then is the time that he thinks: 'I am a poet'. Till then there was a gift of poetry in him, but he did not know it.

The eyes do not become more powerful by looking in the mirror. Only, the eyes know what they are like when they see their reflection. The pleasure is in realizing one's merits, one's gifts, what one possesses. It is in realizing that the merit lies. No doubt it would be a great pity if the eyes thought: 'We are as dead as this mirror', or if in looking in the mirror they thought: 'We do not exist except in the mirror'. So the false self is the greatest limitation.

Question: Is not our *Murshid* our mirror?
Answer: No. The *Murshid* stands in the place of the lion in the fable. But the pool of water is necessary.

Question: Though the soul feels apart from the different bodies, does it not feel one with God?

Answer: Not even with God. How could it? A soul which is captive in a false conception, which cannot see a barrier lifted up between itself and its neighbour, how can this soul lift its barrier to God whom it has not known yet? For every soul's belief in God is a conception after all – because it is taught by a priest, because it is written in a scripture, because the parents have said that there is a God. That is all. That soul knows that somewhere there is a God, but it is always liable to change its belief, and unhappily the further it advances intellectually, the further it goes from that belief. A belief which a pure intelligence cannot always hold will not go far with a person. It is by the understanding of that belief that the purpose of life is fulfilled. It is said in the Gayan: 'The uncovering of the soul is the discovering of God'.

Question: How does the true self dismiss mind and body in death?

Answer: It is not easy for the true self to dismiss mind and body, when a person cannot dismiss in life his thoughts of depression, sorrow and disappointment. The impressions of happiness and of sorrows in the past one holds in one's own heart: prejudice and hatred, love and devotion, everything that has gone deep in oneself. If that is the case, even death cannot take them away. If the ego holds its prison around itself, it takes this prison with it, and there is only one way of being delivered from it, and that is through self-knowledge.

Question: Does a person immediately after death identify himself with his mental body, or still with the dead corpse?

Answer: The mental body is just as the dead corpse. There is no difference, because the one is built on the reflection of the other. For example, one does not see oneself different in the dream when the mind is in a normal condition. If the mind is abnormal one can see oneself as a cow, or a horse, or anything. But if the mind is normal one cannot see oneself different from what one knows oneself to be. Therefore the mental being is the same as one sees oneself in the dream. In the dream one does not see the loss of the physical body. One is running and eating or enjoying in the dream; one does not realize the absence of this physical body. The same thing is in the hereafter. The hereafter does not depend upon a physical body to experience life fully. The sphere in itself is perfect, and life is experienced perfectly.

Question: Is the ego completely destroyed by annihilation?
Answer: The ego itself is never destroyed. It is the one thing that lives, and this is the sign of eternal life. In the knowledge of the ego there is the secret of immortality. When it is said in the Gayan: 'Death dies, and life lives', it is the ego which is life, it is its false conception which is death. The false must fall away some day; the real must always be. So it is with life: the true living being is the ego, it lives. All else that it has borrowed for its use from different planes and spheres, and in which it has become lost, all that is put away. Do we not see this with our own body? Things that do not belong there do not remain in it, in the blood, in the veins, anywhere. The body will not keep them, it will repel them. So it is in every sphere. It does not take what does not belong to it. All that is outside it keeps outside. What belongs on earth is kept on earth, the soul repels it. The destroying of the ego is a word; it is not destroying, it is discovering.

Often people are afraid when reading Buddhist books, where the interpretation of *Nirvana* is given as annihilation. No one wants to be annihilated, and people are very much afraid when they read 'annihilation'. But it is only a matter of words. The same word in Sanskrit is a beautiful word: *mukti*. The Sufis call it *fana*. If we translate it into English it is annihilation, but when we understand its real meaning it is 'going through' or 'passing through'. Passing through what? Passing through the false conception, which is a first necessity, and arriving at the true realization.

CHAPTER XI

Mind and Heart

THOUGHT, MEMORY, will and reason, together with the ego as the fifth and principal factor, constitute the heart. It is these five things that may be called the heart, but in definitely naming the different parts of this heart we call the surface of it mind, and the depth of it heart.

If we imagine this heart as a lantern, then the light in the lantern makes it the spirit. We call the heart a lantern when we do not think of the light, but when there is a light then we forget the word lantern, and we call it light. When we call the heart spirit it does not mean spirit void of heart, as it does not mean light without lantern, but light in the lantern.

The right use of the word spirit, however, is only as the essence of all things. The essential light and life from which all has come – that is the spirit. But we use the word spirit also in a limited sense, just as light is the all-pervading light of the sun, and at the same time the light in the lantern – which we call light also.

People call a part of the breast heart. The reason is that there is a part in this body of flesh which is most sensitive to feeling, and naturally – as man cannot grasp the idea of a heart outside the body – he conceives this idea of the heart being a part of his physical body.

The ego stands separate from the four faculties of thought, memory, will and reason. It is just like four fingers and a thumb. Why is the thumb not called a finger? Because the thumb is the whole hand.* These four are faculties, but the ego is a reality. It holds and accommodates within itself the four faculties, and in order to distinguish it as different from them we call it ego.

As the surface of the heart is known by the imagination and thought, so the depth of the mind, which is the heart, is known by feeling.

The difference between thought and imagination is that

* The thumb is seen as expressing the strength of the whole hand.

imagination is an automatic working of the mind. If the mind is fine there is a fine imagination; if the mind is gross there is a gross imagination; if there is a beautiful mentality, the imagination is beautiful. Thought is also imagination, but imagination held, controlled, and directed by will. Therefore when we say: 'He is a thoughtful person', it means that this person does not think, speak, or act on impulse, but behind everything he does there is will-power which controls and directs the action of his mind.

There are nine principal feelings which can be distinguished as mirth, grief, anger, passion, sympathy, attachment, fear, bewilderment and indifference. Feelings cannot be limited to these nine, but when we distinguish numerous feelings we may reduce them to these nine distinct feelings which we experience in life.

There are six diseases which belong to the heart: passion, anger, infatuation, conceit, jealousy and covetousness.

The more one thinks on the subject of the heart, the more one finds that, if there is anything that can tell us of our personality, it is the heart. If there is anything through which we feel ourselves or know ourselves – know what we are – it is the heart and what our heart contains. Once a person understands the nature, the character and the mystery of the heart he understands, so to speak, the language of the whole universe.

There are three ways of perception. One way of perception belongs to the surface: to the mind. It is thought. Thought manifests to our mind with a definite form, line and colour.

The next way of perception is feeling. It is felt by quite another part of the heart: it is felt by the depth of the heart, not by the surface. The more the heart quality is wakened in a person, the more he perceives the feelings of others. That person is sensitive, because to him the thoughts and feelings of others are clear. The one who lives on the surface does not perceive feelings clearly. Also, there is a difference between the evolution of the two: of the one who lives on the surface of the heart and the other who lives in the depth. In other words, the one lives in his mind and the other lives in his heart.

There is still a third way of perception, which is not even through feeling and which may be called a spiritual language. This perception comes from the deepest depth of the heart. It is the voice of the spirit. It does not belong to the lantern, it belongs to the light – but in the lantern it becomes clearer and more distinct. This perception may be called intuition; there is no better name for it.

In order to study life fully these three perceptions must be developed. Then alone is one able to study life fully, and it is in studying life fully that one is able to form a judgment upon it.

Question: Could you explain further how the mind is the surface of the heart, and the heart the depth of the mind?
Answer: There are five fingers but one hand, there are several organs of the body but one body, and there is a universe full of variety but one Spirit. So there is one heart which feels the various thoughts and imaginations which spring up and then sink into it. The bubbles are to be found on the surface of the sea. The depth of the sea is free from bubbles. The commotion is to be seen on the surface, the depth of the sea is still. The mind is the commotion of that something which is within us, that something which we call heart.

The happiness, the knowledge, the pleasure, the love which is stored in our innermost being is in our profound depth; changing emotions and passions, dreams, ever rising thoughts and imaginations all belong to the surface, as the bubbles belong to the surface of the sea.

Question: Can we say that the heart is nearer to the soul, and the mind nearer to the body?
Answer: Yes, in a certain way. But at the same time the soul experiences through the whole being: through the body, through the mind, through the heart, as it happens to be in different planes of existence.

Question: Is the heart one of the soul's bodies?
Answer: Certainly. The heart is one of the bodies of the soul, the finest body. It goes a long way with the soul, even on its return journey.

Question: Is the heart the same as the angelic body?
Answer: Yes, quite true.

Question: Is it therefore that the Catholics have a special devotion for the Sacred Heart of Jesus?
Answer: Of course. The heart is the shrine of God. If God is ever to be found anywhere it is in the heart of man, especially in the heart of that man in whom the divine manifests.

Question: Is the heart the home of the soul?
Answer: Yes, one may call the heart a home of the soul, but I would call it a temporary hotel.

Question: Is the world of feelings higher than the world of thoughts?
Answer: Yes.

Question: What is indifference?
Answer: This is a word that I always find difficult to explain, and I have made many people angry by talking about indifference, for they say: 'Where is the love which you have come to preach to us? Indifference is quite contrary to love, to the message, to the teaching'. And when people read in Buddhism and Yogïsm about renunciation, *nirvana*, *vairagia* – which in the Sufi terms of the Persian poets is *fana* – they begin to ask: 'Have they all taught to become indifferent, have they taught such cruelty?' But in reality it is quite a different thing. Indifference is not lovelessness nor is it lack of sympathy. Indifference is most useful at the time when a soul has arrived at that sensitiveness when every little thing hurts. Then it is only indifference which keeps it alive.

You might say that it is not good to be sensitive. Yes, but without being sensitive you cannot evolve. Sensitiveness is a sign of evolution. If you are not sensitive you cannot feel in sympathy with your fellowmen. If you do not feel the feelings of your fellowmen, then you are not yet awake to life. Therefore in order to become a normal human being one has to develop sensitiveness, or at least to arrive at sensitiveness. And when you are sensitive, then life becomes difficult to live. The more sensitive you are, the more thorns you will find on your way. Every move you make, at every turn, at every step there is something to hurt you. It is only one spirit that you can develop, and that is the spirit of indifference – yet not taking away the love and sympathy you have for another: that is the right indifference. To say to a person: 'I do not care for you, because you have been thoughtless', that is not the right kind of indifference, that is not the indifference that mystics relate as being *vairagia*. The mystical indifference is that a soul retains sympathy and love even at the thoughtlessness of a person, and expresses it as forgiveness. In the Bible we read the words of Christ: 'Turn the other side of your face if a person has struck you on one side'. What else is this than the lesson of indifference? How can a sensitive person, a person of feeling, a spiritual, tenderhearted person live in this world, if he is not indifferent? He cannot live here one moment! There is only this one thing that protects him from the continual jarring influences that come from all sides.

Question: Why not call it detachment?
Answer: Detachment is not really the right word. We cannot be detached, we are never detached. Life is one and nothing can separate it. Detachment is only an illusionary aspect of life. There is no such thing as detachment in truth. How can there be detachment when life is one!

Often in order to make it clearer I have said: 'Indifference and independence': two meanings of that one word *vairagia*. Indifference alone explains it only by half.

CHAPTER XII

Intuition and Dream

INTUITION RISES from the depth of the human heart. It has two aspects: one is dependent upon an outer impression, the other is independent of any outer impression. The former is called impression, the latter intuition. Intuition is a fine faculty. As it comes by responsiveness it is a feminine faculty. Woman therefore is more intuitive by nature than man.

Often one says: 'This person gives me such and such an impression', but there is no reason to prove it. One is perhaps not capable of finding any reason to prove it, nevertheless one's impression is right. There are some persons, and there are some peoples, who are naturally intuitive. For someone who is intuitive it is not necessary to wait till he, so to speak, finds a person out: all he needs is one moment. As soon as his eyes fall upon the person, this gives instantly rise to an impression, which is the former kind of intuition. Someone with a fine mind, and with a still mind, generally has intuition; someone with a gross mind and a restless mind lacks it.

Intuition is a supersense; it may be called a sixth sense; it is the essence of all senses. When a person says he sensed something, it does not mean that there were objective reasons to prove that it was so. It means that, without any outer reasons or objective signs, he has sensed it.

Intuition which is independent of impression is of a still deeper nature, for it comes before one wishes to begin a thing, and so one knows what will come out of it. Before the beginning of an enterprise one senses the result of it. Intuition is sometimes a kind of inner guidance; sometimes it is a kind of warning from within.

How does one perceive intuition? It is first expressed in the language of feeling. That feeling, spreading within the horizon of the mind, shapes itself, and becomes more narrative of its idea. Then the mind turns it into a form, and then language interprets it to one. Therefore it is the feeling heart to which intuition belongs. In order to become clear, so that it can be distinguished, intuition turns into three different conditions: into a feeling, into an imagination, or into a phrase. The person who hears the voice of intuition even when it is in its first process of development, is more capable of perceiving intuition, and it is he who may be called intuitive. Another person distinguishes it when it expresses itself in the realm of thought. Then there is a third person who can only distinguish his intuition when it is manifest in the form of a phrase.

It is the kind person, the loving person, the pure-hearted, the person of goodwill, who is intuitive. Intuition has nothing to do with learning. An unlettered person can be much more intuitive than one who is most qualified, for intuition lies in another domain of knowledge; it comes from quite another direction.

Very often an intuitive person makes a mistake in catching the right intuition, for the intuition comes from one side while his mind reacts from the other side, and he does not know which is which. If he takes the action of his mind for an intuition, and is once disappointed, he loses faith in himself. So naturally he no longer gives thought to intuition, and that faculty diminishes in him more and more every day. To catch an intuition is the most difficult thing, for in a moment's time both are working: intuition on the one hand and mind on the other. It is as if two ends of a stick which is placed in its centre upon another stick were to move up and down, and one did not notice which end rose first and which rose after. Therefore this needs taking a very keen notice of the action of the mind, which is gained by a thorough practice of concentration.

One must be able to look at one's mind just as at a slate placed before one. While looking at it one must be able to shut oneself off from all sides, fixing one's mind solely upon one's inner being. By developing concentration, by stilling the mind, one can be tuned to the pitch which is necessary to perceive intuition. Besides, if one has once been disappointed in perceiving one's intuition, one must not lose courage; one must go on following it even if it continues to be a mistake. If one continually follows one's intuition then one will come to the right perception of it.

The dream is another wonder, a phenomenon of the mind. In the dream it is not only imagination and thought that work, but also intuition. Intuitions which rise in the waking state rise in the dream state and become clearer, for at that time a person is naturally more concentrated, his eyes being closed to the outer world. But then also there is the same problem: no sooner has intuition risen from the depth than imagination rises from the surface, and one does not know which is which. That is why many dreams are confused: a part of the dream is expressive of some truth, and a part of the dream is confused.

There is no dream which has no meaning. If the dream has nothing to do with intuition, it is a purely automatic activity of all that the mind has gone through in one's work during the day; the same activity goes on automatically just like a moving picture before one. Yet even behind that there is a meaning, for nothing is projected on the curtain of the mind which does not take root in the soil of the heart, producing similar flowers and fruits. If in the dream intuition is working, then the dream is narrative of something in the past, or present, or coming in the future.

There is however a kind of dream which shows everything upside-down, just like a mirror which shows a fat person thin and a thin person fat, a tall person short and a short person tall. So there also comes a condition of the mind where everything shows quite the contrary to what it is. This fault can be traced as the fault of the mind. The mind has been turned upside-down, and therefore all that a person sees looks upside-down, especially in that dream state. Sometimes this dream shows quite the opposite to what was, what is, and what is going to be. If a person did not understand this nature of the dream, he would interpret it quite contrarily to its real nature.

There are dreams which may be called visions. They are reflections; reflections of persons, of their minds, of worlds, of planes on which the mind has become focused. If the mind is focused on a certain world, then the dreams are of that world. If a person is focusing his mind upon himself, then his own thoughts come to him. If the mind is focused on a certain person, then that person and what is within him is reflected in the dream. If the mind is focused on a certain plane of being, then the conditions of that plane are reflected upon the mind.

The deeper one goes into this subject, the more one finds that in the understanding of the dream – its nature, its mystery, its character – one understands the secret of the whole life.

Question: Could you please tell us about the difference between impulse and intuition?
Answer: The impulse of an intuitive person is often guided by intuition, but the impulse of a person who lacks intuition may come from another direction; it may come from the surface. Impulse directed by intuition is desirable.

Impulse is just like a little straw floating on the surface of the water. This straw becomes an impulse when it is pushed by a wave which is coming from behind. For a right impulse man gets credit, for a wrong impulse he is blamed. Yet, if one saw what was behind the impulse, one would be slow to express an opinion on the subject.

Question: How do you explain symbolical dreams?
Answer: The symbolical dream is the working of a subtle mind, and it is a most wonderful working. As subtle as is the mentality, so subtle is the symbol in which the intuition or the thought is expressed. Therefore it has been very easy for the mystics to see the evolution of a person from his dreams. The subtler his dreams, the subtler the person is in his evolution. Nevertheless the virtue is not only in subtlety; the virtue is in simplicity. Poets, musicians, thinkers, writers, people of imagination have wonderful dreams, and the splendour of their dreams is in their marvellous symbology.

Question: Is it the study of symbols that develops intuition?
Answer: Not at all. It is intuition that develops insight into symbolism.

Question: Are conditions in dreams the same as the conditions after death?
Answer: Certainly.

Question: Are dreams of suffocation, drowning, and inability to walk and speak a result of one's health?
Answer: No, they are results of impressions which have been

held in the mind. It is a kind of psychological disorder of the mind, a disease of the mind. The mind must be cured from it.

Question: What about dreams that are inspired by a stimulus from the physical body, as for instance a dream inspired by a feeling of pain in the body?
Answer: The mind has a reaction upon the body, and the body has a reaction upon the mind. Therefore it is natural that a bodily disorder may throw its shadow upon the mind and produce the same disorder in the mind.

Question: What about dreams of flying? Many people say they are a bad sign.
Answer: I think this is the most interesting thing in the world. You do not need airplanes! Dreams of flying have much to do with biology. Psychologically they are expressive of the soul's continual effort of rising above the imprisonment and limitation which it experiences in this earthly life. Also dreams of flying signify a journey awaiting one in the future.

Question: Will you please tell us what makes a person sing in his sleep?
Answer: The dance of his soul.

Question: What is the condition of the mind of people who nearly never dream? Are they not imaginative?
Answer: I think that they are better than imaginative: they are happy! The truth is that either a very advanced person does not dream much, or a very dense person, who never troubles his brain to think. He is quite happy and content without troubling to think. He does not have many dreams. Do not think that you seldom find such souls. You often meet with souls to whom thinking is a trouble; they would rather not trouble themselves about it.

Question: What is the difference between the dream which may be called a vision and the real vision?
Answer: Vision is vision. The more one knows reality, the less one uses the word 'real'. There is one vision which is seen in the dream, and there is another vision which is seen in a state of trance, a state between dream and wakefulness.

CHAPTER XIII

Inspiration

INSPIRATION IS a higher form of intuition, for it comes as an idea, as a complete theme with its improvisation, as a phrase creative of a poem. Inspiration is a stream, a stream of wonder and bewilderment. The really inspired person, whether a writer, a poet, a composer, or whatever may be his work, when once he has received an inspiration, has found satisfaction – not with himself, but with what has come to him. It gives his soul such a relief, for the soul was drawing from something and that object from which it was drawing has yielded to the soul, has given it what it was asking for. Therefore inspiration may be called the soul's reward.

It is not by being anxious to receive something that one is able to receive it. It is not by straining the brain that one can write poetry. It is not by worrying for days together that one can compose a piece of music. One who does so cannot receive inspiration. The one who receives inspiration is quite tranquil and unconcerned about what is coming. Certainly he is desirous of receiving something, he is passionately longing to conceive it. And it is by focusing his mind to the divine mind that, consciously or unconsciously, man receives inspiration.

This phenomenon is so great and so wonderful that its joy is unlike any other joy in the world. It is in this joy that the inspirational genius experiences ecstasy. It is a joy which is almost indescribable. It is an upliftment. One feels that one is raised from the earth when one's mind is focused on the divine mind – for inspiration comes from the divine mind. What the great musicians, poets, thinkers, philosophers, writers, and prophets have left to the world is always uplifting, although it is not every soul who comprehends their work fully, and therefore not every soul can enjoy it fully. But imagine their own enjoyment of what came to them; there are no words to express it! It is in inspiration that one begins to see the sign of God, and the most materialistic genius begins to wonder about the divine Spirit when once inspiration has begun to come to him.

One might ask: 'Does inspiration come as a finished picture? Does it come as a written letter?' No, it comes to an artist as if his hand was taken by someone else, as if his eyes were closed, his heart was open. He has drawn something, he has painted something, and he does not know who painted it, who has drawn it. Inspiration comes to a musician as if someone else were playing or singing, and he were only taking it down: a complete melody, a perfect air. And after he has written it down then it enchants his soul. To a poet inspiration comes as if someone were dictating and he were only writing. There is no strain on his brain, there is no anxiety in receiving it.

It is therefore that many confuse inspiration with spirit communication. Many inspirational people are glad to attribute inspiration to a spirit, knowing that it does not come from themselves – but it is not always spirit communication. It is natural that inspiration should come from a being living just now on earth or from someone who has passed; yet the most profound inspiration comes always from the divine mind, and to God alone the credit is due. Even if an inspiration comes through the mind of a person living on earth or through a soul who has passed on to the other side, it still has come from God, for all knowledge and wisdom belong to God.

It is a fault on the part of mankind to attribute inspiration to some limited being, who is nothing but a shadow covering God. When a person believes that an old Egyptian comes from the other side to inspire him, or that an American Indian comes to lead him on his way, he builds a wall between himself and God. Instead of receiving directly from the source which is perfect and all sufficient, he is picturing his limited idea making it a screen between himself and God.

The best way for the genius is to make himself an empty cup, free from pride of learning or conceit of knowledge, to become as innocent as a child who is ready to learn whatever may be taught him. It is the one who becomes as a child before God, at the same time longing and yearning to express music through his soul, who becomes a fountain of God. From that fountain divine inspiration rises and brings beauty before all those who see the fountain.

There is one step further, and that is when the person no longer remains a poet or a musician or a philosopher, but becomes God's instrument only. Then God begins to speak to him through everything, not only in music or verse, in colour or line: he begins to communicate with God in all forms. Everything he sees above or below, before or behind, right or left, either heavenly or earthly is communicative. He then begins to speak with God, and it is this step which is called revelation.

There is a story of Moses which relates that, when he was looking for fire to bake bread, he happened to see a light on the top of a mountain. So in order to take this fire he climbed to the top of the mountain – but there the fire became lightning. Moses could no longer withstand that great flashing and he fell to the ground. When he woke up he began to communicate with God.

This story is allegorical. The idea is that Moses was looking for light to make it his life's sustenance. But he had to climb on to the higher planes. It was not possible to get it on earth where he stood; it was necessary that he should climb to the top. And then there was not only a light, but it was lightning. It was a light which was beyond the power of Moses to withstand, and he fell down. What is this falling down? To become nothing, to become empty. When he reached that state of emptiness, then his heart became sonorous, and he found communication with God through everything in the world. In the rock, tree or plant, in the star, sun or moon, in whatever he saw he found communication with his soul. So everything revealed its nature and secret to Moses.

It is in connection with this revelation that Sa'adi says that every leaf of the tree becomes a page of the sacred scripture once the soul has learned to read.

Question: I quite understand that inspiration comes from God, but would you kindly explain how one receives inspiration from a person on earth whom one does not know?
Answer: Inspiration comes through the mediumship of a living being in three forms: when you are in the presence

of someone who is inspiring, when you are in the thoughts of someone who is inspiring, and when your heart is in a state of perfect tranquillity and inspiration flowing through the heart of an inspirational genius comes into your heart. It is just like the wireless: sometimes you connect it with a certain station from which you are to receive the music, and sometimes you do not connect it – but it remains a wireless machine. If anything passing through is not received, it is not heard – but the sound is there just the same. In the same way one receives inspiration from these three different sources.

Question: When inspiration comes originally from the divine Mind, must it always be vehicled by someone who has passed on, or who is on earth?

Answer: There are different processes. It all depends upon how the heart of the person is focused on the divine Spirit. There is a person whose heart is focused directly on the divine Spirit; there is another to whom the divine Spirit it too remote. His heart is focused on a centre, and this centre is focused on the divine Spirit from where it receives the message. So it all comes from the divine Spirit just the same.

THE POWER OF THE WORD

CHAPTER I

The Power of the Word

1

WE FIND in the Bible the words: 'In the beginning was the word, and the word was God', and we also find that the word is light, and that when that light dawned the whole creation manifested. These are not only religious verses; to the mystic or seer the deepest revelation is contained in them. Here is a thought which may be pondered over for years, each time with fresh inspiration. It teaches that the first sign of life that manifested was the audible expression, or sound: that is the word.

When we compare this interpretation with the Vedanta philosophy, we find that the two are identical. All down the ages the Yogis and seers of India have worshipped the Word-God, or Sound-God, and around that idea is centred all the mysticism of sound or utterance. Not alone among Hindus, but among the seers of the Semitic, the Hebraic races the great importance of the word was recognized. The sacred name, the sacred word, were always esteemed in the Jewish religion. Also in Islam, that great religion whose mysticism the West is only beginning to discover, one finds the doctrine of *Ismaïsm* which, translated, is the 'doctrine of the mystical word'. The Zoroastrians, who had their religion given to them long before the time of Buddha or Christ, and who have lost many of their teachings through the changes of time and conditions, have yet always preserved the sacred words. Sanskrit is now considered a dead language – but in the Indian meditations called Yoga, Sanskrit words are still used because of the power of sound and vibration that is contained in them.

The deeper we dive into the mystery of life the more we find that its whole secret is hidden in what we call words. All occult science, all mystical practices are based upon the science of word or sound. Man is a mystery in all aspects of his being, not only in mind and soul, but also in that organism which he calls his body. It is his body of which the Sufis say that it is the temple of God, and this is not a mere saying or belief, for if man studies his body from the mystical point of view, he will find it to be much more subtle and far-reaching, and much more capable of doing, understanding and feeling, than he believes it to be.

There are faculties of the soul which express themselves through certain centres in the body of man. As there are parts of lands to which water never reaches – and therefore they never become fertile soil – so it is with these centres when the breath never reaches them. They are intuitive, they are full of peace and balance, they are the centres of illumination, yet never have they been awakened, for man has breathed only in those parts of his body by which he can eat, and live, and perform action. He is only half alive, if his existence is compared with the fullness of life that can be obtained by spiritual development.

It may be compared to living in a great town and not knowing that there are many beautiful things that one has never seen. As there are many people who travel to distant lands and do not know their own country, so it is with man. He is interested in all that brings beauty and joy, and yet does not know the source of all such things in himself.

Man breathes, but he does not breathe rightly. As the rain falls on the ground and matures little plants and makes the soil fertile, so the breath, the essence of all energy, falls as a rain on all parts of the body. This also happens in the case of the mind, but man cannot even perceive that part of the breath that quickens the mind; only that felt in the body is perceptible, and to the average man it is not even perceptible in the body. He knows nothing of it, except what appears in the form of inhalation and exhalation through the nostrils. It is this alone which is generally meant when man speaks of breath.

When we study the science of breath, the first thing we notice is that breath is audible; it is a word in itself, for what we call a word is only a more pronounced utterance of breath fashioned by the mouth and tongue. In the capacity of the mouth breath becomes voice, and therefore the original condition of a word is breath. Therefore if we said: 'First was the breath', it would be the same as saying: 'In the beginning was the word'.

The first life that existed was the life of God, and from that all manifestation branched out. It is a manifold expression of one life; one flower blooming as so many petals, one breath expressing itself as so many words. The sacred idea attached to the lotus flower is expressive of this same philosophy, symbolizing the many lives in the one God, and expressed in the Bible in the words: 'In God we live and move and have our being'. When man is separated from God in thought, his belief is of no use to him, his worship is but of little use to him; for all forms of worship or belief should draw man closer to God, and that which makes man separate from God has no value.

Now rises the question: What is it that makes a word sacred or important? Is not every word as sacred and important as another? That is true – but for whom is it sacred? For the pure and exalted souls to whom every word breathes the name of God, but not for the average man. There are souls who are at that stage of evolution in which every word is the sacred name. But when a teacher gives a method, it is not given to the exalted souls but to beginners, and therefore words are selected and given to pupils by the *Guru* or teacher, as a physician would give a prescription, knowing for which complaint and for what purpose it is given. Hafiz says: 'Accept every instruction thy teacher giveth, for he knoweth which is thy path and where is thy good'.

Great importance is given by the mystics to the number of repetitions, for numbers are a science and every number of repetitions has a value. One repetition means one thing and a few more mean something quite different, as in medicine one grain of a drug may heal and ten may destroy life. When Christ commanded to abstain from vain repetitions he was not, as is often thought, referring to the sacred name as used in worship or religious practices. There was a custom among the Semitic peoples, and it still exists in the East, of the constant use of the name of God by people in the street or market place. They would bring it continually into commerce or business, into quarrels and disputes, and it was against this abuse of the most holy name that Christ was speaking.

In repetition lies the secret of power, therefore it is a great mistake when people take the ways of spiritual culture lightly as an everyday interest, as a little hobby, and learn from a book or from some slight instruction given to them. If they attempt to practise from such knowledge only, they are risking their lives. Imagine, a centre which should be awakened at a certain time of evolution being awakened before that time is reached. It would be a disaster!

There are certain words which attract a certain blessing in life. Some attract power, some bring release from difficulties, some give courage and strength. There are words which can heal, others which give comfort and ease, and again others which have greater effects still. Now when a person in need of peace and rest uses words that bring courage and strength, he will become even more restless. It is just like taking medicine which is a tonic to cure a high fever.

Then there is another question, namely: what makes a word powerful? Is it the meaning, the vibration, the way it is used, or the knowledge of the teacher who teaches the pupil to repeat it? The answer to such a question is that some words have power because of their meaning, others because of the vibration they produce, others for their influence upon the various centres. And there are some words given by saints, sages and prophets which have come inspirationally from God. In them is all blessing and the mystery of how to acquire all that the soul desires in life. If there exists any phenomenon or miracle it is in the power of words. But those who know of this power and who possess it never show it to others. Spiritual attainment is not a thing to be brought before people to prove that it is real, or as a show. What is real is proof in itself, what is beyond all price or value does not need to be made much of before people. What is real is real, and the precious is precious in itself; it needs no explanation nor pleading.

The greatest lesson of mysticism is to know all, gain all, attain all things and be silent. The more the disciple gains, the more humble he becomes, and when any person makes this gain a means of proving himself in any way superior to others, it is a proof that he does not really possess it. He may have a spark within himself, but the torch is not yet lighted. There is a saying among the Hindus that the tree that bears much fruit bows low.

Words have power to vibrate through different parts of man's body. There are words that echo in the heart, and there

are others that do so in the head, and again others that have
power over the body. By certain words definite emotions can
be quickened or calmed. There is also a science of syllables
which has its own particular effect.

Wagner did but repeat the teaching of the mystics of the
East, when he said that he who knows the law of vibrations
knows the whole secret of life.

2

The word is in itself a mystery in every sense, and all scriptures
have considered the mystery of the word – even compared to
all other secrets of life – as the most profound. In the scripture
that is best known to the Western world we read that first was
the word, and the word was God, and then again one reads that
it was the word which was first and then came light. These
sentences convey to us two things. The first conveys to us
that, if anything existed, and if we can express what existed,
we can only express it by the term 'word'. And when we come
to the second sentence it explains another phase of the mystery
which is that, in order to enable the soul surrounded by the
darkness of the world of illusion to come to the light, first the
word was necessary. This means that the original Spirit was in
the mystery of the word, and that by the word the mystery of
the Spirit was to be found.

When we come to the *Vedantic* scriptures, which existed
many thousands of years ago, there also we realize the same
thing. For instance, there is a phrase in Sanskrit: *Nada Brahma*,
which means: the mystery of creation was in *nada* – in the
word. In the Qur'an one reads in the Arabic words *Kun
fa-yakūn* that first was the exclamation 'Be!', and it became.
The One who said 'Be' – and it became – was not a mortal
being. He was and is, and will be all the life there is. If
that is so, then the word was not the mystery of the past,
but the word is a continual and everlasting mystery. And
at this time, when man has engaged himself in the material
phenomena and has progressed very far, compared with the
past, in industry and commercial activities, this aspect of
discovering the might which lies hidden under the word is
still unexplored.

The mystic who knows the value of the word finds that word first in himself; for the secret of all knowledge that one acquires in the world, whether worldly or spiritual, is the knowledge of the self. For instance, music is played outside oneself. But where is it realized? It is realized within. A good word or a bad word is spoken from outside. But where is it realized? It is realized within. Then where is the realization of the whole manifestation, of all this creation that stands before us in all its aspects? Its realization is within.

At the same time the error of man always continues: instead of finding realization within, he always wants to find it without. It is just like a man who wants to see the moon and looks for it on the ground. If a man seeks for the moon for thousands of years by looking on the earth, he will never see it. He will have to lift up his head and look at the sky. So it is with the man who is in search of the mystery of life outside himself; he will never find it, for the mystery of life is to be found within: there are the source and the goal, and it is there that, if he seeks, he will find.

What is sound? Is sound outside, or is it something within? The outside sound only becomes audible because the sound within is continued, and the day when the sound within is shut off, this body is not capable of hearing the outside sound.

Man, living today the life of externality, has become so accustomed to the outside life that he hardly thinks of just sitting alone. When he is alone he busies himself with a newspaper or something else, always working with the life which is outside, always occupied with the life outside himself. In this way man loses his attachment to the life which is within. So his life becomes superficial, and the result is nothing but disappointment. There is nothing in this world in the form of sound, visible or audible, which is so attractive as the sound within; for all that the senses touch and all that is intelligible to the mind of man has its limitation. It has its limitation in time and effect; it makes no effect beyond that.

Life's mystery lies in the breath; it is the continuation of breath and pulsation that keeps the mechanism of the body going. It seems that people of ancient times had a greater knowledge of this mystery than man has today. For what is meant by the lute of Orpheus? It means the human body;

it is a lute, it is meant to be played upon. When this lute is not realized, when it is not understood, when it is not utilized for its proper purpose, then that lute remains without the use for which it was created, because then it has not fulfilled the purpose for which it was made.

The breath goes not merely as far as the man of material science knows. He knows only the vibrations of the air, going out and coming in, and he sees no further. Besides this there is pulsation: the beating of the heart and head, the pulse, all these keep a rhythm. Man very rarely thinks about what depends upon this rhythm. The whole life depends upon it! The breath which one breathes is certainly a secret in itself; it is not only a secret but the expression of all mystery, something upon which the psychology of life depends.

The science of medicine has for thousands of years to some extent depended upon finding out the complaints of the body by its rhythm and by the breath. Ancient medicine knew that health depends upon vibrations, and now again a time is coming when in the Western world physicians are striving to find out the law of vibrations upon which man's health depends. But man, absorbed in the material life, goes so far and no further. The mystery of vibrations does not concern the material plane only: it goes still farther.

If the human body is a lute, then every word man speaks, every word he hears, has an effect upon his body; it not only has an effect upon the body, but also upon the mind. For instance, if a person hears himself called by the name 'foolish' and repeats it, even if he were wise he will in time turn foolish. And it is also true that if one calls a man who is simple wise, in time he will become wise. The effect of a man's name has a great deal to do with his life, and very often one sees that a man's name has an effect upon his fate and career. The reason is only that he is so often in the day called by that name. Is it not true that a man saying a humorous thing bursts out laughing, and a man saying a sad thing breaks into tears? If that is so, then what effect has every word that one speaks in one's everyday life upon oneself and upon one's surroundings!

The superstition that has existed in all times about not saying an unlucky word, an undesirable word, has a meaning. In the East a child is trained to think before he utters a word, since it has a psychological meaning and effect. Very often people reading a poem or singing a song with great love, a song of sorrow or tragedy, are affected by it, and their life may take a turn as a result.

A person who speaks of his illness nourishes his illness by speaking of it. Often I have heard people say that if a pain exists it is a reality, 'and how can one deny it?' It is so amusing to hear them say this, because reality is so far away, and our everyday life is such that from morning till evening we do nothing but deny it. If one could only know where the truth lies, if one could only know what truth is – if one only were to know it and see it – one would think that all else is non-existent in reality. If one studies the depth of this idea, one must admit the power of the word. But then, it is a science, a metaphysics that must be studied.

Yet the depth of the word of each person is very different. If a person has spoken a hundred words in one day, do you think that every word has the same power? No, the power and effect of a particular word depend upon the state in which that person was, and from what depth the word rises. Upon this depend the power and light of that word. For instance, with a person who has a habit of telling a lie, who is insincere, you will always find that his words are dropping down; his words have no force, while the one who speaks with conviction, who is sincere, who tells the truth – his word has a light, his word penetrates. Sometimes, from a person full of sadness and heartbroken, a voice comes, a word, full of sincerity; it has all the power to penetrate; it has such an effect upon the listener! Then there is another person who is lighthearted, who is not deep, not serious enough in life; everything he says and does is always on the surface; he inspires no one with confidence, for he himself has no confidence.

Besides that, there is a power of the word which is in accordance with the illumination of the soul, because then that word does not come from the human mind, that word comes from the depth, from behind; that word comes from some mysterious part that is hidden from the human mind. And it is in connection with such words that one reads in the scriptures of 'swords of flame' or 'tongues of flame'. Whether it was from a poet, or whether it was from a prophet, when that word came from his burning heart, then the word rose as a flame. In accordance with the divine Spirit which is in the word, that word has life, power and inspiration. Think of the living words of ancient times, think of the living words that one reads in the scriptures, the living words of the holy ones, illuminated ones! They live and will live for ever. It is as a music which may be called a magic, a magic for all times. Whenever such words are repeated they have that magic, that power.

What the sages of all ages said – those words were kept by the people, by their pupils. In whatever part of the world they were born or lived, what they let fall as words was taken up as real pearls, and kept as scriptures. Therefore, wherever one goes in the East one finds that the followers of different religions keep the words of the illuminated ones whenever they pray, and they do not need to put them into their own language. One finds that in this way the words said by the great ones have been preserved for ages to be used for meditation.

There is a more scientific and still greater mystery in the word. It is not only what the word means, it is not only who has said the word, but the word in itself has also a dynamic power. The mystics, sages and seekers of all ages, knowing the mystery of the sacred word, have always been in pursuit of it. The whole meditative life of the Sufis is built upon the mystery of the word. For the word 'Sufi', according to the explanation of the initiates, is related to *sophia* which means wisdom. But not wisdom in the outer sense of the word, because worldly cleverness cannot be called wisdom. The intellect which man very often confuses with wisdom is only an illusion of it. Wisdom is that which is learned from within; intellect is that which is acquired from without. The source of wisdom is above, the source of intellect is below, and therefore it is not the same method, it is not the same process which one adopts in order to attain wisdom, as that which one adopts to acquire intellect. In short, the attainment of that wisdom is achieved in various ways by various people, but the great mystery of attaining divine wisdom lies in the mystery of the word.

3

The idea of the power of the word is as old as the *Vedas* of the Hindus. The modern world is now awakening to it through what is called psychology, and since there is an interest in psychology there is a possibility of exploring that ancient treasure which seekers after truth have developed for a thousand years in the East. The race that established itself to make its life in the tropical country called Hindustan was occupied in the study of human nature and its source, leaving aside all things of the world.

Man today looks at psychology as something that can help medical science as a side-issue, but certainly there will come a day when mankind in this modern world will look upon the science of psychology in the same way that the people in the East have looked upon it: as the main thing in religion and spirituality.

As to the power of the word, a new idea has been coming from various places under different names, and it is that the repetition of a certain word or phrase is of great use in curing oneself of certain illnesses. This is new because psychology in the Western world is discovering it today. But what about the Buddhists who, sitting in their temple, have repeated the different *mantras* for so many centuries, repeating them two thousand, three thousand times a day? And what about the Hindus who have kept their sacred *mantras*, the sacred chants which came down to them from thousands of years ago? Even if the language is different, they have still kept their ancient *mantras*. And what about the Jewish people who still have stored the sacred chants which they inherited from the prophets of Beni Israël? And what about the Muslims who for ages have repeated the Qur'an daily for so many hours, and who still continue to repeat the verses of the same book every day? And think what secret there is behind the repetitions of the priests and Catholic mystics! The Zoroastrians – the Parsis whose religion dates from ages ago – have maintained even up to the present time their sacred words, and they chant their prayers several times a day, always repeating the same words.

Does a man, who reads a newspaper today and throws it away tomorrow asking for another one, think about this: that there is something worthwhile in the fact that these millions of people have been clinging to those *mantras*, repeating them day after day all their lives, never becoming tired of doing so? If it were, as it is sometimes called, a religious fanaticism, then nobody could continue those repetitions, as no intoxication can continue longer than its influence lasts; then it goes and a person is disillusioned.

This shows that behind the repetition of words a secret is hidden, and the day when man has fathomed it he will have discovered a great secret of life. Leaving all religions aside and coming to material science, a person who has really touched the great height of science will never deny for one moment that behind this whole manifestation – if there is any secret which can be found as the mystery of the whole creation – it is movement. You may call that motion a vibration, or you may call it by a religious name.

One side of the understanding of the power of the word is to keep in mind that, as a reflector in the form of a globe is needed behind the light in order to throw the light fully, so a reflector is needed for the voice, as every voice-producer knows. The voice-producer will always give exercises to his pupil to repeat over and over again in order to get this reflector into the right condition, so that all the possibility of producing a full voice may be brought out.

That is the material side of the question, but then there is the psychological side of it. This is that not only the organs of the physical body have this reflector, but the mind, or what we call feeling, can also be a reflector. We very rarely explore this question; we cut it short every time we are faced with it. For instance, when a person is telling a lie it is natural that it is weak, and we cannot readily believe it. However loud his voice, however strongly he speaks, since it is a lie it is weak because, psychologically, the power of mind must act as a reflector, and in this condition it does not act, for the mind is not behind it. Take an ordinary phrase such as 'thank you' or 'I am very grateful to you'. If during the day ten people say it to you, each one of them will have a different power of conveying it; for if the reflector is not giving power from behind, a person may tell you a thousand times 'I am so grateful to you', but it will make no effect.

There is another way of looking at the same question: one person may tell you something, and you readily believe it, and another person may tell you the same thing fifty times over, and you do not feel inclined to believe it. What does this show? It shows that we must prepare ourselves before we say anything. It is not always what we say, but how we feel it, how we express it, and what power is hidden behind our expression, what power pushes it out, so that the word may pierce through the heart of man.

Then there is also a thought connected with this idea: how can one best prepare oneself to utter a certain word effectively? Symbolically speaking, a person may pronounce the same word a hundred times before people, but it is an iron word. A person may say it fifty times, but it is a copper word. A person may say it twenty times, but it is a silver word. And another person may say it only once, and it is a golden word. For instance, a person may talk and talk and talk in order to convince you, he may dispute and discuss and argue and show a thousand examples to make you believe, and the more he wants you to believe, the more he pushes you off. There is another person who tells you something perhaps only once, and you cannot help saying: 'Yes, I believe it, I understand it, I am convinced'.

How does one prepare oneself? How does one make the reflectors ready in order to make the impression of the word? Yogis and Sufis have found certain practices by which a kind of psychological development is brought about. Through these a person becomes naturally more and more sincere and earnest, and everything he says bears that influence, that power. Perhaps these practices have no value according to the science of voice production, but they have very great value according to the psychological point of view. It is such practices which have been considered as concentration, meditation, contemplation, realization.

Regarding ancient words, any student of ancient languages will find that different languages can be traced back to one and the same source. The closer you approach the ancient languages the more you will find a psychological significance in them, and the languages of today will seem like corruptions of them. If I were to give you the derivation of words of several languages spoken today, such as French and English, you would be surprised to see how many words exist that are derived from ancient languages; very often they have the same meaning. Also, many names of persons are derived from these languages. In the ancient languages these words were obtained through the intuition; modern languages are based on the grammar one learns. But because its words have come purely from intuition, the language made from man's experience of life, as an action and reaction, has certainly more powerful words than the languages we speak today. Therefore they have a great power when repeated, and a great phenomenon is produced when a person has mastered those words under the guidance of someone who understands that path.

Every vowel, such as *a* or *e* or *o*, has its psychological significance, and the composition of every word has a chemical and psychological significance. The Yogis have certain words which they repeat in the morning or in the evening for so many times, and from saying those words they derive a certain illumination or come to a certain state of exaltation. It is this very science which was called by the Sufis of ancient times *dhikr* (zikar). This means a science of bringing about desirable results by the repetition of the proper words or phrases.

A chemist may have all the medicines, but if every person went and got whatever medicine he wanted, he might cure himself or kill himself. Even more difficult and more responsible is the work of using the repetitions of certain psychological words or phrases. It is the physician's responsibility to give a certain person a proper medicine necessary for his condition, for his purpose. In the East one searches for a *Guru*, or a *Murshid* as the Sufis call him, who has the experience of psychological prescription, and one takes what the *Murshid* has prescribed as an instruction. First the *Murshid* makes a diagnosis of the person's condition, and according to that he prescribes a word or phrase by the repetition of which that person may arrive at the desired goal.

Those who have some experience of voice production will know that in the beginning the teacher does not give any songs; he gives certain words, and a special way of practising by which the voice is developed. In Sufism there are certain words which are considered sacred, and a person of simple faith will only know them as sacred words. But besides that they have psychological significance, and by being repeated they produce a certain effect which helps one to bring about desired results.

It is very interesting to note that science shows every inclination of awakening in the direction of vibrations and their phenomena. During my last visit to the U.S.A. I was most interested to see a new system, known as Dr. Abrams' system. The basis of this method, which as yet is not much developed, is the same: to find out the condition of the vibrations in the physical body in order to treat it in a satisfactory way.[5]

When we see that similar systems were developed by the ancient mystics and occultists and tried for ages, and by numberless people for perhaps all their life, it is clear that those systems must bring about satisfactory results, and give to many a treasure which has always been kept sacred by the seekers after truth.

The Sufi Movement therefore has made a facility for the people of the West, for those who wish to reach that treasure, that source, to obtain by a serious study and practice of Sufism some glimpses of the truth which the ancient mystics possessed.

4

There is nothing more important as a means of raising one's consciousness than the repetition of the right word; there is nothing that can be of greater use and importance in the path of spiritual attainment. When we look at the traditions we find that, from the time of the ancient Hindu teachers who lived thousands of years before Christ, the sacred word was in practice. And so you will find that, in all the great periods when a religious reform came to different countries, the power of the word was considered to be of immense importance: for instance, at the time when the Jewish religion was given, and also when the Christian religion began.

It is the misunderstanding of certain words of Christ which has confused many followers of the Christian religion in their understanding of the importance of the word. For when it is said to keep oneself from making vain repetitions, a person in the Western world, when he reads repetitions, just makes a literal translation; he does not know what is meant by it. The condition at that time was this: the word 'God' had become so much used in common affairs that, whenever a person wanted to convince another about something true or false, he used the word 'God'. If a man wanted to sell something, in order to convince the other person of his own idea, he used to attach the name of God to the object he wanted to sell. And when the other did not believe him the custom was to say: 'By the name of God it is true'. It is therefore that it was said: 'Do not make vain repetitions of the sacred name; it is too sacred to be used in trade or business'. But then those who could not understand the idea behind it said that it was the repetition itself that Christ did not want. If they would only think that even at the last moment the Master repeated the sacred name!

It is the same sacred words which from ancient times up to the present are given from teacher to pupil. Mystical words may be used in different languages, but they do not exclusively belong to any language. Take, for example, the phrase used in the practice of *dhikr* (zikar). It is found today in the Arabic language, it came from Arabia. But then it is used in the Persian language also; one who does not know its existence in Arabia might think that it came from Persia. It also exists in the Hindustani language; one who does not know of its existence in those two other languages might think that it was Hindustani. That divine name also exists in the other Semitic languages. It is the same word which was repeated by Christ himself as his last word. Those who were before Christ, mystics whose origin was the ancient school of Egypt, also repeated the same word. There are sufficient proofs of this fact: during the time of Abraham, who was initiated in the school of Egypt, this word was used.

In the Buddhistic and Vedantic religions and philosophical schools we find that the same words which were used for thousands of years are used even today. For the Hindus it was a kind of science – a science which they called *mantrayoga*, the science of the word, of the dynamic power, the vital power that lies in the repetition of certain words.

Modern psychology is beginning to awaken to the same idea, although it is still searching in darkness, and has not yet found the secret of the use of words. Nevertheless, what little it now perceives, its believing in the power of words and their repetition gives a hope that psychology will come some time to the realization that the ancient people had.

The work of the Sufi Order is to give the combined theory of the Semitic line of mystics and of the Hindu line of mystics, the two joined together. By Semitic I mean not only the line of Moses, but it included Christ also. There are also two distinct mystic lines, and both are joined in what is called the Sufi message. Besides this, to interpret this in a modern form is the meaning of the message.

Now one might ask: 'What is it in the word that helps, and why does it help?' In answer to this I would say that there is no expression of life more vital than words, because the voice is an expressive manifestation of breath, and breath is the very life. Therefore the word that one says not only has an effect upon another person, but also upon oneself. Every word one says has its effect not only upon one's body but upon one's mind and one's spirit. A tactless word not only offends another – a foolish word uttered can prove to be of great disadvantage to oneself.

Many times a person in a pessimistic mood, in a kind of disturbed condition may wish for death, wish for failure, wish for anything. If he only knew what an effect it has, he would be frightened. Even in pain, if a person could refrain from saying: 'I am in pain', he would do a great deal of good to himself. If a person who has met with misfortune would even avoid saying: 'I am experiencing misfortune', it would be a great thing. For when a person acknowledges the existence of something he does not want, he only gives it a greater life. In the same way when a person acknowledges something that he wants, he gives that life too. But when a person says: 'Oh, I have waited and waited and waited; my ship will never come', he is keeping his ship back in the sea. His ship will never arrive in the port, while the one who does not even see the ship, but says: 'It is coming, it is coming' – he is calling it. It will come.

What I have said concerns the psychological meaning of the word, but the mystical word has a greater value than the words that one uses in everyday language. Mystical words have come from three distinct sources: intuitive, scientific and astrological.

Intuitive words have come as sudden expressions from God-realized souls, souls who have become tuned to the whole universe. Whatever word comes from their mouth, that word or phrase is something which has a much greater power than the words that everybody uses. But apart from a spiritual person, do you not even see in your everyday life that there is perhaps one person among your friends, among your acquaintances, whose one word has weight, has power, whereas another person says a thousand words that go in at one ear and out at the other? In one person his mouth speaks, in another person his heart speaks, in another his soul speaks. There is a great difference.

One might ask: 'How can a spiritual person intuitively bring forth a word which has power?' The answer is that there is a possibility of a soul's becoming so much in tune with the whole universe that he hears, so to speak, the voice of the spheres. Therefore what he says comes like the echo of the whole universe. The person who is in tune with the universe becomes like a wireless instrument; what comes from him is the voice of the universe.

Leaving aside the personal aspect and coming to the scientific aspect, I would like to say that a deep study of human anatomy will explain that there are delicate nerve-centres that can only be affected by certain vibrations; upon these centres the equilibrium and the health of mind and body depend. Very often people have even been cured of illnesses by the use of such scientific words, because this has given to a certain centre that vibration which was wanted to bring about the life it needed. If one goes deeper into the science of the word one will find that every vowel and every consonant has its certain effect upon one's mind and body. Often you will find, before seeing a person, that by knowing his name you get an impression of what that person is like. It shows that the name makes such a great difference in a person's character.

When we come to the astrological aspect, it is a very vast subject, for it has a connection with every existing art and science. Vowels and words have their connection with the astrological science. By invoking a certain word one invokes a certain planet, either in order to diminish its influence if it is unfavourable, or to increase its power if it is favourable. Therefore in the astrological science of the Hindus every name given to a person is given in accordance with the astrological science.[11].

5

Many holy scriptures give evidence of the power of the word. But a science so well known to the prophets of all times – where has it gone? That science has been lost to the view of the generality. The reason for this is that man engaged himself in the things of the earth and the knowledge of material things, and in this way he lost the art of the ancient times. By losing that great science, that mystical secret, what has the soul attained? The soul has attained an increasing deafness, and this increasing deafness prevailed with the prevailing of material life. Nevertheless, at every time there have been some thinkers, and in every period there have been some servants of God, working known or unknown to the world, who have admitted that the word was lost. It was not lost for them – they saw that for the generality that word was lost. By the loss of this word is meant that the secret of the whole life was lost. This is however an exaggerated saying. The word which is existent cannot be lost, but man has lost his capability of knowing, of hearing that word.

Besides this, man did not hear that word from the sky: he heard that word from the earth, the outcome of which is the great progress and awakening of material science. All the great inventions of this time, which are like miracles, have come to the great minds who have, so to speak, communicated with matter, and matter has spoken with them face to face. All such great inventions are answers from the earth to the communication of these minds with matter. In this way the word was not lost, but the direction was lost.

Man learned continually from the objective world things that he could touch, and make intelligible, and he always disbelieved in things that were not intelligible to him. So he became far removed from the main part of life's mystery. Nevertheless, if at any time in the world's history man has probed the depth of life, he has found it in artistic expression by communicating with the inner life, by communicating with the heavens. And what is that communication? It is the word.

The Prophet Muhammad, when he thought that Someone existed with whom he could communicate, went away from town and remained in solitude on the top of a mountain, sometimes fasting, sometimes standing, and staying there night and day for two or three days. What did he find in the end? He found that a voice began to come to him, a voice in answer to his soul's cry. His soul, so to speak, went forth, pierced through all the planes of existence, and touched the source of all things. How did the answer come? In what form? The answer came from everything: from the wind, the water, the sphere, the air – everything bringing the same answer. But this is not limited to a certain person or to a certain time. In our everyday life there are times when a sadness comes, and it seems as if everything in the world, even the voices of beasts and birds, cause sadness. Then again comes the hour of profound joy. At that time the sun helps to give joy, and the clouds covering the sun also give joy. The cold, the heat, the friend, the enemy, all help to give joy.

This world to a mystic is like a dome, a dome that gives a re-echo of all that is spoken in it. What is spoken from the lips reaches only as far as the ears, but what is spoken from the heart reaches the heart. The word reaches as far as whence it has come; it depends from what source it has come, from what depth it has risen. The Sufis of all ages have therefore given the greatest importance to the word, knowing that the word is the key to the mystery of the whole life, the mystery of all planes of existence. There is nothing that is not accomplished, there is nothing that is not achieved or known through the power of the word. Therefore in esotericism or mysticism the word is the principal and central theme.

What is the word? Is the word just what we speak? Is that the word? No, that is the word of the surface. Our thought is a word, our feeling is a word, our voice, our atmosphere is a word. There is a saying: 'What you are speaks louder than what you say'. That shows that man does not always speak, but his soul speaks always. How do the fortune-tellers read the future? They hear it. They say that they see it from the action of man. But what is it all? It is all a word. For word means expression, expression in voice, in word, in form, in colour, in line, in movement: all are united in one thing and that is the esoteric side of mysticism.

Of course many people in the Western world have said: 'For us it is very difficult to have a meditative life in the activity of this world. We have so many responsibilities and occupations'. But my answer is that for this very reason they need more meditation. Then a person may say: 'I have things to do. How can I go into a meditative life? I have weaknesses to overcome'. But the answer is that the way of getting above weaknesses is to go through meditation. When there are many responsibilities in life, one's very reason tells one that it is better to meditate and make the responsibility lighter. It is not getting worried over one's responsibilities that helps man. It is being responsible, but at the same time being strong enough to lift one's responsibilities.

There are words – the words which are known to the mystics – which do not belong to any language, but the words of many languages seem to have sprung from these mystical words. It is by the help of these words that one develops two faculties: seeing and hearing.

By seeing I do not mean seeing through the eyes, as everybody does. By seeing I mean penetrating. It is the penetrating quality of seeing that makes man a seer; it is that which was really meant by clairvoyance. Nowadays people have used this word so much that one would not even like to use it any more. But then, people have not left any word that exists in this world without having misused it. If one were so sensitive about words, one would have to leave all language alone.

Then there is hearing. By hearing I do not mean listening, I mean responding; responding to heaven or to the earth, responding to every influence that helps to unfold the soul. By such responding and penetration, that one gains by the power of the word, one attains in the end to the goal, that goal which is the yearning of every soul.

Question: When one has the desire to go into these things, what should one do if one's life is too busy?
Answer: I have heard many persons say that they have the greatest desire to give their time and thoughts to spiritual things, but because they have not attained a manner of living that leaves their mind free to keep to these things, they think they cannot take up anything spiritual. I saw the reason of their argument. It is quite true that in this world, as life is today, it is difficult to move without money. Material things apart, even in spiritual things one cannot do without money. If I were to give you the same lecture and I would not be sitting in a room, it would not become a lecture! If the newspapers had not given the advertisement, if a notice had not been printed, you would not have known about it, and perhaps only two or three persons would have been kind enough to come and listen to me to oblige me.

It is therefore natural that a person should think like this, and he is not to be blamed. But at the same time, when we look at it from a different point of view, we still see that every moment lost in waiting for spiritual attainment is the greatest loss conceivable. Besides, one may go on thinking: 'The day will come when I shall change my life and give in to something higher, something spiritual', and that day will never come! One has to do it today, just now, instead of saying: 'Tomorrow I will do it'. Otherwise one repents.

Life is assimilating; time passes. Hours, months, years slip by before one realizes that they have slipped by. To the one who understands the value of time, spiritual attainment comes first. As Christ said: 'Seek ye first the kingdom of God and all these things shall be added unto you'.

I do not say: 'Let all things go in order to pursue spiritual things'. Spiritual attainment does not deprive one of material gains. One has only to fix the spiritual things before one first. In order to become spiritual it is not necessary to give up worldly things, or all that is good and beautiful and valuable from the point of view of the material world. Solomon, with all his wealth, was not less wise.

You need not give up all you have in order to become spiritual. If you think that, it is a great pity. But to wait and say: 'I shall wait till my ship comes. Then I shall become spiritual' – who knows when the ship will come! It is never too late to go onto the spiritual path, but it is never too early. The best thing therefore is that, the moment you think that it is already too late, you should begin and go through all the tests and trials of this path, confident that there is nothing that cannot be accomplished once the spiritual path is taken.

CHAPTER II

The Power of the Sacred Word

A TIME is coming in the present age when both spiritual and material people are realizing the power of the word. For instance, Couéism is talked about among spiritual and material people and they are beginning to see what a word can do. But when one goes a step further one will find that a sacred word has a greater importance and a greater phenomenon. Everyone who discovers some new idea feels at the time that he is the discoverer of it, but when we look back we find in the history of the world that it had been known already. Thus we come to realize and believe in the saying of Solomon that there is nothing new under the sun.

A great Persian poet has said that the repetition of the sacred name will not add sacredness to the Sacred, but it will make your own soul sacred. Those who understand from a psychological point of view the value of autosuggestion and the value of repetition, and how this works upon their body and their mind, are beginning to understand the elementary aspect of it. But before them is a large world of sound and mystery which is still closed, because they do not know that by repeating one word or one thing this may bring about a particular result – but it may do harm to something else.

The secret of language is that in all different languages that we find today in the world there seems to be a central one that can be traced as the mother language of them all. No doubt it is difficult to distinguish that language as such or such, but the relation that exists between one language and another shows that the human race had only one to begin with. Many linguists have said that it was Sanskrit; there are others who say that before Sanskrit there was another language.

Historians will have different opinions, but metaphysics teaches us that there was a language that was the one language of the human race, then many others came from it. An historian cannot be an historian if he does not give a name to a certain language as being the first; for a metaphysician this does not matter. He only understands, he knows for certain that there was one language. He does not mind if he does not know its name.

When we come to that language we understand that it was much more natural than the languages we know today, which are most complicated. Take for instance the language of birds and animals. These languages are not made from grammar, they are not mechanical; they are natural expressions of their real sentiments, of their real needs. It is by that natural expression that other animals of the same kind understand the warning they give to move, the warning they give to protect themselves, to leave their places; the warning of death or danger, or of a change of climate, of storm or rain coming. They have a certain way of expressing affection, passion, wrath, anger, and yet it is not a mechanical language, it is a natural expression, a natural language.

The primitive language of mankind was a language of feeling, of natural expression, just like the primitive figures. If we trace back thousands of years we shall find that the name of every object was written in a sort of picture which suggested that object. Now that thousands of years have passed those figures and forms have changed, and the words of primitive language have changed. Yet the one who can see into life can trace back at least some forms and some sounds and words that come from the origin of the human race.

The outcome of the language which was the original language of humanity was that every word, every sound that was expressed not only conveyed a meaning to the mind of the person who said it, but created a sensation in the person who heard it, a sensation of a particular expression, of a particular feeling or sentiment. As the ancient people cultivated this domain of science they began to understand that sound, which is called voice, is the main principle in man's life.

It is the voice of man which shows whether a person is hard or tender, wilful or weak-willed; every characteristic of man can be perceived through his voice. The grade of the person's evolution, his tendency and his condition at that moment can be realized by his voice. This shows that, before the face, the expression or the movement, the word can convey a feeling or a condition. It shows that the real being of man, the central point of his life is to be found in the breath, for voice is only an expression of breath. When this voice is expressed outwardly, it is in the form of words.

This expression has a kind of reaction inwardly which has an effect upon a person's body, upon his mind, upon his soul. There are certain parts in the human body which may be considered as the factors of intuitive senses, and when by voice, by word, by breath these parts are brought into action, brought to life, man begins to experience a fuller life. If that person is an artist, a musician, a writer, a creative genius, whatever he is, by cultivating all the natural faculties which are within him he can express his art or his science to the full.

It is by taking this secret into consideration that the ancient people developed the science which they called *yoga*. By the repetition of certain vowels, of certain words and of a particular way of breathing they touched within themselves those centres which are connected with intuitive faculties. This is not only a story of the past. The schools of the Sufis, whose origin is the ancient school of Egypt where Abraham was initiated, still exist and there are words you use, which have that power. But these schools have not made of this sacred idea an ordinary thought. They have not spread it among people who would take it and abuse it, because if you give a sharp sword into the hands of a child, the consequences will be fatal. A person who has not yet risen above his angers and passions, who has not yet risen above greed and above pride and conceit – if all the power there is is given to him, how will he use it? It is therefore that the schools first arranged that people might be taught moral culture and the attitude they should have towards their fellow-men. For they believed – and they still believe, that any power that is ever attained must be used for one purpose only and that purpose is nearing God. If it is not used for that purpose, if it is used for selfish ends, then it is just as well that man remains without powers. Therefore, in the ancient schools, which have tradition behind them and which are meant to serve humanity, initiations must be taken.

What does initiation mean? Initiation means confidence on the part of the teacher and trust on the part of the pupil. Initiation is not given to the one who is curious, who comes to examine the teacher, or who comes to find out if in this particular culture, in this cult, there is truth or not. If by any chance such a person received an initiation, he would go through it all and come back by the same door that he had entered without having found anything. For this treasure house, which is so great a treasure, is a magic house; a house wherein is every treasure, and yet the thief cannot find it. He will go through the house, he will go all around it, he will not see anything and he will go back with his hands empty. For truth is the portion of the sincere one. It is the one who is hungry who must be given food; it is the one who is thirsty who must be given water. He who is not hungry, to him food will do no good, and he who is not thirsty, water will not satisfy his need.

If a person wants to know these things in order to develop magnetic power, to accomplish his way, to gain power, or a name, or more things than he can get in his daily life, it is useless. For the word, and especially the sacred word, is the key. As it is said in the Bible that first was the word, so the last key is also the word. It is the word which was the beginning of creation, and it is the word which opens the mystery of creation. The different centres of intuition, of inspiration, of evolution are touched by the sacred word.

If nowadays science has discovered how the wireless can reach through space without any intermediary, one day the truth will be discovered which has been known to mystics for thousands of years: that man himself is the instrument, the receiver and the sender of that wireless which is above all other ways of wireless. The wireless can explain to us many of the possibilities which are otherwise difficult to comprehend, for it explains to us that every word once spoken is not lost. It is there and it can be caught. This supports what I have brought today before you: that the sacred word has such power that nothing, whether distance, space, air, or sea can keep it back from entering and reaching the hearts that can catch it. Only the difference is that the wireless is known to those who communicate from one country to another country, but this mystery of the word is known to those for whom communication with the world is nothing; their aim is the communication between this world and the other world. For as the word was first and was at the beginning, therefore at the beginning there was not this word or that word: there was only one life, there was only one existence.

In reality there is one life and there is one existence. What we call this world or that world is for our convenience. It is our speculation, it is our way of distinguishing between the different dimensions. What is a dimension in reality? A dimension is rather a conception. There is only existence. It is just the same with time. There is no such thing as time; it is we who have a certain conception of it. But there is only existence, there is an eternal continuity of life. In the same way 'this world and that world' is only our conception of all that hides the other world from our material physical eyes with which we have always been accustomed to look at life.

There is one existence, there is one life, eternal, everlasting. In short, if by the wireless words can be transferred from one place to another, this gives us the proof that, if there is one existence and one life, then in this world or in that world, here or in the hereafter, communication is possible for us – possible only if man has tuned himself, has wound himself, as it were, to that condition where he lives fully.

Since the world contains so much falsehood, every good thing is imitated and every writing is falsified. And as there is such a great desire in the mind of every person to do and to know something about reality, it seems that many different institutions, societies and groups wish to try and speak of things about which they themselves do not know. We could count today hundreds of institutions working in order to give belief in God by teaching what they call spirit communication. By doing this they spoil that sacred science and that great phenomenon which one realizes by attaining to the kingdom of God.

CHAPTER III

The Word that was Lost

1

'THE WORD that was lost' is a symbolical phrase, a paradox of the mystics which has existed in the East and among the wise for ages. Many schools of spiritual or mystical cult have been formed in order to understand this particular problem, but what happens is that whoever wishes to solve the problem says very little about it after he has solved it.

There is an ancient story in the East which tells that there was a wall of mystery. The tradition was that whenever anyone tried to climb upon the wall to look at the other side, instead of coming back he smiled and jumped over and never came back again. So the people of that country became very curious to know what mystery lay behind that wall. They thought they would arrange something so as to pull the person back when he looked at the other side of the wall and wished to go there. When the next person tried to climb upon the wall, curious to see what was on the other side, the people who saw him climb put seven chains on his feet and held him so that he would not go over. When he looked at the other side he too was delighted with what he saw and he smiled. Those standing at their side, curious to know what he had to say, pulled him back, but, to their great disappointment, when he came back they found that he had lost his speech.

The mystery of the whole life has a great charm. Every soul is curious about it, but when one wants to explain the mystery of life words are not adequate. There are many reasons for this speechlessness, for this silence. The first is that the man who has seen the other side of the wall finds himself among children when he returns. To him all the things to which people attach great importance and value seem nothing. For that person truth and fact are two things; for everybody else truth and fact are the same.

The followers of different faiths and religions, of different opinions and ideas dispute and argue and differ from one another. Do they dispute and differ in the realization of truth?

No, all differences and disputes are caused by the knowledge of various facts which are different from one another. There are many facts and one truth. There are many stars and one sun; when the sun has risen the stars pale. The one before whom the sun has risen, to whom the truth has manifested – for him facts make little difference. The light of truth, falling upon the facts, makes them disappear.

It is very interesting to observe that there are many people who are deaf and dumb at the same time. This shows that deafness and dumbness are connected, and according to a certain point of view it is the same thing to be deaf and to be dumb. It is just like two ends of one line: when you look at the ends you may say 'deaf and dumb'; when you look at the line it is one. In the same way perception and expression are the two ends of one line. In other words, the faculty of speaking and the sense of hearing are the same. If one is lost the other is lost.

The difference between science and mysticism is very light; the difference is only that one goes so far and the other goes farther still. Considering the idea of creation from a material point of view a scientist goes as far as realizing that there are certain elements which cause the creation, and form it into various objects. When he goes farther still, he goes as far as atoms, molecules, electrons, and then he comes to vibrations, and at this end he stands still. He says that the basis of the whole creation must be movement, and the finest aspect of movement is called vibration. The mystic is not much different from the scientist who says that movement is at the basis of the whole creation. The difference is that the mystics of ancient times did not put a limit at the end which they called movement or vibration: they traced the source in the divine Spirit.

According to the point of view of a mystic, what existed before creation was the perfect Being. Perfect not in the literal sense of the word, but in the sense of the spirit of the word; for, in our everyday conversation, the word perfect is used for many things which are limited, and the spirit of the meaning of perfection is beyond words. By divine perfection a mystic means the perfection of beauty, of wisdom, of power, the perfection of love, the perfection of peace. But at the same time when there are eyes there must be an object to look at, to admire; that is wherein the purpose of the eyes is fulfilled. When there are ears there must be a sound to be heard in order to enjoy its beauty; therein lies the fulfilment of the existence of the ears. Therefore it was necessary for the perfect Being, in order to realize His own perfection, to create a limited perfection of His own Being. This is accomplished by the One being divided into three aspects, which is really the secret behind the idea of Trinity: the seer, the seen and the sight.

It is the work of the biologist to explain in detail the gradual development of the creation. But the outline that the mystics of all ages have made is that first was the creation of the mineral kingdom, then that of the vegetable, then that of the animal kingdom, and then that of man; and that through all this process of development there has been a certain purpose that has led the creation on to the fulfilment of a certain object. But when one studies the whole process – the mineral, the vegetable, the animal kingdom and then man – the seer finds something which was missing and which then appears as the development goes on further. And what is it that was missing? It is expression and perception, and it is this which the mystics have pointed out in their symbolical expression: 'the word that was lost'.

What made them say that the word was lost, was that in the beginning the word was there; there was movement, vibration, and there was the consciousness of the perfect Being. The rocks were not made – even from a scientific point of view – before vibrations manifested. First there was vibration, and then followed the rocks. The difference between the mystical and the scientific point of view is this, that the scientist says that from the rock intelligence developed by a gradual process, and the mystic says: 'No, the rock was only a grade of intelligence; intelligence was first, and the rock came later'.

The whole process of manifestation suggests that it is working towards some object, and that object is one and the same. Yes, there are two points of view to look at it. One may say: 'A mountain will some day turn into a volcano', or: 'A tree will some day bear fruits, and therein the object of its being is fulfilled'. But then there is another point of view which is perhaps more perfect: that the stone and tree and animal and man all are working towards one object, and that the whole process of the creation is working towards it. And what is that purpose towards which every aspect of this creation is working? What is it that the silent mountains are waiting for in the wilderness? What is it that the woods, the trees, are silently waiting for? What moment? What object? What is it that all the animals are seeking and searching after – besides their food? And what is it that is giving importance to man's every activity, and after the fulfilment of each activity draws him on to another? It is one object, but covered under many forms. It is the search after that word, the word that was lost. The further the creation develops, the greater is the longing to hear this word.

As there is a gradual process from the mineral to the human kingdom, so is there also a gradual process from a certain state of human evolution to a state of human perfection. What is it that gives man the inclination to hear a word of admiration, a word of praise that satisfies him? What is it that pleases him in hearing the voice, the word of his friend? What is it that charms him in music, in poetry, and gives him joy? It is the same word that was lost appearing in different forms.

Creation – I mean the material creation – in its beginning seems to be deaf and dumb. Who feels that pain of realizing himself to be deaf and dumb? It is that spirit of perfection which once was perfect in perception and expression. The explanation of the soul which the great poet Jelal-ud-Din Rumi gives in the Mathnavi expresses this idea in a poetic form. He says: 'The soul is as a bird in a cage, deprived of that freedom and that joy which it was accustomed to experience'. This also explains the main tragedy of life. Although every man, every soul suffers pain to a certain degree, and every soul will describe the cause of that pain differently, yet behind the various causes there is one cause, and that cause is the captivity of the soul. In other words: that the word was lost.

Souls at different stages of evolution wish to search after this word that was lost, in the form in which they are accustomed to search. Ways have been made to search for this word which have become right ways and wrong ways, sins and virtues. It is therefore that the wise are tolerant to all, for they see that every soul has his own way to follow, his own purpose to accomplish. But in the accomplishment of all these purposes is the one purpose, and that is the finding of the word that was lost. No soul, however, will obtain satisfaction unless he touches that perfection which is spoken of in the Bible: 'Be ye perfect, as your Father in heaven is perfect'. This means that the Spirit of God itself has gone through different phases to realize that perfection which has limited the perfection of God's own Being, but which is intelligible. Therein lies the satisfaction.

Now one may ask: 'What explanation can be given of this perfection? What is it? What experience is it?' This perfection is what words can never explain, except by saying that the eyes of the soul become open, and that from all sides that word which was lost comes to the ears of this soul. The poets of the East have pictured it in a beautiful imagery in the stories like that of Rama and Sita. They have explained the joy of this perfection as a lover who, having lost his beloved, has found her again. No imagery can better explain this idea than this picture of a man who has lost his soul, and has found it again.

Wisdom cannot be called truth. Wisdom is a form in which the souls who have realized have tried to perceive the word in life, or to interpret it to themselves. It is this wisdom which is called in the Greek language *sophia*, and in Persian Sufi. Wisdom is the interpretation of life made by someone whose point of view has become different by looking at life in the sunlight. By Sufi message is meant the message of wisdom. It is more a point of view than any teaching or dogma or theory. One arrives at this point of view not only by study, but by association with those who have that particular point of view. Besides, by diving deep into life one comes to the realization of truth and for diving deep into life there is a way or a process. It is possible that either with some difficulty or with ease one may find a place one is looking for in a town. One may look for it in different directions, and at last find it. But by asking one who knows one can find it sooner. The Sufi Movement therefore gives the facility of studying, of coming into contact with those who have the same point of view, and of knowing the ways through which one comes to the realizations that are necessary on the path.

2

The idea of the word that was lost belongs to the inner cult and the secret teaching of all ages. Very few at present know, or at least seem to know, the meaning of it. There is not much difference in belief between the mystic and the materialist, but there is very much difference in their ideal. For instance, a materialist who seeks for the source of the whole creation comes to the same conclusion as the mystic: that there is only one source of the life of variety. And both mystic and materialist come at the end of their path to the same thing: truth.

It is chiefly in their ideal that they differ. The materialist thinks that all the consciousness and intelligence that one sees in man is the natural development of life. The mystic says that this consciousness or intelligence is the same as the unlimited consciousness or intelligence which is put into different channels, and that from this intelligence that existed in the beginning all manifestation has come. Picturing the unlimited consciousness or intelligence as the ocean, the consciousness or intelligence of man is like a drop. Thus the materialist sees the intelligence of man as the natural development of humanity, while the mystic sees it as the divine essence, as one, as the source of all things.

In the belief of the mystic it is not only man who is seeking for something; plants, animals, even rocks and mountains, are all looking for something. Man who analyses life, distinguishes one object as a thing, another entity as a being. In this way he divides life into so many aspects, so many things, but in reality life is one. Therefore he sees intelligence only in living beings. Although intelligence is especially developed in man, there is mind also in animals, in plants, in trees; each mind is a particle of the unlimited intelligence. Often an animal thinks more than a man; one can only say that the animal is not as much developed as man. According to the mystic, mind exists also in plants and trees; in rocks and mountains mind is hidden somewhere. Mind is working imperceptibly in all things, in things that man only recognizes as objects.

Comparison between two minds shows that there is a vast difference between them, but it is difficult to define it. Some persons may have experienced in life how plants often respond to influences, especially to the human beings around them, how they often wither in a home where there is distress, disturbance, or disharmony, and how they often live longer where there is harmony. When their owners understand plants they become responsive to love, harmony and sympathy; often plants feel the absence of these qualities. The condition of a person's mind can be seen in its effect on the plants in his surroundings.

The human being is so much absorbed in his own affairs that he sees no further than he can see. Generally mankind is too unaware of the condition of others; often man does not even know the condition of those who are near and dear to him. If it were not so, some nations could not be happy and comfortable while people in other countries are starving and dying by millions. Man is unaware of the secret of his own being. What he needs is to interest himself in the life of beings in another phase of evolution, before he can come to the fundamental basis, the consciousness of his own being.

If you have ever been far away in the forests or the mountains, far away from all population, you will know that there comes, consciously or unconsciously, a feeling of romance. The wind that repeats the sound coming from the trees, the rocks, the murmur of water running – all tell you that they are wanting to get back something that has been lost. This feeling comes to human beings even during the pleasures of everyday life, for then there is a joy that opens up something in them, and then comes this yearning, and this yearning one feels on every side, in the wilderness, in the forest. There comes a feeling of longing, of deep yearning of the heart, the searching for something that has been lost. When we look at the beings living around us we see the same thing. For instance, look at the birds and contemplate their restless flight, the ceaseless roaming of animals in the forest. The first thought that might come is that they are searching for food, but he who has a deeper insight into nature will certainly feel their restlessness, their searching for that which is lost.

There is the same tendency in human beings, although the human being has much interest in life through his various occupations and moods. He finds a thousand and one excuses for his restlessness, for his depression, and illusion is so much developed in man that a reason always comes at his command. There is always someone who will say to a poor man: 'It is sad for you that you are not rich', or someone comes and says: 'You look depressed; I know there is so much sorrow, that is the reason'. But reason is always at man's command and is applied outwardly, so man cannot find the real reason which is within. That reason is suppressed beneath all the reasoning, and man seeks – more than the animal kingdom does – to get back something that has been lost. Nowadays life never gives man a moment in which to be quiet, to ponder upon the true cause of his constant unhappiness. Also it keeps him in an illusion; always looking outwardly he can never find the cause outside himself. It is as if he were looking for the moon on the earth!

Now you may ask: 'What has man lost?' The answer is: God himself, that perfect intelligence that is in every being, that intelligence that the *Vedanta* calls light. In the Qur'an it is said that God is light, which means that the light of God is immanent in the world of names and forms, in all that exists in this world of variety. In this world of variety different forms of activity are producing different results. Yet man in this life of illusion has the same intelligence, the perfection of which he can realize in that state of consciousness where he is aware of his own perfection.

The religions, the mystics, the philosophers of all ages have given the key to this secret, and that is what the Sufi message is bringing back to humanity. Christ has said it so beautifully: 'Be ye perfect as your Father in heaven is perfect'. The yearning of every soul is for the realization of that perfection; that is the longing, consciously or unconsciously, of every thing, of every being in this world. There is something in the whole creation which is like an alarm-clock set for a certain time to make a sound, so that one may awaken. That clock sounds through all the activity of evolution, and when a certain point of evolution is touched man is awakened by the alarm: that is the word that was lost. It has its echo in the longing.

Now you may ask: 'How can one listen, how can one find that word?' That word rises from one's own heart, re-echoing in everything in this universe. If it does not rise from one's own heart it cannot be heard in the outer world. You may ask: 'What is the sign? What makes it rise? Who can hear it?' The answer is: as soon as this word rises in your own heart, you touch God, you touch perfection, and then you begin to understand the divine tongue, and the secret that was closed for so long seems to be revealed.

Ancient stories, stories in the Bible, tell of men speaking with trees, with running water, of sounds coming from the rock. A man without patience will not stop to listen, he hurries on. He is ready to laugh at such things, but there is nothing surprising or impossible in it. This world which is around us sounds continually; the word re-echoes in all things. Only man must be aware of his privilege, of this underlying oneness of all life. The whole treasure of the universe is in the understanding of the mystical idea. This lack of religion of today, this increasing materialism – what is its cause? It is caused by the lack of knowledge of religion; it is the spirit of religion that is lost.

Mankind cannot all be turned one way. Form does not matter; form is nothing without spirit. What is needed is the understanding of each other's faith, respect for each other's ideal, regard for that which is dear to our fellow-men and other creatures. The attempt to make the whole world believers of one faith would be – if it could succeed – as if all men had the same face. It would become a very uninteresting world.

The work that the Sufi message has therefore to accomplish is to bring forward this idea of the mystics that it is the spirit, not the form, that matters; that one should understand the belief of others, and come to the realization of the word that was lost, which is the seeking of every soul; that one should reflect that picture of oneness in order to hear again the word that was lost, to hear it sounding in one's own heart.

CHAPTER IV

Cosmic Language

WHAT IS it that makes some people know beforehand the coming of floods, the coming of rain, the change in the weather, all the different changes in nature? No doubt there are signs beforehand, signs which become words for those who read them, and by those signs they understand the coming events of nature. For them, therefore, these are the language of nature; for others who do not know this language it is gibberish. What is it that makes those who understand astrology know about people, their past, their present and their future from the change of the planets and the stars? It is only that there are signs which indicate to them the past, present and future just as words do, and from these signs they learn of coming events. There are phrenologists who can see signs in the muscles of the head. Those who know physiognomy can see from the face of a person things that no one has told them, but which they read from his face. There are others who know a science such as palmistry, of a small part of man; even in that case the signs of the hands are for them just as loud words, just as is the form of the face.

Then there are the natural conditions, such as the mother knowing the language of the little child who is not yet able to speak. His tears and his smiles, his looks explain to the mother his moods, his pleasures and displeasures, his aspirations and his wants. It is also known that the heart of the lover knows the pleasure and displeasure, the change of moods in the beloved without one word having been spoken. There are physicians who, through their experience in life, have become so advanced that before the patient has spoken one word they have already found out what is the complaint, what is the matter with the person. There are businessmen who are so engrossed in business that, as soon as a person has come to their shop, they know whether he will buy or whether he will go away without buying. What does this tell us? It shows us that, whatever be our walk in life, whatever be our profession, our business, our occupation – through it all there is a sense within us, a sense which can understand language without words.

There is also another point closely connected with this, and that is that everything in life is speaking, is audible, is communicative, in spite of its apparent silence. What we call 'word' is only the word that is audible in our everyday language. What we consider hearing is only what we hear with our ears, and we do not know what else there is to hear. In point of fact there is nothing which is silent. All that exists in this world – whether it seems living or not living – it is all speaking, and therefore the word is not only what is audible to us, but the word is all. This is supported by the Bible where it is said: 'First was the word, and the word was God'. But it is not only that the word was first, but always when there was anything it was the word, and always the word will be.

The real meaning of the word is life, and is there anything that is not life, whether silent objects or living beings? For instance a person not knowing the secret of the planets, not knowing their influence, their nature, their character – what do they say to him? Nothing. He knows that there are planets, and that is all. As far as the science of astronomy goes, a person who has studied it may say that the planets have a certain influence upon the weather and upon the season, but the astrologer will perhaps hear a louder sound from the planets; he can say that the planets have a certain influence upon the individual and upon his life. What do we understand by this? That to one the planet does not speak, to another it speaks whispering, and to yet another it speaks loudly.

It is the same thing with physiognomy. To one a person is a mystery; another may know something about him, and to a third he is like an open letter. For one physician it is necessary to make an examination of a patient with all kinds of machines and mechanisms; another physician likes to ask the patient about his condition, and a third physician looks at the patient and knows perhaps more about him than the patient does himself.

Is it not the same thing with art, when we see that one person goes to a picture gallery, looks at different pictures and thinks that there are different colours and lines? He is pleased to see the colours, and that is all; he knows nothing more about it. There is another person who sees the historic facts behind the picture, and is more interested in it, because the picture has spoken a little more to him. Then there is a third person for whom the picture is living. The picture which he sees, which he appreciates, is communicative. He reads in it the meaning which was put into it by the artist; it is revealed to him by looking at it. Therefore through the medium of the picture the thought, the ideal of one person is made known to the other.

In the same way to one person music is a noise, or perhaps a harmonious group of notes. For him it is a pastime, a certain amusement. To another person there is some joy coming from it; he is enjoying some pleasure, he feels the music which is coming to him. Then there is a third person who sees the soul of the artist who is performing the music, who sees the spirit of the one who wrote the music. Even if the music were written a thousand years ago he hears this spirit in the music.

Is it not all communicative? In art or in science, or in whatever form, life expresses its meaning, if only man is able to understand it. The one who does not understand this will not understand life's meaning. His inner sense is closed; it is just like being deaf. In the same way his sense of communication with things has become dull, he does not understand them. But if a person does not hear he may not say that life is not speaking. In the same way, if a person cannot sense the meaning of life, he may not say that life has no meaning. The word is everywhere, and the word is continually speaking.

There is an ancient belief that the word was lost, and then found again. Out of this belief was made a great mystery, a mystery which exists up till now among people of old civilizations. Up till now they are looking for that word which was lost, and they consider that in gaining that word lies the fulfilment of their life. There are many who have tried to mystify this idea, so much so that a person may go on and on and never come out of it again. But the truth is not found in mystification; the truth is to be found in simplicity, for there is nothing more simple than the ultimate truth. The idea is simply that all that exists has come out of the word, and goes back to the word, and in its own being all is a word.

By word is not meant a word which is audible only to the ears; by word is meant all that is conveyed to you, all that is expressed and comes to you as a revelation. It means that what you hear with the ears, what you smell with the nose, what you taste, what you touch, what you perceive through all the different senses and through all that becomes intelligible to you – that is a word. It is life's mission to convey something to you, and everything that it conveys to you is a word. Through whichever sense you experience it, through whichever sense it is conveyed to you, it is a word.

It is not only upon the five senses – taste, hearing, seeing, smelling and touching – that the word depends; we call them five senses because we experience them through five different organs. In reality there is only one sense, a sense which experiences life through the vehicle or the medium of the five external senses. As life is experienced through these five different directions, the experience of life becomes divided into five different experiences, for the word – or life – becomes visible to us, tangible, audible, it can be smelled and it can be tasted. But besides these five aspects in which we are accustomed to hear the word there is another aspect of hearing the word, independently of the five senses, and this way of hearing the word is called the intuitive way.

When a person comes before you, you cannot say – by only seeing or hearing him – that you have recognized him, whether you are satisfied with him or dissatisfied, whether you feel sympathy for him or antipathy; you can only say that you had a certain impression of that person. This shows that there is a language which is beyond the senses, a language which we are capable of understanding if the inner sense is open to a certain degree. There is not one person who has not experienced this; maybe some have experienced it more, others less. Some are conscious, some are unconscious, but when a disaster is coming, a sorrow, a failure, a success, then a feeling comes. No doubt a person with a tender heart, with a greater sympathy, with love awakened in his heart is more capable of experiencing this sentiment. It is this feeling which may be called intuition, something which does not depend upon senses. A woman feels it more perhaps than a man. Often a woman will say to a man: 'I feel it. I feel that it is going to be a success', or: 'It is going to be a failure'. And when he asks her what is the reason – for a man is very reasoning! – she will still say: 'I feel it'. There is a language that she understands; the man has not heard it.

Then there is another experience. It is not only an experience of spiritual or most advanced people, but it is known even to a scientist, to a material person, to an inventor. He may not believe it, but this experience comes all the same. It is a sense of how to work out his invention, or how to form his system, how to make a plan, or how to arrange something he wants to arrange. One may say that these great inventors have studied mechanics and technique, that it is the outcome of this study that gives them their ability, but there are thousands of students who have studied mechanics and not every one of them is an inventor.

The one who accomplishes something surely accomplishes it through the help of inspiration. You may ask all kinds of artists – a painter, a drawer, a singer, a dancer, a writer, a poet –: 'Can you always do the work you wish to do so perfectly, so excellently as you are able to sometimes?' The answer will be: 'No, I never know when it will be done. It comes, and sometimes I am able to do it; I do not know when nor whence it comes'. A poet may try for six months to write a poem – the poem that his soul is longing for, his soul's desire – and yet never finish it. But it is finished in six minutes if that time comes, if the moment comes. The poet cannot imagine how such a thing could come in the space of six minutes, something which is wonderful, which is complete in itself, which gives him the greatest satisfaction, which is living. The great musicians have not written their most beautiful compositions, their masterpieces over a period of six months. What has taken them a long time to write is of little importance; it is what they have written at moments and finished in five minutes which is living and which will always live. It is the same thing with all aspects of art: creative art depends upon inspiration. Mechanical art may be developed, and a person may be most qualified in it, but it is a dead art.

The only living art is the art which comes from a living source, and that living source is called inspiration.

What then is inspiration? Inspiration is that same word which has been spoken of all this time; it is the hearing of that word which comes from within. A person hears it and expresses it in the form of line, colour, notes, words, or in whatever other form. The most interesting and the most wonderful thing in connection with this subject is that the same inspiration may come to four persons. It is the same word which comes to four persons: one draws it in the form of lines, another puts it in the form of notes, a third writes it as words, and a fourth paints it as colours. This shows that artistic inspiration, inventive genius – whatever form in which the meaning of life wishes to express itself within – has another aspect different from what we see in the life outside.

Where does this inspiration come from, the soul of which we know to be the word? It is beauty in itself, it is energy, wisdom, harmony in itself. It is energy because it gives the greatest joy when expressed by an artist, by an inventor; it is wisdom because it comes with the understanding of accomplishment; it is light because the thing that one wants to make becomes clear to one – there is no sign of obscurity; it is harmony because it is by harmony that beauty is achieved.

There is another form of inspiration, a form which a person attains by a greater enlightenment, by a greater awakening of the soul. This can be pictured as a person going through a large room where all things are exhibited, but where there is no light except, in his own hand, a lantern with a search-light. If he throws his light on music, music becomes clear to him, notes and rhythm become clear to him; if he throws his light on words, the words become clear to him; if he throws his light on colour, all colours come near to him; if he throws his light on line, all lines in most harmonious and beautiful forms come near to him.

This searchlight may become greater still and may reach still further. It may be thrown on the past, and the past may become clear, as it was clear to the prophets of ancient times. It may be cast on the future, and it is not only a sense of precaution that a person may gain, but a glance into the future. This light may be thrown upon living beings, and the living beings may become as written letters before him. This light may be thrown on objects, and the objects may reveal to him their nature and secret. And when this light is thrown within oneself, then the self will be revealed to a person; he will become enlightened as to his own nature and his own character. It is this form of experience, it is this way of knowing which may be called revelation. It is by knowing revelation that one accomplishes the purpose of life, and that the word which was lost – as the mystics have said – is found.

Every child is born crying; his crying conveys that he has lost something. What has he lost? He has lost the word. This means that all he sees conveys nothing to him. He knows not what it is, he seems to be lost in a new country to which he has been sent. As he begins to know a little – his mother, those around him, the colours and the lines, and all things of the world – these begin to communicate a little with him. He begins to know things a little with the eyes, ears, nose, mouth, and in this way he begins to know the word which is within. It is this communication which is the sustenance of life. It is not food or drink which keeps man alive, it is this communication through the different senses to the extent that he understands what they have to say. It is this that makes man live.

When we think of our life, and when we compare the pain that we have in our life with the pleasure, the portion of pleasure is so small. Besides, what little pleasure there is, it costs also, and therefore it resolves into pain. If that is the nature of life, how could we live in this life if there were not this communication, if there were not that word which to a smaller or greater extent we hear from all things, from nature herself? It is the fulfilment of this communication that no wall nor any barrier should stand between us, nor between the life within and without. It is this which is the longing of our soul, and it is herein that revelation comes. It is in this that lies the purpose of our life.

CHAPTER V

The Word

IN THE East it is believed by the *Vedantists* that the creation originated from what they called word, or sound. The same idea has prevailed among the Semitic religions from the earliest times. This word is described as *Ismi Azam*.

The fact that the mysterious always attracts, leads some people to make things out to be mysterious which are not, and thus they profess to know a secret which others cannot know. Here there is the greatest opportunity for deluding the unwary, but when one has come to understand the mystery of this word one understands the mystery of all religion, for all religion lies in this one word *Ismi Azam*.

Modern science is coming nearer to understanding this. On the one hand Professor Bose spoke about pulsations and showed that vibrations exist even in the vegetable kingdom, so that they can be recorded in graphic form. On the other hand investigators have demonstrated the forms which different vowels make on a glass plate, so that one sees various designs. The forms of various plants and their leaves can be shown in this way. On a recent visit to Paris I met Professor Frossard, who for years has been investigating the effect of the vibrations of the voice upon different parts of the human body, and has been able to demonstrate scientifically how these effects vary with different vibrations.

However, Yogis had worked with sound before any such researches were thought of or undertaken. The school of *mantrayoga* is concerned with this science. The one belief that started this was that vibration is creative and that the whole universe was produced by sound, by the word; as it is said in the Bible, first was sound and then was light. Herein lies the thought of the mystics that one may understand vibrations in two directions: when audible they become intelligible, and when taking form they become visible. Even if the word were neither audible nor visible it would have the capacity of being both. If our power of sight and hearing is not enough to help us, it is because the reality is beyond and beneath the range of our sight and hearing, and therefore it is not intelligible to us. We are not aware of it, but if our sight and hearing allowed us to hear and see it, we should know that all life is vibration.

There is another consideration. Whatever is continuous disappears from our perception, whereas anything that is momentarily tangible becomes visible to us. This is shown when we start on a sea voyage. At first the noise of the engines is almost unbearable, but as we go on we get accustomed to it, so that after four or five days we find that we do not notice the noise any more, while at the same time we can hear the least whisper of a friend speaking to us. The continuous noise is now no longer audible unless we stop, to pay attention to it.

It is just like this with the whole mechanism of the universe. It is audible all the time; it is visible both externally and inwardly – but we are so concerned with our own activities, with the things we ourselves are interested in, that our consciousness can only retain these and pays no attention to all the other things, loud as they are.

There are two things to consider: the mastery of the mystery itself, and the insight into the mystery, its perception. To gain insight into things the mystic enters into the depths of the whole mechanism of the universe by educating his senses to be keen enough to see and hear the working through it all, throughout the whole cosmic system. Taking these two senses as his means of investigation he dives deep into the universal life. But there is another way to take, and that is by the power of the word that one utters, which by means of its vowels and consonants enables the mystic to master life. How is it that he can master life by this means? It is because this is the only source of creation. Everything that has been created, and then constructed or destroyed, has come into being through vibration and through sound. So the mystic considers that this is the chief means for accomplishing everything.

All the religions of the past have used this, but they have only given the outcome to the world without making its mystery known. It has been a cult in every religion. The great mystics who understood it did not impart this knowledge to the masses. It would not be wise to give a loaded revolver to a person who might lose his temper in a moment of time. One needs to be sure that he has such control that he will only use it in the best way. So it has been with the mystics. They do not give initiation until they know that they can trust a person that he will make the best use of it. It is not that they are afraid of somebody stealing the mastery they possess. If it were only that, the mystic would be no different from any worldly man who is clinging to his possessions. The mystic must be more generous with his knowledge than anyone else. He is aware that everyone can attain to his knowledge, and he must always help others. Out of the goodness and kindness of his heart he will deny no one his help in every possible way.

As to the word, we see that there are vowels and consonants. Each vowel represents one of the five elements: earth, water, air, fire and ether; and there are the companions of the vowels which together with them make words. Every letter is related to the planets and the planetary influences. Besides, words have a practical effect, a scientific power working on the body, especially on its different centres as recognized by the mystics: the head, the breast, the solar plexus, et cetera. The consciousness must be awakened to each centre. For instance, a musician accustomed to the piano seems to have his consciousness in his hands; the violinist has his in his finger-tips, so that it seems as if the whole of life comes through them. This shows how our consciousness, energy, and life can be directed to a certain place, so as to make the best use of that part of our being. Every centre of man's being is a vehicle for perceiving the life within as well as the life without. Thus it is possible at will to send this consciousness and energy to that particular centre. One can then gain more insight into life, and one can gain more hold, more control over life. Then, when the person repeats the word, its vowels and consonants have some connection with a particular part of the body.

When we consider the part played by the mind we come to see that every word spoken with the mind has a greater action and effect. Furthermore, there is the value attached to the meaning of the word. A person may continually call his son or daughter 'Wise'; if they keep on hearing him call them 'Wise', they really will become wise. If, however, he calls them 'Stupid', the very fact of hearing this makes them stupid in the end. The repetition of the word suggests it to them. That is why it is a great mistake to give nicknames which either have no meaning or only a silly meaning. Even when given in fun, as a joke, they still exert their influence.

We see then that the meaning of a word has a great deal to do with its action, and when both the word itself and its meaning are used for contemplation they become very powerful.

You may ask: 'Has the language any relation to the power of the word? Does it matter which language one uses? Must the word be Latin, or Hebrew, or Zend, Eastern or Western?' The answer to this is that in the East each keeps to his own language. Brahmins offer their prayers in Sanskrit, although this is no longer in everyday use; all the same they use Sanskrit for their *mantras*. A Parsi may live outside his original country, but he repeats his *mantras* according to the tradition of ancient Persia, though their religion almost passed away a thousand years ago. So you see it does not matter to a mystic what language he is using. He sees the source of all languages in the human heart. Whatever the language – Arabic, Sanskrit, Persian, Hindi – it is still human. The more you study this subject, the more you will see how the source of all languages is one. Even the English language contains words related to Sanskrit, Persian and Arabic. Many names would never be suspected of being Persian in origin, and yet they are. So many names are Semitic, so many are Sanskrit. People never suspect how many of their own words belong to other languages. No language in the world today can claim to be so pure as to have no admixture from others. Any language is really a mixture of many languages. It is unfortunate that every later language is just a corrupted form of a former one. Hardly anyone would understand me if I spoke of *Dar-es-Salam**, but if I say Jerusalem everyone can. We see how true this is when we study some words of the Bible. *Alleluia*, for instance, is really *Allahu*. The order of the letters is changed, and this makes it seem a different word; the spelling is altered because different countries spell their words differently. The vowels and the vibrations, therefore, change to a certain extent, and so the mystics prefer, when possible, to adhere to the original form of the word. It is not because it belonged to a certain language of the past, but because there is actually more benefit to be obtained by using the word in its original form.

* The Gate of Peace.

There are also words which no language can claim for its own. This is true of the word *Ismi Azam*, which means: the word of power. No one can claim this word as belonging to his language. It is a word which belongs to no language. Why is this? It is because it is a word of nature. Art has reproduced it, but art has not produced it. All other words have been made from it, for *Ismi Azam* is the spirit of all words; it is the root of all other words.

While the different schools of Sufism understand all this and use different methods in teaching it, they do not restrict themselves to one particular practice. The Sufi regards practices as prescriptions which are not given indiscriminately to everyone, but are chosen separately, one for this pupil, another for that. These practices are only preparations for receiving the truth. There is no such thing as giving truth to one person, and then his giving it to another, for truth by its very nature cannot be uttered, cannot be given. One cannot give that which cannot be put into speech. So the teacher gives a method for finding the truth, for unfolding it, for unlocking that which seems to be in one's heart. No real teacher, no true mystic, has ever claimed to be able to give one anything like this. It is clearly impossible for anyone to impart his knowledge to another person; he can only show him how to unfold his own knowledge to himself. Everybody possesses a kingdom, but he has to find it. The seeker will find it easy to find the truth when he has the help of someone who has himself trodden the path towards it.

In the story from *The 1001 Nights* about Ali Baba and the Forty Thieves we find the mystery of the word portrayed by Ali Baba. It was at a time when Ali Baba was in great distress for lack of money; he badly wanted a change of circumstances. He was even wondering whether he should commit suicide, and then he thought he would try to obtain what he needed, try if he could find a place where his desire could be fulfilled. After travelling some time he arrived at a certain place where a dervish was sitting. He began a conversation with him, and the dervish said: 'Yes, I will give you the key to what you want. Go to such and such a place, and there you will find a rock. Then, standing in front of this rock, repeat such and such a word'. So Ali Baba went to the place indicated by the dervish and, after he had found the rock, he repeated the word before it. Then the rock broke open and revealed a path opening up before him.

The rock is the heart of man. The dervish is the *Murshid*, the spiritual guide, and the word he gives you to utter is this mystery: that by the help of the word the treasure can be found and a door opened by which one can enter into the kingdom in one's heart.

Self-confidence, faith, trust, perseverance and patience are all necessary. As long as you tell yourself that it is not possible for a dervish to give you a word, or that this word cannot possibly do what he says, then, even though you were to go near that rock, you might just call out the word and find that the rock would not open. So then you might think: 'It is no use. I shall go home again', or you might think: 'This is a rock. How can it possibly be opened or split?' True, it will never be opened in this case: the word has no power. The word is the sword, and the sword needs an arm to wield it. The arm to wield it is faith. If there is no faith there is no arm either. The sword is there, but there is no one to wield it. Someone must be there to hold the sword, and it is faith that will hold it.

The power of the word has shown itself to me throughout all the experiences of my life. Every moment has been full of wonder; every successive moment a greater and greater wonder. It is true that some people may achieve various phenomena in another way, but this is not the way of the sage. The way of the sage is: to understand for oneself. It is as when a person turns over on to the other side in his sleep – then he wishes to live with a different purpose. To such a person only the sage might say: 'Would you like to observe the phenomena? Then come with me'. The sage would never go about indiscriminately saying to people: 'Look at these phenomena which I have learned!' No, even to his own pupils he will say: 'I will show you how to see for yourself what the phenomena of life can reveal to you. If I were to show you these phenomena it would still not be you who is producing them. Even if my showing the phenomena were to give you faith, it would be a much stronger faith if you could observe the phenomena yourself. If you were only trusting in my phenomena you would only believe it to be true for a few moments'. This cannot be spoken of before anyone or everyone; it is only understood in the heart and kept there. That is why it is called mysticism.

So let me impress this on my *mureeds*: You must all keep in mind during the time of your initiation, when you are practising your exercises, that you should keep all your experiences to yourself. Whatever you come to understand, whatever you think of during this time, keep all this in your heart. Do not open your heart before persons not capable of understanding, persons who would argue with you, would disapprove of your way of thought and thus hinder you instead of encouraging you. Keep all this close to your heart, and only open your heart to those in need, who are able to understand. Throughout all this you must be patient in your practices, with what you have to learn, and with all that you will have to face in everyday life.

Never expect that the events of life are favourable all through. You will have to make a continual struggle and fight with others, whether you like it or not, whether you love them or not. You will find that this fight must be encountered on every side. So you must face it patiently. Do not turn your back to it. Face the conflict with courage and bravery and tranquillity. Since you know that you are on the path of truth you can go on trustfully. Although there is a great responsibility in this worldly life, it is through this responsibility that you are enabled to evolve spiritually. In fact your evolution will become much greater even than that of the saints who have renounced the world. The reason for this is that, when you pursue your life's journey steadily and with tranquillity through all the struggles and conflicts you have to undergo, success will surely come in time. This success will perhaps enable you in your turn to bring great success to the lives of many other souls too.

CHAPTER VI

The Value of Repetition and Reflection

FOR THOUSANDS of years the secret of repetition has been known to the mystics. They found that the greatest mystery was hidden in the form of repetition, and on that science *mantrayoga* was founded by the Yogis in India, while the Sufis worked for ages in the lands of Syria, Palestine and Egypt with the science of the repetition of words.

What attracts us most is the repetition of any experience that we have had. If you are in the habit of going to the park, you have perhaps made an association with a little bench there, and you will always be attracted to it whenever you go to the park. You have experienced the magnetism of the place. There may be a better place, but on the place you once sat you will sit again, and the oftener you sit there, the oftener you will be attracted to it. Then there are simple songs that you have heard in your childhood; they are already lost from your memory. You have become a great lover of music, but when that song is sung that you once heard in your childhood, it brings you a new joy and a desire to hear it again; you cannot compare it with the best music in the world! There are also things that one eats or smells – that have a perfume, and after having experienced them once, twice or thrice they grow on one. One begins to like them so much that the one who has never experienced them is surprised to think what joy there is in liking such a thing. This also is the effect of repetition.

Friendship, familiarity, acquaintance, all these are repetitions. Sometimes one feels very uncomfortable in the train finding oneself among people one does not know, but after having seen them for a while one becomes so accustomed to their presence that sympathy awakens and one becomes friends. So the whole life is based upon the principle of repetition. Therefore things that help one to be illuminated and to attain spirituality are prescribed by the wise for repetition.

It is through misunderstanding that in the Protestant religion people stuck to that one hint of Christ against 'vain repetitions'. But this was not meant against repetitions, it was against vain repetitions. The Protestant clergy, however, took this idea up and made out of it a saying against repetition. So in countries like Switzerland, and other places where there is a Calvinistic spirit, people very often do not understand this. Yet on repetition the whole of life is based. Even going to church and saying prayers is repetition.

Nowadays a wave is coming in this material age when people are beginning to recognize from a psychological point of view an idea, as used by Coué, that by repeating: 'You are well, you are well, you are well', one becomes well. People come home with this idea about which the mystics of all ages have thought, and they say: 'Somehow it is useful'. The more they understand it, the more they will find that there is much in repetition, if once they will explore it.

In India there was a maid in our house who got a fancy to sing a song, the words of which were: 'How my fate has changed today'. During a week she sang it the whole day long, and at the end she fell from the balcony and died. Fate changed for the worse.

There was a Moghul emperor, Bahadur Shah, who was an exquisite poet under the name of Zafar, the greatest poet of his time. He wrote sad poetries and he died in utter sadness.

Then I may tell you about my own experience. While travelling in Holland I went with a friend – a very practical man and wide awake – to have lunch in his country house. In the train I told him how once I had lost my station, and so went away from the place where I should have got down. While telling this we actually lost our station, and instead of arriving for lunch we arrived for dinner. This shows that everything we repeat has a psychological action.

Good omen and bad omen also depend upon repetition. If you tell a person about an accident when he is just getting into his automobile, it means that you put the wheels of his automobile on the track leading to an accident.

Why does success repeat itself, and why does failure repeat itself? There is always success after success, and failure after failure. This is repetition too; it forms a rhythm. There is nothing that succeeds as success, and once you have failed, you will fail again and again. If I were to go deeper into this subject, I would say that the moving of the world is also repetition by which a rhythm is formed. The rising and setting of the sun, the waxing and waning of the moon, the changing of the seasons, the rhythm that the waves take, and the speed with which the wind blows, all this works according to the law of repetition. Since repetition is movement – a mobile movement because it goes forward – so it is used even by the mystics as the greatest secret for spiritual progress or material success.

There are many ways of concentration, but the best way is the repetition of a word. For instance, if a person wants to concentrate on balance, he cannot make a form of it before his mind because it is an abstraction. But if he closes his eyes from all other things and repeats to himself: 'Balance, balance, balance, balance, balance', naturally each time he repeats 'balance' it makes a picture in his innermost, a picture of balance, and in everything he does he sees that picture reflected. So his life becomes balance.

Very often parents, not knowing this, call a child 'naughty'. The child is impressed by it; it knows that it is naughty, so it goes on being naughty. So it is with friends and relations and with all those around us. Not knowing the psychological effect of our speech we may turn them from bad to worse. If you say to your business partner: 'Is it not dishonest what you did?', that means that you have made that person dishonest. The first thing he did was less dishonest; you have completed it by saying so. Every kind of accusation of dishonesty, of lack of kindness, or affection, or love, makes a person that of which you accuse him. Ignorant of this people often rejoice saying to another something they want to see changed in him. If you say to someone: 'You have been very unkind to me', or: 'You have not been just', or 'very cruel', you have made that person more unkind, more unjust, more cruel, and that person cannot help it. It would have been much better not to have said anything, not to have taken a chance of making that person better! For all that you acknowledge you make worse by the repetition of words.

Acknowledging is giving life to something. If you do not take notice of things, they die because you have not given them life. By noticing them you give life to things which may not be profitable to you. There is the simple one, the clever one, and the wise one. The simple one does not see into human nature; the clever one sees it and what he sees he says; the wise one sees and does not say anything, and it is that which makes him wise.

In the East they give great consideration to the names given to children, to horses, to animals, because that word is repeated so many times, and that repetition brings about the same result as the name indicates. When you give a person the name Lucky, and he is always called so, he must become lucky. By this I do not mean to say that Mr. Armstrong is always a strong man. I only wish to say that the name has a great effect for the very reason that it is repeated.

There are sages, there are those who have concentrated and whose mind is powerful and, when they give a certain name to someone with a certain meaning, that name has a great effect. It is like giving the life which is in the name, and that life beginning to grow in the person; it is like sowing a seed in the ground, and that seedling bearing flowers and fruits. The meaning which is in the name works after days and years, and brings about most wonderful results. From the moment the name is given the whole life is changed. If it is given by a person with power and inspiration it has a wonderful effect.

As to spiritual development, there are different influences which may be considered as spiritual influences, and such we need in our life; such as the influence of kindness, of compassion, the influence of Providence, inspiration, cure, health, wisdom, power, and so forth. These being spiritual influences the mystics have names for them – for each of these influences – and they call them the sacred names of God. There are perhaps a hundred of such names or more which the mystics use, and each of these names has been practised by them for thousands of years. The effect of these names works sometimes most wonderfully.

In Hyderabad it so happened that a sage wanted to meet the king, and he could not. The secretary said: 'The king is too busy to meet everyone who comes'. The sage said: 'All right. As the king will not receive me, I shall receive the king'. By the repetition of a certain sacred name for about six weeks such a condition was brought about that the king came to visit the sage. I have seen this myself. There was just a few months ago a case where a young man was to be engaged to be married to a princess. But it was all in his mind; nothing was outside. The State was against it, the Church was against it, the family was against it, and the man's own financial condition was against it. So there was no chance from anywhere. This person in utter despair wanted to commit suicide. Then he came in contact with a spiritual teacher; the young man said to him: 'There is no other way in the world except suicide'. The teacher said: 'There is a way. Repeat this word and it will all be well'. In three months time all difficulties and troubles fell away. He got his heart's desire. There is nothing that cannot be accomplished if a person has faith. When he takes that direction, he will know the benefit that comes from the law of repetition.

When a person repeats something to himself, whether a good word or a bad word, whatever it is, he is engraving that idea in his innermost, and that idea is reflected in the *akasha*, in the space. On every person he meets it will be reflected. For instance, if a person who repeats 'kindness, kindness, kindness', meets the most cruel man in the world, the kindness that is engraved upon his heart will be reflected upon the man, and that man cannot but act kindly. Besides, a person who has repeated 'kindness' so many times in his life – whoever he will meet will say: 'That is a kind person', because by saying 'kindness' he has become kind.

Of course one may overdo it; one may do it wrongly, and that must be avoided. One may try to experience it before one is ripe enough to experience it. For instance, one may hear this lecture and go before a bank and say: 'Money, money, money, money, money', and then come to me and say: 'I repeated "money" a thousand times, but money has not come!' That person has not proceeded rightly. Besides that, to make use of such a wonderful thing for the attainment of earthly things is very foolish, because life is an opportunity, and when that opportunity is lost, it is lost for ever. When we use this knowledge for things that are not worthwhile, then the time is lost. Therefore this only proves worthwhile if it is used for the attainment of spiritual knowledge. If we use this secret for the attainment of earthly things, we do not know whether they are good for us or bad. Very often we would love to have this or that, but if it is not good for us we may just as well not have it. Best is the moral principle which we read in the Bible: 'Seek ye first the kingdom of God, and all those things shall be added unto you'.

In order to seek the kingdom of God it is not necessary to give up the things of the world. Whether we have them or do not have them, the first thing is to seek the kingdom of God. I heard many people say: 'If my financial situation will be right for the remainder of my life, I will set to work on spiritual lines; if the money situation is all right, I will do it'. I quite understand that it is necessary to think of the financial situation; it is reasonable. But at the same time, when we look at life which is passing – this moment we have will never come again! – when we think that we let our life pass in the pursuit of earthly things alone, and wait before looking at something higher, perhaps it will be too late. Earthly things last only as long as the life of the body lasts: in a moment it has gone. Who knows into whose hands the wealth one has collected will go. At the same time we must remember that Solomon with all his wealth was not less wise. We need not give up all those things; by pursuing God we need not lose the things of the earth; they all follow. But one should not say: 'After I have finished my acquirements, then I shall take the spiritual path'. This is a dream which may never be accomplished. If you want to take the spiritual path, you must take it right now, at this moment, and at the same time think about worldly obligations. One may just as well earn money and profit by it and experience all the comfort that is there. It does not matter, as long as one pursues the spiritual path.

Now you may ask: 'In what way does one attain to spiritual knowledge by repetition? Is it by repeating the name of God that one comes to spiritual knowledge?' Not necessarily, but by repeating a certain thing you forget yourself. Forgetting yourself you are forgetting the false self, and it is in forgetting the false self that lies the secret of spiritual attainment. Spiritual attainment apart, even the secret of the great works of musicians and poets was that they forgot themselves in their work. In order to give life to something one must make a sacrifice, and in spiritual attainment it is by the sacrifice of the false self that one comes to the real self. There are many who are afraid and say: 'If we lose ourselves, what do we gain? It is only a loss!' It is not losing the real self, but the false conception of oneself. It is like a person who is dreaming. He is so interested in the dream that, if somebody comes to wake him up, he says: 'No, no, let me sleep'. He forgets that awaking will be another experience; his great interest is in the dream. So it is with some people; they are afraid to lose themselves, and they forget that it is only the false conception of themselves that they lose.

At the imagination of the spiritual ideal, many people are very afraid, as someone is afraid on the top of a high mountain when looking back on the immense space. It makes them fear, because they have always seen narrow horizons. The wide horizon has an effect which gives them a shock. It is the same with those who are accustomed to the false conception of the self. The best way of losing the self is by the repetition of a certain sacred word which gradually makes one lose the conception of the false self, expressing at the same time the idea of the real self, a foundation upon which life will be built for ever and for eternity.

PHRASES TO BE REPEATED

PHRASES TO BE REPEATED

The following sentences were composed by Hazrat Inayat Khan to be used, according to the needs of each person, as 'phrases to be repeated ten or twenty times' at fixed times every day.

Bless, Lord, my life with Thy divine blessing.

I am well and happy in the life and light of God.

Guide me to the purpose for which I am born on the earth.

My balance is secure in the hands of God.

Grant me, Lord, Thy wisdom, joy and peace.

Providence has blessed me.

Success is my birthright.

Bless my life with every bliss.

Help my life to fulfil its purpose.

Complete my life by the grace of Thy divine perfection.

My body, heart and soul radiate the healing spirit of God.

Balance my life, that I may know and act aright.

May my life become powerful and harmonious.

I seek my supply in God.

Grant me to have all power and wisdom, that I may best fulfil my life's purpose.

Give me, Lord, Thy divine influence which I may spread among my dear ones.

Help me to serve Thy cause.

O Spirit of Guidance, throw Thy divine light on my path.

Open my heart, that Thy spirit it may reflect.

My life is changing and taking a better turn.

My mind is still, my thought is steady, my sight is keen, my life is balanced.

Harmonize my soul, Lord, with all people and with all conditions.

My body is healed, my mind is fortified, and my soul is illuminated by the grace of God.

Fortify my heart. Give me a new life and new inspiration, that I may see in life Thy divine inspiration.

Make my heart Thy divine temple.

NOTES

1. In ancient times it was very difficult to speak openly of the truth; the governing authorities were so strict, the religions were so narrow in their interpretation, in their understanding. It was especially difficult for the Sufis. Many of them were beheaded for speaking the truth. The mystics, therefore, invented a way of speaking the truth in music, in words such as: tum – dim – tarana – la, that had apparently no meaning, so as to be understood by the initiates, while to the uninitiated it seemed to be nothing more than a meaningless song. At the present time, even in the East, there are many who do not know that such words have any meaning. They know that the song is called Tarana, but they do not know what it means.
(Words of Hazrat Inayat Khan, found in a manuscript called 'Art and Music')

2. In the East, and especially in India, composition has been considered as a picture. If a painter makes a picture of a forest, the appearance of the forest will change in ten minutes: the light, the shades will alter; in time the fruits will be different. If a photograph is taken and the camera is moved around in ten different positions, there will then be ten different pictures. If the picture of the material object varies so much, how much more varied will be the picture of the imagination, the picture of the thought! Therefore, very little is given by the composer – the outline only – and the rest is the expression of the singer, of his feeling at the time of singing. First he listens to the *Raga*, and the picture of the *Raga* is impressed upon his soul. Then he is given the outline of the composition, and he improvises upon that, as a design is given to an embroiderer, and the embroiderer chooses whether to fill it in with silk or with gold, and how to fill it in. He listens to what his soul tells him, and he produces that. When he has mastered this, he may improvise without any outline.
(From 'Art and Music')

3. There are certain *Ragas* which must be played or sung at particular times and seasons. This idea still exists in India. Many cannot tolerate a *Raga* sung untimely. However, few are those who realize the reason why a *Raga* should be sung at any particular time. No doubt, it is a matter of habit. As untimely food is often distasteful to many, so the *Raga* which our ears have been accustomed to hear at a certain time sounds inharmonious when sung at a wrong time. It is like taking a stroll on a midsummer morning wearing an evening dress! But those who have introduced this idea intuitively found out the connection between the modes and their relative times and seasons,

which is often felt by the keen student of Indian musical cult. The inner reason is that every time of the day has its atmosphere, has its influence upon us, and at that time certain *Ragas* are beneficial for bodily health, the state of mind, and the condition of the soul. (From 'Art and Music')

4. In this book and elsewhere Hazrat Inayat Khan is briefly alluding to Dr. Abrams' medical system. It will interest readers to know that since the death of this eminent scientist further developments have constantly been achieved in this realm by outstanding personalities such as Ruth Drown, George de la Warr, Malcolm Rae, and many others. But this research work has always been treated without sympathy by the medical establishment and many pioneers have been prosecuted or ridiculed. Thus it has been very difficult to advocate such systems – now called Radionics – and many have ruined their career in doing so. The work has, however, been going on underground up to now and some thousand or more practitioners in many countries all over the world are today using Radionics very successfully.

These techniques are in fact close to spiritual healing enabling the physician to treat the patient either through energized medicines or at a distance through the means of an instrument. In this work one has recourse to the extra-sensory perception faculties in form of dowsing. Basic to the radionic theory and practice is the concept that man and all life forms represent definite vibration patterns within the electro-magnetic field of the earth, and furthermore that each life form has its own peculiar rate of vibration which, if sufficiently distorted, will in time result in disease of the organism.

The intentional thought of healing can be expressed in numerical values or geometrical configurative energy patterns which, when submitted to magnetism through adequate instruments, will affect the patient very efficaciously. (Editor)

5. There is another story of Tansen. Once he was asked by Akbar the Great to sing *Dipak-Raga*. The influence of that *Raga* was on fire. Tansen refused at first, but as Akbar urged him to sing, he sang it – and was burned. When his whole being was in flames he left the court and went to Marwar where two maidens were drawing water from a well. He went there and asked them to give him some water to drink. 'Oh', one of them said, 'poor man! He is burned by *Dipak*. What can we do for him?' The other maid sang *Malhar*, the *Raga* of rainfall. The clouds gathered, and the lightning cracked, and there was a shower through the midsummer day. The fire that had burned Tansen was then extinguished, and he became well again. There are many stories of that character told, showing the mystical power of music. (From 'Art and Music')

6. The first edition of Hazrat Inayat Khan's 'The Mysticism of Sound' contained a long passage wherein Hazrat Inayat gave an interpretation of certain words from different mystical terminologies. As has already been noted, these explanations should not be taken in a linguistic sense. The real explanation is to be found further on in this book – for instance in the chapter 'The Power of the Sacred Word' – where it is said that the source of all languages is one central mother language, that 'the human race had only one language to begin with', and that 'every sound, expressed, not only conveyed a meaning, but created a sensation'. With this central language Inayat Khan did not mean the concrete, complete language as we know it today. Rather one should think of sounds and expressions communicating feelings. These sounds, still to be found in syllables of different languages, are meant in the following passage.

(We have preferred to produce this passage in a note rather than in the text of the book, producing thus the exact words of the first edition, issued during Hazrat Inayat Khan's lifetime, without trying to correct the spelling of words from Oriental languages, or to adapt it to the one currently used in the present edition.)

Truth, the knowledge of God, is termed by a Sufi *hak*. If we divide the word *hak* into two parts it becomes *hu ak*, *Hu* signifying God or Truth, and *ak* in Hindustani meaning one; both meanings together expressing one God and one Truth. *Hukikat* in Arabic means the essential truth; *hakim* means master and *hukim* means knower – all of which words express the essential characteristics of life.

Aluk is the sacred word that the *vairagis*, the adepts of India, exclaim as their sacred chant. In the word *aluk* are expressed two words: *al* meaning from, and *huk*, truth, both words together express God the source from which all has come.

The sound *Hu* becomes limited in the word *hum*, for the letter m closes the lips. This word in Hindustani expresses limitation: *hum* means I or we, both of which words signify ego.

The word *humsa* is the sacred word of the Yogis which illumines the ego with the light of reality.

The word *huma* in the Persian language stands for a fabulous bird. There is a belief that, if the *huma* bird sits for a moment on the head of anybody, it is a sign that the person will become a king. Its true explanation is that, when man's thoughts so evolve that they break all limitation, he becomes as a king. It is the lack of language that it can only describe the most High as something like a king.

It is said in the old traditions that Zoroaster was born of a *huma* tree. This explains the words in the Bible: 'Except a man be born of water and the Spirit, he cannot enter the kingdom of God'. In the word *huma hu* represents spirit, and the word *mah* means water.

In English the word human explains two facts which are characteristic of humanity; *Hu* means God, *man* means mind, which word comes from the Sanskrit *mana*, mind being the ordinary man. The two words united represent the idea of the God-conscious man; in other words *Hu*, God, is in all things and beings, but it is man by whom He is known. Human therefore means God-conscious, God-realized, or God-man.

The word *humd* means praise, *humid* praiseworthy, and Muhammad praiseful. The name of the Prophet of Islam was significant of his attitude to God.

Hur in Arabic means the beauties of the heaven; its real meaning is the expressing of heavenly beauty. *Zhur* in Arabic means manifestation, especially that of God in nature.

Ahur Mazda is the name of God known to the Zoroastrians. In this first word *Ahur* suggests *Hu* upon which the whole name is built. All of these examples signify the origin of God in the word *Hu*, and the life of God in every thing and being.

Hai in Arabic means everlasting, and *hai-at* means life, both of which words signify the everlasting nature of God.

The word *huwal* suggests the idea of the omnipresent, and *huwa* is the origin of the name of Eve, which is symbolic of manifestation – as Adam is symbolic of life. They are named in Sanskrit *Purusha* and *Prakriti*.

Jehovah is really *Yahuva* and originally was *Yahu*: *ya* suggesting the word oh!, and *Hu* standing for God, while the 'A' represents manifestation.

Hu is the origin of sound, but when the sound first takes shape on the external plane, it becomes 'A', therefore *alif* or *alpha* is considered to be the first expression of *Hu*, the original word. In Sanskrit as well as in most other languages 'A' begins the alphabet as well as the name of God. The word 'A' therefore expresses in English one or first, and the figure of *alif* gives the meaning one, as well as first. The letter 'A' is pronounced without the help of the teeth or tongue, and in Sanskrit *A* always means without.

The 'A' is raised to the surface when the tongue rises and touches the roof of the mouth when pronouncing the letter *l- lam* – and the sound ends in *m – mim* – the pronunciation of which closes the lips. Therefore these three essential letters of the alphabet brought together as the mystery in the Qur'an form a word, *alm*, which means knowledge. *Alim* comes from the same and means knower. *Alam* means state or condition, the existence which is known.

When *alif*, the first, and *lam*, the central letter, are brought together they make the word *al*, which means from and may be interpreted to be 'the latter derived from the former'. In English 'all' suggests the same meaning of entire or absolute nature of existence.

The word *Allah* which in Arabic means God, if divided into three parts, may be interpreted 'the One who comes from nothing'.

El or *Ellah* has the same meaning as *Allah*. The words found in the Bible – *Eloi*, *Elohim* and *Alleluia* – are a corruption of the word *Allah-Hu*.

The words *om, omen, amen* and *ameen* which are spoken in all houses of prayer are of the same origin. *A* in the commencement of the word expresses the beginning, and *M* in the midst signifies end; *N* the final letter being the re-echo of *M*, for *M* naturally ends in a nasal sound, the producing of which sound signifies life.

In the word *Ahud*, which means God, the only Being, two meanings are involved. *A* in Sanskrit means without, and *hud* in Prakrit means limitation. The Persian word *Khuda* has its origin in *huda* which signifies 'the limit and end of all things in Him'.

It is from the same source that the words *wahadat, wahadaniat, hadi, huda* and *hidayat* all come. *Wahadat* means consciousness of self alone; *wahadaniat* is the knowledge of self; *hadi* the guide, *huda* to guide; *hidayat* means guidance.

7. In the original report of this lecture the following words were deleted with the annotation 'omit':

This was a wonderful experience for me when I visited Germany after the war (1920), because of the contrast between the voice that was there before the war – the voice at the bottom – and the voice of the people which is just now going on. It seems as if there was a lake or a river which has become land. That running water which was life itself has become buried, and there is earth covering it. Yet one feels that underneath there is still water to be found – but there is earth covering it. One feels that one just walks over the ground, but that perhaps there was some water before. So one feels how the voice of the whole country can change with the changing of conditions.

8. The following words were deleted in the original report:

The Prophet Muhammad came with a revolt to clear the whole of Mecca of all its gods, but nothing would induce him to take away this one stone. After having swept away all the gods from there, it was his intention to take away all the stones, but he did not touch that one stone set up by Abraham.

If Abraham had been alive he could have defended it, but now the stone would defend itself.

9. There is still another question and answer in the original report with the annotation 'omit':

Question: Do we leave our impressions on pet dogs, and do we so hurry our dog's evolution?
Answer: Yes, certainly – but I have doubts about our own evolution.

10. The following question and answer – inserted in the text of previous editions – has been omitted, as after a study of the original reports the text is not clear:

Question: During the time that someone has lost his memory are the impressions received during that time recorded? Do they come back later on?

Answer—according to one report—: Yes, they do too. The time when one has lost one's memory — at that time the memory is not actively taking the record of things given to it.

Answer—according to the other report—: No, because the time when a person has lost his memory — at that time the memory is not actively taking the records of what is happening.

In the first edition we find:

But the impressions during the time that a person has lost his memory are also recorded; they come back later on. Only at the time when a person has lost his memory, the memory is not actively taking the record of things given to it.

11. The following words were still added by Hazrat Inayat Khan to this lecture:

Now only a few words of advice that I should like to give to my *mureeds*. It is most essential that initiation in the Order be not mentioned before others. Besides, all the exercises given to them are given individually, and must not be told to another. Its action upon you, upon your life, upon your character even, must not be spoken of before others, for others cannot understand it, and it would be of no advantage in any way. The mystical path is a secret path, and a *mureed* is more and more to be trusted on his proving to be worthy of the trust — which he can prove by developing the power of keeping a secret. For with every desire of the teacher to help a *mureed*, he cannot do much if the pupil does not show depth in himself. Therefore the two great qualifications necessary to be developed are: to keep in secret all teachings that are given, and to be sincere in the path every day more and more. For, as I have always said, the truth is the portion of the sincere ones.

LIST OF LECTURES AND ARTICLES
THAT ARE THE SOURCES OF VOLUME II

MUSIC 1 – Ville d'Avray (France), 12th August, 1922

MUSIC 2 – Paris, 5th December, 1922

MUSIC 3 – Suresnes, 29th July, 1922

ESOTERIC MUSIC – 'The Indian Magazine', July, 1913

THE MUSIC OF THE SPHERES 1 – San Francisco, 2nd May, 1923

THE MUSIC OF THE SPHERES 2 – Paris, December, 1922

THE MYSTICISM OF SOUND – date unknown

THE MYSTERY OF SOUND – England, between 1914 and 1919

THE MYSTERY OF COLOUR AND SOUND 1 – San Francisco, 25th April, 1923 (the questions and answers were exchanged on another occasion)

THE MYSTERY OF COLOUR AND SOUND 2 – England, between 1918 and 1919

THE SPIRITUAL SIGNIFICANCE OF COLOUR AND SOUND – Geneva, January, 1924

THE ANCIENT MUSIC – Paris, 16th February, 1924

THE DIVINITY OF INDIAN MUSIC – Hagen (Germany), 14th December, 1921

THE USE MADE OF MUSIC BY THE SUFIS OF THE CHISHTI ORDER 1, 2 date unknown

THE USE MADE OF MUSIC BY THE DANCING DERVISHES – Suresnes, 20th July, 1923

THE SCIENCE AND ART OF HINDU MUSIC – San Francisco, 8th March, 1923

THE CONNECTION BETWEEN DANCE AND MUSIC 1 – 2 – 3 – a compilation composed with an old manuscript called 'Art and Music', undated, and an unfinished manuscript for a book called 'Sangeet Vidhya, Hindustani Musical Series'

RHYTHM 1, 2 a compilation from the same documents

THE VINA 1 and 3 – a compilation from the same documents

THE VINA 2 – Burlingame (U.S.A.), 10th April, 1926

THE MANIFESTATION OF SOUND ON THE PHYSICAL SPHERE – Suresnes, 21st June, 1926

THE EFFECT OF SOUND ON THE PHYSICAL BODY – Suresnes, 12th July, 1926

THE VOICE – Suresnes, 28th July, 1926

THE INFLUENCE OF MUSIC UPON THE CHARACTER OF MAN – an article from magazine 'The Sufi', April, 1918

THE PSYCHOLOGICAL INFLUENCE OF MUSIC – San Francisco, 4th April, 1923 (the questions and answers were exchanged after lectures on 'The Art of Personality', Suresnes, Summer 1923)

THE HEALING POWER OF MUSIC – San Francisco, 11th April, 1923

SPIRITUAL ATTAINMENT BY THE AID OF MUSIC – San Francisco, 18th April, 1923

APHORISMS – those aphorisms which were not published in Volume XI of the Series 'The Sufi Message of Hazrat Inayat Khan' are taken from his personal notebooks and from reports by his disciples

THE MYSTICISM OF SOUND – the only available document is the first edition of this book: 1923

COSMIC LANGUAGE – Summer 1924, a report in shorthand by Sakina Furnee, a typescript report by Murshida Sharifa Goodenough, with corrections dictated by Hazrat Inayat Khan

THE POWER OF THE WORD 1 – an article from magazine 'Sufism', December, 1921

THE POWER OF THE WORD 2 – 13th November, 1923

THE POWER OF THE WORD 3 – 22nd November, 1925

THE POWER OF THE WORD 4 – 7th March, 1924

THE POWER OF THE WORD 5 – 15th December, 1923

THE POWER OF THE SACRED WORD – 20th January, 1925

THE WORD THAT WAS LOST 1 – December, 1922

THE WORD THAT WAS LOST 2 – 15th January, 1923

COSMIC LANGUAGE – 22nd December, 1924

THE WORD – England, 25th April, 1920

THE VALUE OF REPETITION AND REFLECTION – 22nd February, 1926

PHRASES TO BE REPEATED – from a document kept by Murshida Sharifa Goodenough

INDEX